THE BOOK OF

Derby County

THE BOOK OF
Derby County

Breedon Books
Publishing Company
Derby

First published in Great Britain by
The Breedon Books Publishing Company Limited
44 Friar Gate, Derby, DE1 1DA.
1994

ISBN 1 873626 89 4

Printed and bound by Hillman Printers, Frome, Somerset.
Covers printed by BDC Printing Services Limited of Derby

Contents

Dedication

This book is dedicated to the memory of
Frank Broome, who died in September
1994. A player with Aston Villa and
England before the war, he joined Derby
County in 1946 and was so proud of his
association with the club. He also
happened to be one of the nicest and most
helpful of men.

Introduction

IN 1983, Breedon Books published their first book on the Rams, *The Derby County Story*. It was well received and the following year Gerald Mortimer's *Derby County: The Complete Record* took the story a stage further with his massive work of reference which detailed the full statistical story of the club as well as looking at the biographies of over 100 of the club's greatest players, all the managers and many other aspects of the Rams. The *Derby County Story* was eventually republished in a more permanent case-bound edition — and, of course, the story had by then taken many more dramatic turns — and *Derby County: The Complete Who's Who* and *The Great Days of Derby County* also added to the Rams' literature.

The Book of Derby County looks at various aspects of the club's history, either not covered in the previous books or given only the barest mention because of lack of space. It has enabled the compilers to dwell upon certain episodes in the Rams' history, to look at the careers of a few players in greater depth, and to present statistics which did not find their way into any of the previous works. Also, new photographs have recently come to light and they are included, some in a large format which we hope readers will enjoy.

At the time of writing, in September 1994, there is again turmoil at the Baseball Ground. On the pitch, the Rams got off to an indifferent start but looked as though results might now be going their way. Behind the scenes there appeared to be strife — no stranger to the Baseball Ground boardroom over the years — and local newspapers and radio daily reported the latest developments.

Of course, all Derby County supporters wish for is that their team makes headlines only for its successful playing performances. It seems a forlorn hope that, in the near future, we shall again see anything like the breathtaking days of the 1970s, upon which so much of the legend of Derby County is based. But nowhere does hope spring more eternal than in the thoughts of football supporters. In the meantime we hope that *The Book of Derby County* revives some golden memories, answers some questions and generally informs and entertains.

The articles in the book were contributed largely by Pip Southall with contributions from Anton Rippon and Andy Ward. Two of Andy's articles, 'The Game of Three Halves' and 'The Missing 78 Seconds, first appeared in *Soccer's Strangest Matches* published by Robson Books. The statistical sections are entirely the work of John Grainger.

Derby County in 1895. Back row (left to right): J.Methven, A.Staley, J.Leiper. Middle row: W.D.Clark (secretary), J.Cox, A.Goodall, J.Robinson, G.Kinsey, J.Staley. Seated: J.Goodall, J.Paul, J.Miller, J.Stevenson. On ground: S.Bloomer, J.McMillan. Rams skipper John Goodall lost the toss twice in the 'game of three halves', while goalkeeper Jack Robinson complained that he hadn't had his rice pudding and that had contributed to him conceding 11 goals.

The Game of Three Halves

O N the first day of the 1894-95 soccer season Sunderland were at home to Derby County. The official referee, Mr Kirkham, was late. The game started with a deputy in charge, later named as John Conqueror of Southwick. The teams played for 45 minutes and then Mr Kirkham arrived. What should he do?

Mr Kirkham made an incredible decision. He offered Derby County, who were losing 3-0, the option of starting again. Naturally they took it. Two more halves followed, and the game became known as 'the game of three halves'.

more than Derby. After kicking against the wind for 90 minutes the visiting players were, to say the least, weary. Sunderland scored five more in the third half. The result was recorded as an 8-0 win although Sunderland had scored 11 goals during the three halves. A pattern was set for the season. Sunderland sailed to their third Football League Championship, while Derby were fortunate to hang on to their First Division status.

The 'game of three halves' assumed a legendary place among the folklore of Derby County players, none more than England-international goalkeeper Jack Robinson, who conceded 11 goals that afternoon. Robinson had previously boasted that he would never concede ten goals in a game (adding as a joke that he would come out of goal when the opposition reached nine) and his team-mates debated whether the Sunderland game counted as eight or 11.

Robinson explained the débâcle by his failure to eat rice pudding before the match at Sunderland — the only time he missed with his superstition. 'No pudding, no points,' Robinson would tell his teammates, who would go to great lengths to indulge their temperamental goal-keeper. One day at Burnley, when a hotel waitress announced the rice pudding was 'off' John Goodall went searching for an hour before he came up with a plate of something which would pass for the same dish. Derby County won at Burnley that day, and they played just two halves.

Derby County legend John Goodall pictured in his later years in Watford, where he had managed the local club. Goodall had a great love of wildlife and is seen here with a fox which he had tamed.

Derby were captained by England international John Goodall, who lost the toss twice. Derby were forced to kick against a strong gale for the first two halves. But the biggest panic was among the pressmen present at the game. They had already dispatched messages all over the country to the effect that Sunderland were winning 3-0 at half-time. Fortunately, Derby obliged by conceding three more goals during the 'second' first half.

Perversely, the decision to start the game *de novo* probably favoured Sunderland

Steve Bloomer (extreme right) in typical pose, waiting to pounce as an opposition defence gets itself into a tangle.

Playing Alongside Steve Bloomer

by Ivan Sharpe

*Ivan Sharpe, 40 Years In Football
The Sportsman Book Club,
London 1954.*

T HE goalscorers always steal the stage. So do batsmen. Stephen Bloomer became the English football hero of his time because he so often got the winning goal. That's why Scotland feared him. When I met him in season 1911-12 he had just returned from Middlesbrough to his beloved Derby County, the club which had brought him out. He had received from the crowd at Derby a welcome home such as no other footballer has known.

Again the star did not look the part. Bloomer was called 'Paleface'. In the dressing-room his limbs lacked the ruddy glow of the players around him. His build was slim yet, at inside-right, he was master of them all. He was the driving-wheel of the Derby County eleven. Returning in 1910-11, he led them back to the First Division, as Second Division champions, in 1911-12.

I was the outside-left of that eleven, and so was able to study his methods. He was not a subtle or really scientific player. But he had the golden gift of splitting a defence with one arrow-like, pin-pointed pass. Just as he could make this pass while the ball was moving, so he could shoot with sudden touch. He scored most of his goals by *sudden* shooting. His great haul of 380 goals in first-class football — then a record — came principally from first-time shots. His was instantaneous marksmanship aimed at beating the goalkeeper's *eye*. It follows that he could use both feet.

But our Stephen was a tyrant. He said what he thought, and if things were going wrong his partner had no pleasant Saturday afternoon. "What d'ye call that? A pass? I haven't got an aeroplane!" This was a fair sample of a Bloomer explosion.

He would extend his activities to the opposite flank of the forward line. I was there. I know.

If, after a breakdown in attack, one studied the crowd, the sky, or any other useful object out of the line of Bloomer's glare — as was the rule in the Derby ranks of that day — he would stand stock still, in the centre of the field, strike an attitude by placing his hands on his hips, and fix the offender with a piercing eye. If the glare, as was the rule, etc., was still ignored, he would toss up his head, as if beseeching the recording angel to make a note of this most awful blunder, then stamp back to his position in a manner intended publicly to demonstrate his disapproval.

Quite wrong, of course. Not good for the side. Not good for the alleged offender. Not good for the game. But those who knew Bloomer knew that he was really quite harmless, quite a peaceable person, who meant well and got the best out of the players because of his inspiring example, his great unselfishness and his tremendous devotion to his team on the field of play. So harmless, in fact, that within a week or so of joining the ranks of the great Bloomer's club the budding juniors selected Bloomer for their dressing-room pranks.

A curious personality, but genius runs that way.

How did he shoot? With power, of course, but the shot came from nearer the toe than the instep. This gift enabled him to make the effort a moment quicker than the man who has to raise the foot a few more inches in order to bring to bear the curve and fuller power of the instep.

A magnet, but not a magician. Bloomer

Steve Bloomer in his 'Sunday best'. In fact, the great Derby star had dressed up to pose for photographs which accompanied an interview he conducted in 1905 with J.H. 'Jimmy' Catton, editor of the *Athletic News* and the doyen of Edwardian football writers.

had few tricks, and plenty of players have excelled him in the dribble. Rare judgement, inspired raiding and passing, and sudden shooting sum up the story of Steve Bloomer in football. When he was asked to explain it all he said: "That's an easy one. I try to get there first." Most people do, but Bloomer usually succeeded.

I was in the Midlands because I had reverted to my parents' business — boots and shoes — and was writing football articles in my spare time. And the Derby team hit the headlines. It was because of Bloomer's cross-field passes to feed my speed that Derby were able to knock out of the Cup the great Newcastle team captained by Colin Veitch and containing the off-side expert, William McCracken. By 3-0 we beat them . . .

The Rams pictured just after the end of World War One. Standing: (left to right): A.Quantrill, Sgt H.Curzon (trainer), J.Bagshaw, J.Atkin, G.Lawrence, H.Wightman, J.Kidd, J.H.Walker. Seated: G.Thornewell, J.Moore, H.Leonard, N.Burton, W.Baker. On ground: T.Barbour, B.Martin.

The Game That Shouldn't Have Started

TOWARDS the middle of November 1921, Derby County sat in the bottom half of the old Second Division, having been relegated the previous April, and for the Rams, this too was turning into a season of struggle. They had opened it with a 4-2 defeat at Blackpool and then been beaten 1-0 at home by Sheffield Wednesday. True, there had been some better afternoons — a 5-1 home win over Bristol City for instance — but overall this third season of post-war football was becoming increasingly worrying for Derby.

On 5 November, the Rams entertained fellow strugglers Coventry City, who were in only their third season in the Football League after seven seasons of Southern League soccer. At the Baseball Ground on Guy Fawkes' Day, some

11,000 spectators saw the Rams win 1-0, their goal coming from a Harold Wightman penalty.

A week later, the Rams travelled to Highfield Road for the return — in those days clubs played each other back-to-back on successive Saturdays — but on this occasion those fans who risked their money on admission saw practically nothing. The game lasted for barely half an hour — and 30 minutes of farce it was too.

As 'County Onlooker' reported in the *Derbyshire Football Express*, it was a fruitless journey and 'the proceedings were merely farcical'.

The journalist told his readers: 'Coventry was enveloped in fog when Derby arrived for the return match in the city shortly after one o'clock today.

'The fog was not experienced on the journey until Coventry was approached. Enquiry showed that it had been over the city all the morning, and this afternoon it showed promise of lifting, but later became almost as bad as ever. The gates were not opened until the arrival of the referee, and the crowd was then allowed admittance, half an hour before the advertised time for the kick off.

'Derby made one change compared with the winning side of a week ago, Birdsall displacing Pattison at outside-left, and making his debut in Second Division football. It was his first appearance since his recovery from ptomaine poisoning. Coventry had the misfortune to be without their custodian, Best, who was absent through influenza. Findlay, who deputised, was making his first appearance, as also was Swindale, both of whom joined Coventry from Blyth Spartans.

'The fog was still so thick that it was almost impossible to discern the band which was discoursing music in the centre of the field. In fact, it was impossible from the stand to see more than a yard or two beyond the touch line.

'One was very much surprised that the game was started under the conditions, for the fog was as bad as ever. How many people were present it was impossible to say; It was also impossible to say who won the toss, for it was impossible to see the referee when he sounded the whistle for the game to commence.

'Cheers were heard from different portions of the ground, and all that could be gathered from the first ten minutes or so was that the play was being concentrated in the vicinity of the Derby goal.

'Gradually the fog screen began to lift and one could see half the players instead of four or five. The Derby goal posts appeared just as Coventry forced a corner, which Lawrence was seen to fist away. A few minutes later the stand on the opposite side of the ground loomed into view, and after the game had been in progress some 20 minutes it was possible to have some idea of what was actually happening. Coventry apparently were the more aggressive.

'A free-kick was given against Ritchie, but Lawrence saved, and with Derby attacking on the right Storer met the ball as it came across, and his shot was not very wide of the mark.

'A nice forward movement, initiated by Storer, led to Moore volleying, only for Findlay to stop the ball somewhere near the foot of the post.

'The sun tried to clear the air, but it had not this power, and it was very difficult to follow the game; in fact, the fog began to creep over the field, again, and once more I had to be content with watching a couple of players — one on each side — running up and down the touch line. Their movement gave some idea as to which end of the field the ball was. Once Swindale forced a corner on the Coventry right, which must have been cleared, for I just discerned Wightman dribbling away from the centre of the field before punching the ball out to the right.

'Findlay was cheered for a save from one of the Derby forwards, and with Storer and Ritchie unable to check the home right, Swindale swept the ball across and Lawrence in the mist was noticed to run out several yards.

'He had to do the same thing a moment later. Moore and Birdsall tried to make progress without success, but what the Derby right wing was doing cannot be stated, for although the game had been in progress half-an-hour they did not come into my view nor that of several hundred other people on the stand where the best seats are situated.

'At the half hour the players left the field, and on enquiry I ascertained that the game had been abandoned, and that there was no score.

'As far as it went it was a complete farce from a spectator point of view, for at no period did the fog completely lift, although the referee stated that he followed the game until he blew his whistle to stop the proceedings.

'I understand it is something unusual for Coventry to have a match abandoned through fog, and that it was the first time it had happened within the knowledge of the oldest supporter (*in fact it was on 28 November 1903 that a game had last been abandoned through fog at Highfield Road*). It was decided to play the match on Thursday next, kicking off at 2.45pm.'

When the game did get under way again five days later, the Rams won 2-1 with goals from Scotsman Bill Paterson (who later joined Coventry) and Frank Keetley, one of nine Derby brothers who all played professional football.

At the end of the season the Rams had climbed to 12th place, whilst Coventry just avoided relegation in 20th spot. By then Rams manager Jimmy Methven, their former player, had disappeared from the scene following illness and his place was taken by Cecil Potter, hitherto the Hartlepool boss. Within 16 months of the farce at Highfield Road, the Rams were taking part in an FA Cup semi-final and a revival was under way at the Baseball Ground.

The Baseball Ground in the early 1930s, showing the Popular Side and Normanton End terraces before the double-decker stand was built.

New Ground for Derby County – A Continuing Saga

HE Taylor Report following the Hillsborough disaster has made all Football League clubs think very seriously about the future of their stadiums. The top two divisions were initially to have converted to all-seater grounds by the beginning of the 1994-95 season and as capacities have been reduced, new stands have been erected a pace and new stadiums considered by many including Derby County.

For the Rams, the chance arose to move to a purpose-built all-seater stadium on Chaddesden Sidings as part of the Derby City Challenge Scheme at 'Pride Park'. And as uncertainty continued over many months it is interesting to reflect on an earlier proposal which the club almost accepted 70 years before.

After 28 years at the Baseball Ground, growing attendances forced the club to

15

Cup-tie crowd on the old Popular Side of the Baseball Ground in 1902. In those days that side of the ground was uncovered. Note the buildings of the old Ley's factory behind. and below: The Municipal Sports Ground on Osmaston Park Road, pictured here in 1982, was built as part of a Government job-creation scheme for unemployed Derby men between the wars. It was to here that the Rams might have moved in the 1920s.

consider its options regarding development, and in October 1923, after months of negotiation, Derby County offered to take over the tenancy of Derby Corporation Sports Ground — the Municipal Sports Ground on Osmaston Park Road. Seating room was planned for 4,000 spectators and two covered wings to hold 10,000 more. Up-to-date dressing-rooms, offices, gymnasium and a billiard room were also scheduled.

But the move seems to have been dogged by misunderstanding as the Town Council confidently expected the Rams to be in residence for the 1924-25 season and that all work would be complete in time. Doubts were growing in the minds of Derby's directors, however, with the other consideration to redevelop the Baseball Ground to mind. (It does sound a familiar tale!).

An article in the *Derby Football Express* at the time revealed some disquiet, for even in 1923 supporters thought the Baseball Ground outdated: 'A new and more modern ground would be much more acceptable to the supporters and there are sites in or adjacent to the borough boundary which might be urged to suit the purpose . . .if ways and means can be devised to assure a holding capacity of 40,000 . . .'

Sites mentioned for a new home for Derby County included the then disused prison in Vernon Street, later to become Derby Greyhound Stadium in 1930, and a plot of allotment land between Cotton Lane and St Thomas' Road. Indeed the original site for the Municipal Sports

Ground was to be on Manor Road. Doubts too were expressed on the purchase of the Baseball Ground along the lines of 'where is all the money coming from'.

The directors dragged their heels on the matter until, forced by the supporters' club to make a statement, on Wednesday 5 March 1924, Alderman Oswald Ling, chairman of the Derby Council Sports Ground Committee, received a letter informing him that the Rams board had 'after careful consideration . . .come to the conclusion that it would be unwise to accept a lease at the present time . . .and would be obliged if you will accept this letter as a withdrawal of our offer'.

The *Derby Evening Telegraph* reported on the 'fiasco of the Derby Sports Ground'. The paper told its readers: 'Over £63,000 had been incurred in constructing a ground which the town's premier club declined to occupy.' The ground was also deemed unsuitable for motor-cycle and pedal-cycle races, (another intended purpose) and was handed over to the Parks Committee for tennis and athletics.

An interesting observation from the

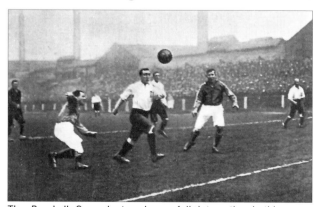

The Baseball Ground staged one full international, this game between England and Ireland in February 1911. An England-Ireland game had also been held at the County Ground on Nottingham Road, as had an FA Cup Final replay and several semi-finals. The Baseball Ground also staged FA Cup semi-finals. Again, note the uncovered Popular Side and Ley's factory buildings and chimneys. The smell of the foundry was familiar to Rams fans for decades.

The Osmaston Stand at the Baseball Ground, damaged in the heaviest air-raid on Derby of the war, in January 1941.

After World War Two there was a renewed call for Derby County to move home to the Municipal Sports Ground and this model of how the new stadium might have looked was on display at the Council House in Derby. It was proposed as a 'Wembley of the Midlands', built on the Derby ring-road with great advantages of access by motor cars, although in those days, of course, most Rams fans would have travelled to the games by bus.

Telegraph that day is that it ran an item of national news stating that a decision on whether or not to construct a Channel Tunnel had been deferred!

Following their 11th-hour turnabout, Derby County announced on 4 July 1924, at their annual meeting at the Royal Hotel, that the club had purchased the Baseball Ground from Sir Francis Ley for £10,000 and that £2,000 was available to develop the ground.

In the close season of 1926, a new stand was erected to the design of famed football ground architect Archibald Leitch, utilising the labour of Ford and Weston builders of Derby. The order for the stand was delayed until promotion to Division One was confirmed, foundations starting on 25 May and the 'B' Pavilion opening, albeit incomplete, on 4 September for the 2-1 home victory over Liverpool.

The stand seated 3,000 with tip-up seats in the centre and benches on either wing. The *Derby Evening Telegraph* expressed a wish that 'Derby spectators will be quite as sporting as others in not climbing over to the higher-priced seats.'

Capacity was thus raised to 30,000 and the club continued its development into the 1930s, spending £40,000 in the eight

April 1969 and one of the last games to be played at the Baseball Ground before the Ley's Stand was built. The 'Offilers Ales' sign had been a prominent feature on the roof of the Popular Side for many years. Ley's factory, behind, was still in full production.

DERBY COUNTY FOOTBALL CLUB LTD.

Floodlit Football Match

Baseball Ground - - Derby

Wednesday, 24th March, 1954

Kick-off 7.15 p.m.

DERBY COUNTY

versus

EAST FIFE

Official Programme

2d.

Printed by Derwent Press Ltd. Derby, for Friary Publicity Ltd. Derby.

In the 1950s, the Rams installed floodlights but League and Cup games under lights could still be vetoed, so Derby arranged a series of friendly games against Scottish League clubs.

Normanton End received a similar complement.

In 1946 there was once again talk of a move to the Municipal Sports Ground and plans were drawn up for a 75,000 capacity stadium, a 'Wembley of the north', by the end of that decade, but again they dissipated and the next major development was not until 1969 with the construction of the Ley Stand.

Improved floodlights — the Baseball Ground had first staged night games in the mid-1950s when lights were perched on the corners of the Osmaston and Normanton Stands — executive boxes and more seats gradually chipped away at the capacity at the Baseball Ground throughout the 1970s and beyond, to the current situation where only the Popular

years since purchase. In 1933 a new double-decker stand was erected at the Osmaston End and in 1935 the

Side retains terracing in an overall ground capacity of just below 20,000. If the last bastion of terrace banter were to become seated then the figure would reduce still further to around 14,000. Obviously that capacity would be far too low for top-flight football and the suggested capacity for the new ground varies between 25,000 and 30,000.

The reduced attendances and installation of so many seats has made the old ground a much quieter place than it has ever been, removing for ever the so-called 'cauldron of noise' for which the Baseball Ground was famous in the early 1970s

Many supporters travelling away to Molineux, Filbert Street, the City Ground and even Meadow Lane, seeing impressive new stands springing up everywhere, have become impatient as Derby County have at times appeared totally committed to move to the Pride Park site and at

For many years the Baseball Ground pitch had caused concern. Even in the late 1970s it was infamous throughout football as a thick carpet of cloying mud in the winter months. By the end of the season there was hardly any grass on the pitch which was simply a large brown diamond with four small patches of grass by each corner flag. Many treatments had been attempted – the pitch being below street level hampered drainage – and in the early 1980s, when this picture was taken, a heavy fall of snow followed by a rapid thaw wreaked havoc. Happily, after another troublesome spell when the pitch actually appeared to dry out too quickly, causing an uneven bounce, the problem now seems to have been solved.

others stated no that final decision has been made. As the 1994-95 season opened it was announced that the Rams might yet play at a new stadium but would effectively be tenants of a football ground owned by another company and part of a larger leisure complex. The planning application to develop the Baseball Ground had also gone ahead leaving Rams fans as uncertain today as they were in days gone by as to whether or not the 99-year 'permanent' home is to remain Derby County's stadium into the next millennium.

The Rams pictured in 1924, at a Baseball Ground which was still largely undeveloped. They are standing with their backs to the Osmaston End, which comprised simply of an uncovered cinder terrace. Note Colombo Street to the right of the picture. Back row (left to right): J.McIntyre, Steve Bloomer (coach), J.Hardy, H.Thoms, Cecil Potter (manager), B.Olney, T.Crilly, H.Whiteman, S.Plackett, Laurie Edwards (trainer). Front row: F.Keetley, G.Thornewell, J.Lyons, R.Galloway, J.Moore, L.Murphy.

The Rams Longest Cup Tie

IN 1923-24 Derby County were a Second Division side that had struggled since the war even for the club's very existence, but now they were pushing hard for promotion back to the First Division and, having disposed of Bury with a last-minute goal in the FA Cup first round, were drawn at home to First Division Newcastle United. It turned out to be a tie that was to last 420 minutes and produce a record 20 goals, quite simply the most extraordinary FA Cup tie in Derby County's history.

Their Geordie opponents stood seventh in the First Division and neither club had taken its players away to the 'hydro or seaside'. The Rams had indulged in brine baths at Stafford whilst both sides relaxed with golf before the first game.

As early as 8.30am spectators began arriving in the town. Bus services were frequent and busy, resulting in the gates at the Baseball Ground being closed half an hour before kick-off. The *Derby Evening Telegraph* reported that 'balloons, streamers, horns and bells were very much in evidence and the teams turned out and faced a cinematograph operator'.

A ground record 27,873 had turned up and they witnessed a highly entertaining 2-2 draw, full of incident. Initially the Newcastle backs looked weak and 'nothing superior by way of construction was displayed by the First Leaguers'.

However, they became livelier and took the lead on 24 minutes. Following a skirmish on the right, McDonald headed the ball goalwards. Rams goalkeeper Olney shouted "Right!" to Crilley, but fumbled the ball which went through his legs into the net.

After half-time Newcastle went two up when McDonald shot Low's cross past Olney. All looked bleak for Derby until, on the hour, hope arrived as Galloway nodded a Whitehouse lob across to Storer, who headed on downwards in a prelude to whipping a shot home past Mutch. A frantic finale followed and Storer earned the Rams a replay at St James' Park with an 88th-minute equaliser.

On Wednesday, 6 February 1924, Newcastle drew their season's biggest crowd so far when 50,393 watched the Rams valiant Cup fight continue. The Magpies again rushed into a two-goal lead with Harris and Cowan scoring, but with it they 'lost most of their brilliance'. Derby's hero in the fight back was Lionel 'Spud' Murphy from Melton Mowbray, who produced a superb display of left-wing trickery despite several scathing tackles by Newcastle full-backs.

The first Rams strike was an own-goal by Mooney with a miskick and the leveller, again two minutes from the end, came courtesy of Galloway — just desserts for a splendid second-half rally.

Half an hour of extra-time was goalless. After the game the directors of both clubs met in the boardroom to discuss arrangements for the second replay.

United turned down Shef-

George Thornewell, who thought he had scored the winner in what turned out to be an epic FA Cup tie against Newcastle United.

Goalkeeper Harry Wilkes, centre-forward Harry Bedford and full-back George Collin off to enjoy a round of golf in 1928.

field as a venue, saying that the Yorkshire town was 'too near Derby for our liking'. Maine Road was next choice but again proved unsuitable as Manchester City were involved in a replay at nearby Old Trafford. Newcastle suggested Leeds but finally Burnden Park, Bolton, was decided upon. Referee Mr S.Rothwell of St Annes on Sea had never been once absent from work until that day, when he decided that he would again take charge of the next match as he had developed 'a keen interest in the tie'.

The following Monday the two teams reconvened at Bolton for a third attempt to settle the outcome. Yet again there was to be late drama but on this occasion it was to be the First Division side who scored in the dying seconds of extra-time.

The Rams outplayed Newcastle at Burnden Park, having much the better of all exchanges. Again Chandler was in fine form, effectively taming England winger Stan Seymour for long periods. The Magpies had luck on their side, however, and took the lead through a disputed penalty award when Chandler gave Seymour a 'fair shoulder charge' before putting the ball into touch for a corner.

The Newcastle winger went to take the flag-kick but the referee made all Rams followers wish he had not taken another day off work as he awarded a penalty for 'violent charging'. Hudspeth converted the kick and then Galloway equalised with a powerful drive to ensure more extra-time, during which Derby appeared to have scored the winner with a Thornewell beauty from 20 yards.

Alas, Seymour again reaped the benefit of the referee's misjudgement. The Newcastle man and Harry Thoms both stumbled in a by-line challenge and the Rams defender was adjudged to have committed a foul. From the free-kick Seymour levelled with seconds remaining.

More strong protests ensued in respect to the next venue for the tie. No agreement could be reached, so a coin was spun. Lady Luck again smiled on the Geordies and Derby had to travel to St James' Park once again two days later. Both sides protested over Mr Rothwell's handling of the games and the services of Mr J.T.Howcroft were secured for the third replay.

Thornewell was injured for the Rams and replaced by Frank Keetley, but it seemed to matter little as Derby swept into a two-goal lead through Randolph Galloway's double. Newcastle battled back in a fine, flowing game and Neil Harris netted a hat-trick inside 24 minutes to send United into a 3-2 half-time lead.

On 53 minutes, Seymour made it 4-2 but Derby weren't done for yet. Storer pulled one back on the hour and there were visions of more extra-time or even a fifth meeting as the Rams pressed forward. Eventually Willie Cowan ended those hopes when he shot home Newcastle's fifth goal to end a tussle which had lasted seven hours and was illuminated by 20 goals before it produced a victor in the shape of the First Division outfit.

The four games were watched by over 128,000 people with receipts exceeding £9,000. Derby's share was £3,000 which, as 'County Onlooker' reported, was 'beyond the dreams of the most sanguine Derby director'. Newcastle, incidentally, went on to lift the FA Cup, beating Aston Villa 2-0 in the second Wembley Final, without conceding another goal in the competition after their epic struggle with the battling Rams.

Derby had a League match at Bury to play before the second replay on 11 February. Bury were promotion rivals but the Rams rested four players from the Cup team, Chandler, McIntyre, Thoms and Storer.

The consistent team in 1923-24 had been a significant factor in Derby's success. Indeed, 11 players made 31 or more appearances each during the season and the same 11 played in 21 League and Cup games.

Derby lost by the only goal at Gigg Lane and at the end of the season Bury and Derby were level on 51 points as joint runners-up to Leeds United, with the Lancashire side being promoted on goal-average by 0.015 of a goal. Perhaps the Cup battles with Newcastle had more than a little to do with that, giving the Rams five matches to play in 11 days in early February. It was enough to see them miss promotion by a whisker.

Jack Kirby gathers the ball at White Hart Lane in February 1935, when the Rams drew 2-2 with Tottenham Hotspur with goals from Hughie Gallacher and Dally Duncan. The Rams defenders watching are Jack Barker (left), Ted Udall (obscured) and Jack Nicholas. Derby were wearing their change shirts of black and white stripes. That season the Rams finished sixth in Division One.

The North of England Schoolboys side which played in the 1927 final trial at Bournemouth. Raich Carter is fourth from the right. After the game a spectator gave Carter half-a-crown (13p), his first 'wage' for playing football. Other boys who made the grade in League football were George Farrow (Blackpool) who is on the extreme right, Albert Geldard (Everton, Bolton and England) who is next to Farrow, and, fourth from left, George Pinder of York City.

Raich Carter – The Man They Never Forgot

TO ANYONE who began their Rams watching in the 1950s, the names of Derby County's finest stars were but the stuff of legend. The club's greatest era so far was over, the 1946 FA Cup-winning side broken up and, further back, the men of Jobey's great team of the 1930s now of golden memory. Small boys taken to the Baseball Ground by their fathers now saw Rams decline and fall into the Third Division North. And as they trailed out of yet another home defeat, older supporters would speak yearningly of 'Carter and Doherty'. For of all the great Derby players of the previous two decades and more, there were two who stood out from the rest.

Raich Carter and Peter Doherty graced the Rams colours for only a short time. Yet the mark they made was indelible. In particular, Carter was the man who older fans still recalled with awe and affection. True, Doherty — 'the most complete footballer the game has ever seen' — made a massive contribution to Derby County's most glorious day, but his Baseball Ground career was so very fleeting. Carter, though, stayed on to thrill the crowds post-war, just as he had on Wearside all those years before.

Raich Carter was born in Sunderland on 21 December 1913, the son of 'Toddler' Carter who had played on either wing for Burslem Port Vale, Fulham and Southampton and was licensee of the

Ocean Queen public house in Sunderland when his son, named Horatio Stratton, first saw the light of day a few months before the outbreak of World War One.

Surprisingly, young Raich was never encouraged to play the game by his father, who had been forced to retire due to a blow on the head and who died from a brain tumour when the boy was 14. Indeed, Raich did not play organised soccer until he was 13, but thereafter he blossomed into one of the most brilliant footballers of his age.

From the local Hendon School team, he graduated quickly to Sunderland, Durham County and England School-boys. Inevitably, an offer to join Sunderland as an amateur soon followed, the plan being that Carter would work on the Roker Park office staff and play as an amateur until he could sign professional forms when he was 17. But an uncle who had watched over him since his father had died, advised the boy to get a trade first and when he left school he began as an apprentice electrician with the Sunderland Forge and Electrical Company.

Carter continued to play football for the works team and for a side called Whitburn St Mary's. Just before Christmas 1930, he celebrated his 17th birthday and when Leicester City visited Roker Park on Boxing Day, young Carter sought out their Wearside-based scout, George Metcalfe, who was a neighbour of the Carters, and asked for a trial with the Midlands club.

On 27 December 1930, on a bog of a Filbert Street pitch which had just staged two matches in successive days, Carter turned out against Watford Reserves in the unfamiliar position of outside-left. By his own admission, Carter had a nightmare afternoon and as he trudged off at the end, the Leicester manager told him, "Son, you're too small to be a footballer."

Undaunted, Carter approached the Sunderland manager Johnny Cochrane and reminded him of his offer to sign the lad as an amateur. Cochrane agreed and Carter was farmed out to Esh Winning FC, who played in the Northern Amateur

League. Huddersfield innocently offered him a trial, thinking that he was unattached, and when Carter asked Sunderland to release him they responded by giving him a game in their Reserves in the North-Eastern League.

On 12 November 1931, the Roker club signed Raich Carter as a full-time professional on £3 per week with an extra £4 when he played in the Reserves. With his firm suffering from the national economic depression and all the workers on short-time, Carter gladly accepted. Clutching ten one-pound notes — his signing-on fee — he left the Roker boardroom to launch a new career.

Raich Carter's League debut came at inside-left against Sheffield Wednesday — he replaced Bob Gurney who had 'flu — on 15 October 1932 at Hillsborough, where the Owls won 3-1. He retained his place for the following week's game, a North-East derby at Middlesbrough, and was to be a regular in the Sunderland first team until the League was suspended when war broke out in September 1939.

By then, Raich Carter had won every major honour then open to an English footballer — full international caps, League championship winners' medal and FA Cup winners' medal. He was 20 when he made his England debut, against Scotland at Wembley in April 1934, and afterwards he chose £6 rather than a commemorative medal — a player could have one or the other but not both and Carter was still his family's breadwinner.

When Sunderland won the championship in 1935-36, Carter scored 31 League goals which made him the First Division's joint leading scorer alongside his teammate Reg Gurney and Grimsby Town's Pat Glover. And Carter would probably have been leading scorer outright but for the fact that he had to miss the last two games of the season after being suspended for seven days following a sending off at Middlesbrough in a stormy North-East derby match

Appointed skipper of Sunderland at the start of the following season, Carter led the Wearsiders to victory in the 1937 FA Cup

Final, when they beat Preston 3-1 at Wembley with Carter scoring the goal which gave his side the lead after they had fallen behind.

On the Monday before the Cup Final, Raich Carter had been married, coincidentally as it turned out, at Derby, where his childhood sweetheart Rose Marsh now lived with her parents. The Marshes had moved to Chaddesden and it was that happy coincidence which was to bring Carter to the Baseball Ground during the war.

When Carter and the rest of his Sunderland teammates travelled to London for a First Division game against Arsenal on Friday 1, September 1939, their train was full of army reservists, for the international situation was worsening by the minute as Europe stood on the brink of another war. The following day the Gunners won 5-1 — Derby beat Aston Villa 1-0 at the Baseball Ground that same afternoon — and the Sunderland players were at the Russell Hotel on the Sunday morning when they gathered around the wireless to hear Prime Minister Neville Chamberlain announce that Britain was now at war with Germany.

So Raich Carter's Sunderland career was all but ended. Including those three games of the aborted 1939-40 season he had made 279 senior appearances for the Roker club and scored 130 goals which included three hat-tricks. He was to make another 26 appearances in wartime football, scoring 33 goals, before his Sunderland days were finally over.

When war was declared, the Football League closed down and Carter, along with the rest of his Sunderland colleagues, was given half a week's wages and told that he was finished with the club, at least for the duration of the war. With no income he had to act quickly and so he

Raich Carter at the wheel of an Auxiliary Fire Service engine. He joined the AFS when war broke out and served for two years in Sunderland, which was badly bombed, before transferring to the Royal Air Force.

In the summer of 1946, Carter had a brief excursion into county cricket. Here is the Derbyshire team which met Worcestershire at Stourbridge. Back row: Walter Fulwood, Bert Rhodes, Charlie Elliott (who also played football for and managed Coventry City), Alan Revell, scorer, Cliff Gladwin, George Pope, Arnold Townsend. Front: Raich Carter, Denis Smith, Stan Worthington, Albert Alderman (who also played for the Rams), and Bill Copson.

joined the Fire Service, although the wages of £3 per week did not go far. As a professional footballer he had been earning £8 per week.

Carter's decision to join the Fire Service rather than one of the Armed Services earned him the scorn of football fans and when he resumed playing in the early days of the war, his ears burned as taunts were directed at him from the terraces.

He said later: "I'm not proud of my war service and admit I made a mistake. I should have tried to get into one of the services as soon as possible."

He sells himself short, though. For a start, the Fire Service was uncomfortable and dangerous work as the German blitz on the North-East began. And although many big-name professional sportsmen did join up immediately, the majority had relatively comfortable jobs as PT instructors well away from any kind of danger. Two exceptions were Derby's Jack Stamps and Tim Ward. As a gunner in the Royal Artillery, Stamps was one of the last men to be lifted off the Dunkirk beach in 1940 as the BEF retreated in the face of a German onslaught; and Ward, in the Royal Army Medical Corps, was wounded in Normandy shortly after D Day in 1944.

Carter guested for Huddersfield Town before finally joining up in October 1941, when he reported to Blackpool for basic training in the RAF. After passing a PT instructor's course at St Athan he was posted to a fighter operational training

Scotland goalkeeper Crozier dives at Carter's feet during a wartime international at Wembley in 1944.

Overshadowed by goalkeeper Frank Swift, Carter shakes hands with Mr Ernest Bevin before the start of the international against France at Highbury on 3 May 1947, when England won 3-0.

unit near Sunderland and began playing for his old club in wartime football. In 1942 he played for the RAF against Hibernian and renewed his pre-war England partnership with Stanley Matthews.

When wartime internationals began, the 'England' team was drawn half from the Army and half from the RAF. Carter considered it possibly the best England team ever, because the players, instead of being drawn from several clubs, actually played alongside each other most weeks in Services football.

In 1943, Carter's home in Sunderland was badly damaged during an air-raid and his wife moved to her parents' home in Chaddesden. Her health had not been good since the birth of their daughter Jennifer, that year and, naturally, Raich Carter wanted to see more of his family, so he asked permission to play for the Rams.

Soon afterwards he was posted to RAF Innsworth Lane in Gloucestershire and in October 1943 he made his debut for Derby County as a guest player. His first appearance was against Birmingham in a Football League North game at the Baseball Ground, where 8,000 fans saw him make a memorable first debut, scoring a hat-trick as the Blues were beaten 5-3 with Jack Stamps scoring the other two. By the end of the season, Carter had made 14 appearances and scored 13 goals.

Each week the Rams organised free seats for two coach loads of airmen recuperating at RAF Loughborough. It struck Carter that helping them back to full fitness would be worthwhile work and in the summer of 1944 he was posted there, to the No.3 Medical Rehabilitation Unit.

Already working at the Loughborough rehabilitation centre was another airman, the brilliant pre-war inside-forward of Manchester City and Northern Ireland, Peter Doherty, Carter suggested that Doherty, too, guested for Derby and on 26 August 1944, in a goalless draw against Nottingham Forest at the City Ground, arguably the best inside-forward pairing ever to appear in English club football turned out for the Rams for the first time.

By the end of that season the pair had helped Derby to win the Midlands Cup. In those topsy-turvy wartime days there were several regionalised competitions, some games in the league also counting towards two and even three other competitions. The Midlands Cup was sandwiched into the last month of the 1944-45 season and for the Rams began with a 2-1 defeat at Northampton Town. But each tie was a two-legged affair and back at the Baseball Ground, goals from Carter (two), Duncan (two) and Doherty (from the penalty spot) helped the Rams to a 6-2 aggregate victory.

The semi-final saw Leicester City beaten 5-2 on aggregate, on 19 May 1945, a Carter hat-trick gave Derby a 3-0 win over Aston Villa in the first leg of the Midlands Cup Final at Villa Park. For the second leg, Carter was on England duty but Doherty more than made up for the absence of his partner, scoring five of the Rams' six goals in the second leg at the Baseball Ground. In all, Carter (29) and Doherty (35) had scored 64 goals for the Rams in their first season together as Derby players.

By now the war in Europe was over — both Carter and Doherty played in the VE Day celebration match against Nottingham Forest at the Baseball Ground when Doherty's goals earned the

Rams a 2-2 draw — and on the eve of the following season, Japan surrendered but the Football League decided to carry on with the guest player system for another season to allow clubs to retrieve their players from the services and generally regroup.

The FA, however, decided that the FA Cup should restart and it was that which led both Raich Carter and Peter Doherty to be officially transferred to the Rams in December 1945, in time to be eligible for the third round of the Cup in January, when the Rams were due to meet Luton Town over two legs.

Both men had fallen out with their respective clubs. Carter, now 31, wanted to safeguard his financial future and asked Sunderland for his accrued share of a second benefit from 1936 to the outbreak of war, and then for a ten-year contract which would ensure him two more benefits. Remember these were the days of a maximum wage for footballers.

Carter explained: "I didn't think I was asking for the moon. Without any false modesty, I had done a lot for Sunderland and I thought they would meet me. Instead they agreed to place me on the transfer list.

"From the viewpoint of personal convenience, apart from the fact that I had guested for them during the war, the club I naturally hoped to go to then was Derby County; and I was very pleased when I saw a newspaper report that they had made an offer for me.

"Sunderland, however, sat on the offer for some weeks and I didn't know what was going to happen until I was leaving Loughborough on 14 days' Christmas leave. It was the morning of 21 December 1945, my 32nd birthday as it happened, when an airman caught me up with a message that I was to meet the Derby directors in a hotel in Derby as soon as possible.

"They told me that my transfer to the Rams was almost complete and that they were just waiting for a telephone call from Sunderland, confirming a couple of small points. Midnight that night was zero hour for transfers so far as the FA Cup was concerned.

"Eventually it was agreed that Jack Catterall, the Derby secretary, and I should set off for Sunderland with the transfer forms in any case. We reached York just after eight o'clock that evening and telephoned Derby. The deal had been finalised and now we had to get to Sunderland and get the forms signed before midnight.

"It was a 90 minute run, which left us plenty of time, but to our dismay we found the platform crowded and we couldn't get near the Sunderland train. Despairingly we watched it steam away and then Catterall went outside the station and began bargaining with the taxi drivers until he found one who had enough petrol — remember these were still wartime conditions — and who would be prepared to race through the night on roads far removed from today's dual carriageways.

"We drew up at the Grand Hotel in Sunderland with an hour to spare. The Sunderland officials were waiting for us and the forms were signed. Then the taxi took us back to York so that we could catch a train back to Derby and I could travel with the Derby team to Birmingham the following day.

"We lost 1-0 at St Andrew's and I had a bad game, not surprising after the trials of the previous 24 hours. I think I cost £6,000 and Sunderland were silly to let me go for so little, just as Derby were lucky to get me. Still, I felt that, overall, things had worked out alright for me, considering Sunderland's attitude."

Peter Doherty also cost the Rams around £6,000 after being officially transferred from Manchester City the same month. Doherty, too, had fallen out with his club, who, astonishingly, had at one point refused him permission to guest for Derby County — but told him that he could play for their bitter rivals Manchester United! Doherty pointed out that if he could get back to Manchester that easily, then he might as well play for City.

Four months after being transferred to the Rams, Raich Carter and Peter Doherty had helped the club to their first-ever FA Cup Final success, when they beat Charlton Athletic 4-1 after extra-time at Wembley. On the eve of the Final, Carter's father-in-law passed away but Carter's wife insisted that the news was kept from her husband until after the game.

There had also been controversy when Carter and Doherty, two experienced men in the Rams camp, led a threat to strike after the Rams board tried to palm the players' wives off with cheap tickets in a uncovered part of the stadium while the directors' wives sat in comfort. "No tickets, no game," said Carter. And the tickets were quickly produced.

Outside-right Reg Harrison, the young replacement for the injured England star Sammy Crooks, will never forget Raich Carter's influence on the Rams camp. "We got off the coach and he just shouted, "Cup winners in town!' He said, "Don't worry, we'll beat this lot!" And I thought, well if Raich says we can . . .

Doherty scored one of the Rams' goals that day, his tenth in the Cup that season, and although Carter did not manage to get on the score-sheet at Wembley, he was top scorer overall with 12. It was arguably the greatest day in the Rams' history and the pinnacle of what became known as the 'Carter-Doherty' era, although by Christmas 1946, Doherty had left. After only 15 peacetime League games he was transferred to Huddersfield Town after the Rams board refused him permission to take over the licence of the Arboretum Hotel near the Baseball Ground.

For Raich Carter, the summer of 1946 was a particularly enjoyable one. An excellent cricketer, he had made his Minor Counties debut with 44 runs in an hour for Durham at Headingley, against a Yorkshire 2nd XI for whom a young opener called Len Hutton made 48 in two hours and ten minutes. Playing for the Hendon club he was known as 'the Gilbert Jessop of Durham cricket' as he smashed runs all over the Durham League. Against the 1934 Australian

tourists, however, he was out cheaply to Fleetwood-Smith and was then told to clear off when he went to the Australian dressing-room to get their autographs after the game.

In the first peacetime County Championship season of 1946, Carter made three appearances for Derbyshire, against Worcestershire, Surrey and Northamptonshire, and took two wickets in the first game, against Worcestershire. But first-class cricket was a different proposition to Minor Counties and league, and after that Carter restricted his summer activities to turning out for the Rams cricket team.

In 1946-47, Carter won his first full England caps as a Rams player — he had been capped twice in Victory internationals after joining Derby — and altogether he won seven caps as a Rams player to add to the six he had gained with Sunderland before the war. It was scant reward for a player of his talent and, to add insult to injury, all his pre-war caps had been destroyed during a German air-raid on Sunderland.

At the end of the season, in which the Rams finished 14th in the First Division, Carter had scored 19 goals in 33 League games to finish as the club's leading scorer ahead of Jack Stamps and Frank Broome, who each had 17 goals to their credit. He also scored twice in the Cup but the Rams' defence of the trophy came to an end in the fifth round at Anfield.

The following season of 1947-48 proved to be Raich Carter's last with Derby County. He was nearing the end of his career and although the Rams board had hinted that they might find him a job when his playing days were over, when he saw an advertisement inviting applications for the post of manager of a League club, he replied.

The club was Leeds United and Carter was invited for an interview. Things seemed to be going well until Carter said that he was looking for a five-year contract. Leeds were offering only a three-year deal and said they would think about it. A week later, Carter received a letter telling him that the Leeds directors

Carter, in Derby's colours, watches as Chelsea goalkeeper Harry Medhurst collects a cross at Stamford Bridge in 1947.

had decided to leave the matter until the end of the season.

The player, meanwhile, was still playing regular First Division football for the Rams, who were to finish fourth that season and reach another FA Cup semi-final. But after news that he had been interviewed by Leeds, Carter was the target of several clubs and it was clear that he would soon be leaving Derby. The most lucrative offer came from Notts County — Tommy Lawton accepted a similar one to join the Meadow Lane club — but Carter was still undecided. Nottingham Forest and Hull City both wanted him as player-assistant manager to Billy Walker and Major Frank Buckley respectively, and those jobs excited Carter more.

The pressure from other clubs was now intense and the Rams board decided to rest Carter from the team to meet Liverpool at the Baseball Ground on Monday, 31 March 1948. When he arrived at the ground he was greeted by representatives form Hull City and the deal was struck for him to move to

Boothferry Park as a player and assistant to the legendary Major Buckley.

It meant that Raich Carter had played his last match for the Rams. It had come 48 hours earlier against Blackpool at the Baseball Ground and, fittingly, Carter had scored the only goal of the game in front of 34,896 spectators.

In all he had scored 50 goals in only 83 League and FA Cup games for Derby County, with another 55 goals in wartime League and Cup games. His contribution had been remarkable, not just in statistical terms but in the entertainment and delight he had given Derby supporters who had flocked to see him play.

He had dominated almost every game in which he had played, a supremely confident performer — some said arrogant was a better description — who could dictate the pattern of play, who strolled the field like a true general directing his troops and who possessed a superb, powerful shot. He once said, "I liked to help everybody but I wasn't one for the goalmouth. I liked to hit them home from

One of Raich Carter's last appearances in a Derby County shirt, in the 1948 FA Cup semi-final against Manchester United at Hillsborough. Back row (left to right): Stuart McMillan (manager), Tim Ward, Bert Mozley, Leon Leuty, Jock Wallace, Don Howe, Chick Musson, Jack Poole (trainer). Front: Reg Harrison, Raich Carter, Jack Stamps, Billy Steel, Angus Morrison.

outside the penalty area. People remember those sort of goals."

With Hull, Carter continued in glorious fashion. Taking over from Buckley he steered the Tigers to the Third Division North title in front of huge crowds at Boothferry Park. Then came a short spell with Cork Athletic, with whom he gained an FA of Ireland Cup winners' medal.

Ironically, when he went back into League management it was with Leeds United, the club who had turned him down in 1948. He spent five years at Elland Road, taking Leeds back to Division One in 1956 after building his team around the brilliant John Charles. He was surprisingly dismissed in May 1958, after Leeds had slipped to 17th place in the top flight, but then he set Mansfield on the road to promotion from the Fourth Division before his final move, to manage Middlesbrough in January 1963. Alas, his time at Ayresome Park was the least successful of his football career

and 'Boro were on the brink of relegation to the Third Division for the first time in their history when he was sacked in February 1966.

Carter went to work in the sports department of a Hull store and then lived in semi-retirement in a delightful bungalow at Willerby near Hull. Visitors could always be assured of a warm welcome and he needed little bidding to bring out his carefully kept scrapbooks which contained practically every cutting from his debut as a Sunderland schoolboy footballer to more recent appearances at celebrity dinners.

Alas, in recent times his health has failed him and he now lives in a nursing home. But still his entrance into any room will turn heads. As someone said of the

Raich Carter leads out his new club, Hull City, shortly after joining the Tigers from Derby County.

articles which wrongly suggested that he was living like a pauper, looking to sell his international medals and cup winners' medals to make ends meet. None of it was true, just the all-too-familiar trend nowadays, a journalist looking for a sensational headline and never mind if it wasn't true, never mind who it hurt.

Raich Carter deserved better, not least for the enormous pleasure he had given to thousands.

But his epitaph should not be what he achieved in the game, but his great sensitivity. Tears would well into his eyes when he recalled his days at Sunderland, when thousands of out-of-work, hungry men would hammer their encouragement on the side of the bus carrying him to Roker Park early on a Saturday afternoon.

"They had no job, little food, rags to wear. But they scraped together the few pence it cost to come and watch us. It lit up just a little part of their dreadful lives. We had to turn it on for them, had to make that day more bearable than the rest. I was lucky. It could have been me. I'll never

distinguished silver-haired gentleman, "Without knowing what he did for a living, you still knew that, whatever it was, he would still be at the very top of his profession."

He was hurt by insensitive newspaper

Raich Carter with his old Rams colleague Peter Doherty, pictured in October 1984 at the 65th birthday party of Tommy Lawton, the former England centre-forward and a contemporary of the legendary Rams pair.

JACK STAMPS

DALLY DUNCAN

JACK CATTERALL

DAVID McCULLOCH

SAMMY CROOKS

BEN ROBSHAW

JACK HOWE

STUART McMILLAN

PETER DOHERTY

FRANK BOULTON

VIC WOODLEY

JAMES BULLIONS

RAICH CARTER

WALTER MUSSON

JACK PARR

JACK NICHOLAS

ANGUS MORRISON

REG HARRISON

DAVE WILLIS

LEON LEUTY

A local cartoonist produced these caricatures of the Rams staff just before the 1946 FA Cup Final.

Rams wing-half Tim Ward, watched by Billy Steel, is congratulated by Wolves' Billy Wright on being selected to play for England against Wales at Villa Park in 1947. The above took place before the Rams match at Molineux in September that year.

Bert's Baseball Ground Nightmare

Johnny Morris, Jack Stamps and Billy Steel, who orchestrated the Rams' brilliant performance against Manchester City.

WHEN Manchester City arrived at a waterlogged Baseball Ground on the first Saturday of December 1949, they were already a team in crisis after only four victories in their first 19 League games of that season. They also had a goalkeeping problem that was proving difficult to solve.

Their great England 'keeper Frank Swift, who had announced his retirement the previous season, had been called out to play in a handful of games at the start of 1949-50, and then City had given Ronnie Powell, who was later to serve Chesterfield so well, a dozen games before turning to one of the most controversial signings a club could have made in those very early post-war years.

Bert Trautmann, who had arrived in England as a German prisoner-of-war in April 1945, had shown such talent as a goalkeeper with St Helens Town FC that City had taken him on their books, despite howls of protest from many of their fans. It was a difficult time for Trautmann, who had served as a paratrooper in the German army. The majority of City's fans had suffered through the Nazi

Ken Oliver, signed to replace Leon Leuty at centre-half but found time to join in the Rams attack.

blitz on the city, and many of their supporters were also Jewish, so the signing of a German so soon after the end of hostilities was hard to swallow.

Trautmann made his debut in a 3-0 defeat at Burnden Park, then played in a rare victory — 4-0 over Birmingham City at Maine Road — before arriving at the Baseball Ground for only his third game in City's first team. The game turned out to be a nightmare for City, and for Trautmann in particular, as Derby County hammered in seven goals to record their biggest peacetime win since beating West Brom 9-3 back in December 1934.

Like City, the Rams had a disappointing start to the 1949-50 season. After finishing third in Division One the previous season, they had started with a 1-0 home defeat by Manchester United. Four consecutive defeats at the end of September and the beginning of October — including home reverses by Arsenal and Wolves — had dumped them in the bottom half of the table. But then three wins on the trot raised supporters' hopes and by the time struggling Manchester City came to Derby on a rainy day in early December, the Rams had lifted themselves into a midtable spot.

The match kicked-off at 2pm in those days before floodlights and 16 minutes into the match, Johnny Morris, the Rams British record signing from Manchester United, put them ahead, thanks to a fine pass by Jack Stamps and a bad mistake by Trautmann. Morris hit the ball from Stamps first time straight at Trautmann but the novice City goalkeeper could only knock it up in the air and then look back in anguish as it dropped over his head and trickled over the line.

Even then, however, there was no suggestion that this would be the start of a flood of goals and within 60 seconds of the restart, Stamps had missed a penalty for Derby. Nine minutes later, though, Stamps was on hand to make it 2-0 after Tommy Powell laid on a neat centre after previous good work by Chick Musson, who collected a weak clearance out of the City defence.

After 35 minutes it was 3-0. Another poor clearance fell to Johnny Poppitt, who pushed the ball to Tim Ward. The Rams' England wing-half found Morris and he fooled City centre-half Joe Fagan — who was later to manage Liverpool to further European glory — before taking the ball up to Trautmann and then around him and sliding home a neat shot at the near post.

In the second half the rout continued, although City did manage to hold out for half an hour. Then Hughie McLaren wriggled his way past Bert Sproston before squaring the ball to Stamps, who had a simple task to side-foot home the fourth Rams' goal.

Eight minutes from time, McLaren made it 5-0 after Morris went out to the left wing to rob Murray. Morris held the ball while McLaren ran into position and then gave him a direct passage to goal which the Rams winger took well.

It was the sheer persistence of Billy Steel, another British record signing by Derby, which gave McLaren his second goal five minutes later. He held off the combined challenge of Fagan, Phillips and Murray, then feinted to shoot before whipping the ball into the path of McLaren, who was cutting in. Trautmann was completely deceived and McLaren made it 6-0.

The final goal came in the last minute, when Steel dribbled his way down the middle — despite the awful state of the pitch — and then drew Trautmann out of his goal, hooking the ball round the goalkeeper and the coolly pushing it into the unguarded net.

The *Derby Evening Telegraph* opened its Monday evening report thus: 'Sweet music at the Baseball Ground on Saturday. It was goal music, seven-in-a-net rhythm, as played by the Morris, Stamps, Steel trio augmented by the Rampant Rams combined goal-harmonic orchestra — with emphasis on the combined. For Manchester City, the main tune was the "blues" — and did they have to dance to it? The new Derby suite started at 2.16pm, when maestro Morris waltzed his way through to put his men on top form, and

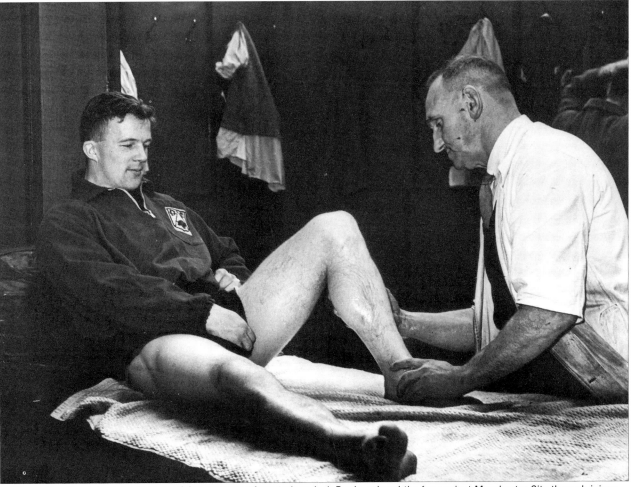

Winger Reg Harrison, seen here receiving treatment from trainer Jack Poole, missed the fun against Manchester City through injury.

from then to the end of the performance 89 minutes later, the "orchestra" never struck a wrong note.'

Rams goalkeeper Billy Townsend scarcely had a shot to save all afternoon, while centre-half Ken Oliver, signed from Sunderland for nearly £7,000 to take over from the classy Leon Leuty, found time to link up with the attack as the Rams surged forward.

At the end of the season, City were relegated while the Rams finished in 11th place. And five weeks after the seven-goal hammering of City at the Baseball Ground, Derby scored another five past them at Maine Road, in the third round of the FA Cup. Bert Trautmann missed that one though and Ronnie Powell was the luckless goalkeeper on that occasion.

Trautmann, of course, went on to become a legend in English football, winning over the fans and making 545 League and FA Cup appearances for City, collecting a Cup winners' medal at Wembley in 1956 when he finished the Final against Birmingham City with a broken neck.

The Rams in 1949-50, when Chick Musson missed only one game. Back row (left to right): Tim Ward, Bert Mozley, Bill Townsend, Jack Parr, Ken Oliver, Chick Musson. Front: Les Mynard, Johnny Morris, Jack Stamps, Billy Steel, Hugh McLaren.

Wonderful Tribute to a Great Clubman

THE year 1955 will go down in Derby County's history as one of the most miserable in the club's history with relegation from Division Two after a truly awful season. But there were far greater tragedies to strike Derby County the year, when Cup winners Chick Musson and Leon Leuty died, both young men and both suffering from leukemia.

Musson, the fierce little ball-winning wing-half from Kilburn, had clocked up 280 League and FA Cup appearances for the Rams before being appointed player-manager of the Loughborough club, Brush Sports, in June 1954. Alas, within ten months he was dead, only 34 years old when he became the first member of that glorious 1946 Cup Final team to pass away.

Musson died in April 1955, and in

Musson files out of the dressing-room ready to do battle for the Rams once more. Behind him are Jack Stamps and Jack Howe.

December the same year, 35-year-old Leuty died of the same illness in Nottingham General Hospital. Leuty, an England 'B' centre-half, had made 158 senior appearances for the Rams before joining Bradford for the big fee of £20,000 in March 1950. Six months later he became a Notts County player for £25,000.

Both names were already writ large in the Rams' history. Not only as members of the Cup-winning side, but as fine players in their own right. Indeed, Leuty had been kept out of the full England side only by the presence of the great Neil Franklin of Stoke City and is universally regarded as the best post-war Rams number-five until the emergence of Roy McFarland.

In the autumn of 1955, when floodlit football was still something of a novelty — the Rams arranged several games under lights against Scottish League clubs — a crowd of well over 21,000 packed the Baseball Ground to see Derby, now a Third Division North side for the first time in the club's history, take on an All-Star team in aid of Chick Musson's dependents.

The game brought several former Rams stars back to the Baseball Ground and *Derby Evening Telegraph* reporter Wilf Shaw told his readers all about it.

'Mrs Ruby Musson and her 11-year-old boy, Melvyn, sat in the stand at the Baseball Ground last night to see and hear 21,350 football fans pay a 100 per cent tribute to a 100 per cent player — her late husband and Melvyn's father 'Chick', the former Derby County wing-half. Gate receipts totalled £2,333 1s 6d, and after approximately £500 has been deducted for tax, Mrs Musson will receive about £1,800.

'Soon after Derby County had won an amazing and highly entertaining game against the All Stars by 9-5, she said a simple and sincere 'Thank You' to members of both teams. Let Raich Carter and Peter Doherty the Rams' inside-forwards of their 1946 FA Cup triumph, reply for everyone concerned with the organisation of the game.

'Peter told me: "Chick was worth it, he was a wonderful clubman."

'Raich said: "He gave Derby great and loyal service. Everyone of us is proud to have played with him, and for Mrs Musson tonight."

'The present-day Rams scored nine of the 14 goals, but they were quick to pay tribute to the old Rams — there were ten former Derby County players in the All Stars side — for the glimpses they provided, the football that carried the world-class hallmark for everything but speed.

'Carter reminded everyone that it is better to make the ball do the work by using it accurately without trying to beat two or three opponents, and promptly nipping into an open space to be in a position to start using it again. So did Doherty, and there was an abundance of defensive artistry too — from Jack Parr and Jack Howe, and wing-halves Tim Ward and Joe Mercer.

'Much of their understanding was as though they were linked by tele-communications; they provided high-stature wizardry but, alas, too often their legs just could not move with the alertness the brain worked.

'The Rams supplied the speed and, to their credit, some of the good football. Powell, in particular, and Pye, I thought were two present-day players who could have changed jerseys and not looked out of place. Powell's goal, a calculated chip over the head of the advancing goalkeeper, was certainly in the tradition of the old masters.

'The opening minute provided a roar the like of which has not been heard on the ground for a long time. Carter had possession of the ball, Doherty received a similar welcome, but after the two of them had provided a back-heel and flicks which are rarely seen today, the Rams' power football brought them six goals in 20 minutes.

'The margin narrowed to 6-3 by half-time, before which an Ackerman shot hit one upright and a Parry drive hit the other within two seconds of each other.

'After the interval, as they had done before it, the Rams made intelligent use of the long ball against the offside trap of Parr and Howe, scoring three more goals in 20 minutes while the Stars replied with two.

'There were moments of comedy especially when the now rotund Carter was vainly appealing for penalties and a remarkable example of penalty kick strategy seconds before half-time when, after Webster had protested in vain that he had not pushed Jimmy Hagan, Doherty took the spot kick, but only rolled the ball a couple of yards to his left for Hagan to dash up and score.

'In addition to Townsend, who replaced Frank Swift (an influenza victim) in the All Stars goal at short notice, Burton Albion player-manager Reg Weston was a last-minute deputy for Blackburn Rovers

Former Rams star Tim Ward leads out the All Star XI for the game in aid of Chick Musson's dependents. Following him are some of Musson's former teammates, Bill Townsend, Frank Broome and Reg Harrison.

manager Johnny Carey, who was unable to travel.

'The crowd was the second biggest the All Stars have played before. The biggest to date is 33,000 at Leeds.

'Most of the turnstile operators and other members of the ground staff gave their services free.'

Derby County: Webster; Barrowcliffe, Upton, Clarke, Oliver, Ryan, Tate, Parry, Ackerman, Pye, Powell.

All Stars XI: Townsend; Parr, Howe, Ward, Weston, Mercer, Harrison, Carter, Hagan, Doherty, Broome.

Referee: Mr F.L.Overton (Derby).

Goals timetable: Derby County: Ackerman (9, 25 and 65 mins), Parry (15 and 29 mins), Pye (30 mins), Weston own-goal (28 mins), Powell (51 mins) and Parr own-goal (53 mins). All Stars: Doherty (35 and 46 mins), Hagan (41 and 44 mins) and Carter (54 mins).

Action from a Forest-Rams game at the City Ground in October 1904 when the Rams won 1-0 with a goal from Fred Barker, who died the following month at a tragically young age. He had scored twice in his four appearances for the Rams, both times against Forest.

East Midlands Rivals

Rams v. Forest Encounters

1892-1994

THE East Midlands 'derby' match doesn't quite have the fervour and passion of a same-city derby such as Liverpool versus Everton, Sheffield's United-Wednesday clash or a permutation of Black Country rivalry, notably Albion v Villa or Wolves. The two cities aren't quite close enough for that, but the Derby County fixture with Nottingham Forest has taken on something resembling this kind of feverish, importance in the eyes of many supporters, heavily beefed-up by the Clough factor in more recent years.

Indeed, there are a lot of Rams supporters who go to great lengths to mock their near neighbours from 16 miles to the east. Some avoid the colour red altogether, even to the point of removing red Opal Fruits from a packet before eating them.

Support, too, for each side had occasionally wavered in those delicate areas around Ilkeston, Alfreton, Heanor, Kegworth and many other settlements along Derbyshire's eastern frontier. In the 1970s the Rams had the

Kevin Hector glides through the Forest defence at the City Ground in October 1971, when goals from Hinton and Robson gave the Rams a 2-0 win.

pulling power but the 1980s saw a reversal in the trend in those areas.

It was all a little different in years gone by, with very moderate attendances at the Baseball Ground, and it wasn't until Forest's 17th visit to Derby for a League game that the attendance rose above 20,000, that in 1921-22.

The sides had first met in the Rams first season, 1884-85 when Derby had a list of friendly fixtures. County ran out winners by a 6-1 margin with a hat trick for a Repton schoolmaster, one John Barrington Trapnell Chevallier at Forest's Lenton ground on 31 January 1885. Derby were founder members of the Football League but the Nottingham club had to wait until 1892 to be accepted and from then the rivals met in earnest. Forest had much the better of those early exchanges, the Rams' first win over their neighbours being a 4-2 victory at the Racecourse in September 1894, the fifth encounter, with Johnny McMillan (2) Bloomer and Raybould on target. The following season Derby scored two big victories, 4-0 and 5-2 at home and away respectively with Bloomer hitting a hat-trick in each game, including the first between the sides.

Another three followed on Easter Monday 1898, a 5-0 home win five days before the sides met at The Crystal Palace for the Rams first FA Final appearance. Alas, the earlier victory over a slightly weakened Forest side, raised false hopes and the Reds won 3-1 in the Final, Bloomer netting the Rams' goal.

For the next few seasons, Derby had a particularly lean time in the fixture, winning only two out of 12 from 1898 to 1904, including a 6-2 home defeat and 5-1 away hammering in 1903-04.

Various promotions and relegations meant fewer League fixtures between the Rams and Forest, and between 1915 and 1969 the two sides were in the same divisions in only four seasons. In the FA Cup, however, Derby's attendance record was broken when 37,830 packed into the Baseball Ground to witness 'Spider' Halford and Jack Bowers score the goals that knocked Forest out in the fourth round in January 1936, when Forest were a Second Division club. (The Nottingham outfit were without top-flight football for 32 years between 1925 and 1957).

There has never been quite so much sustained interest in Nottingham as Derby regarding the importance of the fixture. When the sides met at the City Ground in November 1954, the attendance was only 16,386, (The Notts County match drew in 30,198 six weeks earlier). However, when Derby and Forest met again after a 14-year gap, circumstances had altered dramatically. The Rams were in the ascendancy after storming to the Second Division championship, whilst Forest, after some good years, were about to slide.

Derby were attracting their biggest-ever attendances but, surprisingly, lost 2-0 at home in front of 38,225 on 29 November 1969, the seventh-highest League crowd of the season at the Baseball Ground. Revenge was sweet, however, as 42,074 saw the Rams cruise to a 3-1 triumph at the City Ground with goals from O'Hare, Durban and O'Kane (own-goal). In November 1970, O'Hare scored in Nottingham again, along with McGovern, Wignall and Gemmill as the Rams ran out

John Robertson, later to sign for Derby, scores from the penalty spot at the Baseball Ground in November 1979, but the Rams, on their way to relegation from the old First Division, scored a famous victory over their high-riding neighbours.

4-2 winners, although they lost at the Baseball Ground in the return in March.

The 1971-72 season — Derby's first championship season — saw the rampant Rams do the double on their Trentside rivals for the first time since 1925-26. In October 1971, goals from Robson and Hinton (penalty) gave Derby an away win at Forest for the last time, Steve Powell starting a League match for the first time, aged 16 years 40 days that afternoon.

In February, Derby ran out 4-0 winners, starting a run of five straight League wins as the championship race hotted up. Forest, at the time, were heading for relegation and were not considered a particularly big attraction in Derby, unlike today. A crowd of 31,801 saw the home match, but larger crowds were in evidence against other nearby clubs Wolves, Leicester and Stoke, with the Forest clash only the 13th highest attendance in a championship season.

The Reds dropped out of the top flight in 1972 and faded further from Derby's minds as the Rams basked in glory. Games against Leicester temporarily took over as

the 'big one' locally, until former Rams manager Brian Clough was appointed at the City Ground in January 1975. Many supporters on the eastern side of Derby drifted towards Nottingham as Clough halted the Forest decline and brought them back to Division One in 1977.

The Rams were now slipping as managerial changes and a high turnover of players took hold. The Derby-Forest clash was now definitely the match of the season as the Rams slumped 3-0 in September at Nottingham, before a goalless home draw in front of 33,384 in January 1978. The Rams' rivals won the championship four months later and Derby struggled to hold on to their more fickle fans as Clough scaled domestic and European heights at the City Ground.

Eventually, Derby were relegated in 1979-80 but the performance of the season came at the Baseball Ground in October when the Rams hammered the Reds 4-1. On a sour note it was a Frank Gray goal in the return in April that sealed Derby's fate.

The next local derby was to be in the FA

45

Nearly four years later, the Rams achieved another memorable Baseball Ground victory over Forest, this time in the FA Cup. Brian Clough, returning to the scene of many of his triumphs, studiously ignores the battery of cameras.

Cup, when Derby and Forest were paired in the third round in January 1983. Billed as 'Clough v Taylor' the match was a classic as an unfavoured Second Division Rams outfit played out of their skins to beat their more illustrious neighbours 2-0 with goals from an Archie Gemmill free-kick and reserve striker Andy Hill. It was an afternoon to savour, made all the more spicy by the acrimonious parting between the former managerial pair, a rift sadly never to be healed.

Over four years passed before Derby bounced back into top-flight football but victories over Forest have been hard to come by since then. Only in 1990-91, another relegation season for the Rams, did Derby manage to beat their rivals. This was a 2-1 triumph when Craig Ramage, in perhaps his finest moment for his local side, scored an equaliser before Dean Saunders put Rams fans in jubilant mood with a terrific headed winner.

The 1993-94 season saw both sides in the new First Division, with Forest relegated from the Premiership and Clough retired from football. In August, Derby led through a Micky Forsyth goal at the City Ground, only to be pegged back to 1-1, whilst Forest won by two goals to nil the return in April, tension stifling the Rams play and individual blunders costing dear. In the end, Forest were promoted automatically, as runners-up to Crystal Palace, whilst the Rams failed in the Play-off Final at Wembley against Leicester, other East Midlands rivals.

Steve Bloomer is easily the top goal-scorer in the history of the Derby-Forest encounters. He scored 27 League and Cup goals including three hat-tricks. Alf Bentley hit an FA Cup treble in 1908-09 for the Rams but no Forest player has ever scored a hat-trick against Derby.

Archie Gemmill scores a brilliant goal from a free-kick against his old club and the Rams are on their way to a Cup sensation.

Derby County v Nottingham Forest the Results 1892-1894

	Home			Away	
Season	Result	Attendance		Result	Attendance
1892-93	2-3	8,500		0-1	12,000
1893-94	3-4	6,500		2-4	10,000
1894-95	4-2	6,000		1-2	6,000
1895-96	4-0	6,000		5-2	9,000
1896-97	1-1	5,500		2-1	5,000
1897-98	5-0	12,000		4-3	10,000
1898-99	2-0	3,000		3-3	8,000
1899-1900	2-2	12,000		1-4	10,000
1900-01	0-0	12,000		0-1	17,000
1901-02	1-1	13,000		1-3	8,000
1902-03	0-1	10,000		3-2	20,000
1903-04	2-6	7,000		1-5	10,000
1904-05	3-2	5,000		1-0	15,000
1905-06	2-2	15,000		0-0	12,000
1911-12	1-0	14,000		3-1	33,500
1914-15	1-0	14,000		2-2	15,000
1921-22	1-2	22,803		0-3	28,000
1925-26	2-0	19,076		2-1	19,549
1953-54	1-2	21,961		2-4	31,397
1954-55	1-2	18,772		0-3	16,652

1969-70	0-2	38,225	3-1	42,074
1970-71	1-2	34,857	4-2	30,539
1971-72	4-0	31,801	2-0	37,170
1977-78	0-0	33,384	0-3	28,807
1978-79	1-2	30,156	1-1	34,256
1979-80	4-1	27,729	0-1	32,266
1987-88	0-1	22,394	1-2	25,017
1988-89	0-2	25,174	1-1	24,818
1989-90	0-2	24,176	1-2	24,060
1990-91	2-1	21,729	0-1	25,109
1993-94	0-2	19,300	1-1	26,684

	P	W	D	L	F	A	W	D	L	F	A
Total											
League	62	11	6	14	50	45	10	6	15	47	60

FA Cup

Season	Round	Result	Venue	Attendance
1897-98	F	1-3	Crystal P	62,017
1908-09	4 (QF)	3-0	(h)	16,000
1927-28	4	0-0	(a)	22,594
	4R	0-2	(a)	35,625
1935-36	4	2-0	(h)	37,830
1982-83	3	2-0	(h)	28,494

League Cup

1985-86	3	1-2	(h)	22,226

Peter Taylor is ecstatic as victory over Forest is assured.

Dean Saunders celebrates the Rams' second goal against Forest at the Baseball Ground in November 1990.

Saying Their Last Farewell to the Baseball Ground

FOOTBALLERS' careers vary enormously in length and these days most players will move around several clubs, but eventually they will play their final game. There have been many interesting circumstances behind farewell appearances involving Derby County players over the years and some are detailed below.

SAMMY CROOKS and **DALLY DUNCAN** were 38 and 36 years old respectively when the 1946-47 season opened after seven years without League competition. Two of the greatest of Derby's pre-war stars, they were to make only five post-war League appearances between them and the two Rams legends both bowed out, as it transpired, in a 2-1 home defeat by Blackpool on 28 September 1946.

PETER DOHERTY made only 25 peacetime appearances for Derby County before the FA Cup hero fell out with the Rams directors, who refused him permission to take on the licence of the Arboretum Hotel on Osmaston Road. Doherty felt he had no option but to leave and, after protracted negotiations involving the Irishman's former clubs, Manchester City and Blackpool (where he still lived), a deal was struck with Huddersfield Town. Doherty was named in the programme as a Town player against Aston Villa on Boxing Day 1946, but the deal had not been completed and the inside-forward was instead summoned by police message to the Baseball Ground. Doherty was 'extremely surprised' to be told he must play for Derby against Everton. The directors had hoped that he had a change of heart about leaving, but as he said later, "My Irish obstinacy would never have permitted me to change my mind." He did, however, make that last appearance against Everton, scoring twice in a 5-1 Rams win.

STEVE EMERY's Derby County career was ended by a wild tackle from Rotherham United's Gerry Gow at Millmoor on 2 February 1982. Emery broke his leg, while Gow was ordered off and barracked relentlessly on all his subsequent visits to the Baseball Ground.

JACK FRYER is one of two Rams players to bow out with the club after an FA Cup Final. Unfortunately for the goalkeeper known as the 'Cromford Giant' or 'String', his finale saw Derby on the receiving end of the record score in an FA Cup Final as Bury put six past the beleaguered County at the Crystal Palace in 1903. Fryer didn't let in all six, though, as he left the field on two occasions, permanently after 68 minutes, and grave doubts were expressed for years about whether he should have played at all. He was carrying a groin injury and some colleagues said Fryer was selfishly protecting his star status, although the 'keeper claimed he had been practically forced to play by manager Harry Newbold and his directors. In May 1903, a few weeks after the Final, Fryer moved to Fulham. Five years earlier

Phil Gee, made his last full appearance in a Cup thriller against Aston Villa and scored twice.

JIMMY TURNER made his last Rams appearance in the club's first FA Cup Final when Nottingham Forest beat them 3-1, also at the Crystal Palace.

Although he made one brief further appearance as a substitute, Rams striker **PHIL GEE** last started a match for Derby in the FA Cup fourth-round tie against Aston Villa at the Baseball Ground on 5 February 1992. The former painter and decorator from Pelsall scored twice in the thrilling 4-3 defeat but was about to make way for the expensive signings which Lionel Pickering's cash injection provided.

PAUL GODDARD went into his last game for Derby County on Boxing Day 1989 as the Rams' joint leading scorer with Dean Saunders. Derby lost 1-0 at home to Everton but Rams' supporters would see Goddard in action only five days later, on New Year's Day 1990 when he made his debut for Millwall *against* Derby at The Den after being controversially sold by Arthur Cox to the Lions for £800,000. While the player never settled at Millwall, Derby County plummeted down the First Division table and many fans saw the move as the start of

Jack 'String' Fryer, who last game for Derby was an FA Cup Final which produced a record score and controversy about whether Fryer was fit to play.

Paul Goddard was joint leading scorer when he made his last appearance. Five days later he was lining up against the Rams for Millwall.

the Rams' most recent decline.

RICHARD GOULOOZE was signed by Arthur Cox from Dutch football in 1992. The bald-headed midfield player developed a short-lived cult following with the crowd, a strange chant of his surname accompanying his every touch. However, it became obvious that Goulooze wasn't suited to the pace of the English game and he made some alarming errors, particularly in his own penalty area. The Dutchman made his final first-team appearance, though, on the grand stage of Wembley Stadium in the Anglo-Italian Cup Final against Cremonese on 27 March 1993, during which Cox observed: "He seemed to be on another planet at times."

Diminutive goalkeeper **LES GREEN** was dropped after the 4-4 home draw with Manchester United on the snowy Boxing Day of 1970. It brought to an end an unbroken run of 129 first-team appearances, Green was never selected again and his League career was over.

Record appearance holder **KEVIN HECTOR** marked his last game for the Rams — in his second spell with the club — with the goal against Watford to clinch a 3-2 victory on 15 May 1982, thus ensuring Derby of Second Division survival after a relegation battle.

GORDON HUGHES had been ever-present in Brian Clough's first season at

Gordon Hughes signs for Derby manager Tim Ward. Hughes had survived Brian Clough's arrival to the extent that he was an ever-present until the League Cup semi-final against Leeds. Then Hughes, too, was on his way from the Baseball Ground.

Derby until the League Cup semi-final second leg against Leeds United at Elland Road on 7 February 1968. Elimination from the competition left Clough free to look to the future — some of his star players had been Cup-tied — and the busy winger Hughes was sold to Lincoln City in March with the Rams looking to Alan Hinton for their wing inspiration.

FRANCIS LEE had only two minutes of his Football League career remaining on 24 April 1976 as Derby County led Ipswich Town 4-2 at Portman Road. This, however, was no obstacle to the great former England striker finding the net twice before the final whistle. A fitting finale to Lee's 500th and last game.

DAVE MACKAY's last game for Derby against West Bromwich Albion on 1 May 1971 marked the first time in the long career of the 'iron man' that he had been an ever-present in a League season.

ROY McFARLAND appeared in 530 matches for Derby County, yet his last game was one of the least glorious and is now largely forgotten. He came on as substitute for Graham Harbey during a 3-0 drubbing against Portsmouth at a freezing cold Fratton Park on 10 December 1983. McFarland had originally left Derby in 1981 but was asked to pull on the famous white shirt in nine games of the disastrous 1983-84 relegation season (five of them as substitute). The Rams had re-registered the great centre-half as a player in an emergency during his time as team manager under Peter Taylor.

DON O'RIORDAN scored after coming on as a substitute for McFarland at St Andrew's when Derby lost 3-1 to Birmingham City on 22 October 1977. The Dubliner was never selected again and Tommy Docherty allowed him to leave four months later after featuring in only seven senior matches while at the Baseball Ground. O'Riordan went on to make in excess of 500 League appearances for nine different clubs and was still turning out for Torquay United in 1994. Thus the Rams lost another promising youngster who was to be a consistent

performer, and one the club must have wished it had held on to during the grim times in the early 1980s.

Goalkeeper **FRANK PAYNE** enjoyed an all-to-brief career with Derby County but it was a triumphant occasion when he made his only appearance in the Rams first team. On 4 February 1948, Derby hit a major injury snag. Goalkeeper Bill Townsend damaged his thumb in an accident at the Baseball Ground gymnasium. This came only three days prior to a crucial FA Cup fifth-round tie at Middlesbrough and the only fit 'keeper on the books was Payne, signed from Ollerton Colliery the previous December and with eight Central League games his only experience. At Ayresome Park, however, he did the Rams proud with a string of fine saves contributing greatly to a splendid 2-1 Derby win in front of a 43,000 crowd. Alas, the 21-year-old Payne was discarded immediately as Derby signed the veteran Blackpool custodian Jock Wallace — 16 years Payne's senior — to cover for Townsend and when the Rams played in the next round of the FA Cup against Queen's Park Rangers, Frank Payne was in the 'A' team at South Normanton Miners' Welfare. Payne played five League matches for Lincoln City in 1949-50 before drifting out of the professional game, his fleeting moment of glory already beginning to fade.

WILLIAM RAISBECK came from a family of footballing brothers which included the great Liverpool and Scotland centre-half Alex Raisbeck. William did not play many games for Derby but his last one was in the FA Cup semi-final of 1902 when the Rams drew 1-1 with Sheffield United at The Hawthorns before eventually losing in a second replay. Two years later forward **JOE WARRINGTON** bowed out for Derby in the FA Cup semi-final lost to Bolton Wanderers at Molineux on 19 March 1904.

BRUCE RIOCH played the last League game of his first spell with Derby County in a 2-0 defeat at Everton on 20 November 1976. He was sold to the Goodison Park club two weeks later. In less than a year

Derby bought him back from Merseyside and he made his second debut at the Baseball Ground on 5 November 1977 — against Everton!

PETER SHILTON played his last game in Rams colours against Watford on 29 February 1992, announcing before the 3-1 home win that he would be taking the manager's job at Plymouth Argyle. The Devon club wished Shilton to continue playing but as Derby had two vital League matches still outstanding with the Pilgrims, including one on the following Saturday, the Derby management insisted upon a clause forbidding the former England goalkeeper to play against his old club that season.

JOHN SIMS was a fixture in Derby County's Central League side at a time when there was little chance of a breakthrough into the first team. The last of only four senior appearances at Derby, however, was in one of the most important games in the Rams history when the Belper-born forward came on as a late substitute for Peter Daniel in the European Cup semi-final second leg at home to mighty Juventus on 25 April 1973.

There have been many instances of players making only one appearance for Derby County. Four of these characters scored on their solitary outing and can therefore consider themselves a little unlucky not to be selected again. The first was **R.J.Jardine** whose goal gave the fledgling Derby County a famous 2-1 win over champions Preston North End — only the second League defeat inflicted upon the Lilywhites — on 19 October 1889 at the County Ground.

In December 1898, **James Rutherford** scored in a 3-3 draw at Nottingham Forest. He moved on to Darwen, then a Second Division club, the following month.

For the last game of the disappointing 1953-54 season, manager Jack Barker fielded a largely experimental side. Given his Rams debut was forward **Ted Lowell**, who scored Derby's only goal in a 1-1 draw with Rotherham United. Lowell, who was born in Cheshire and joined Derby as a junior, never figured again and a little more than a year later he had moved to Stoke City.

On 24 September 1955, former England schoolboy international **Geoff Tate** scored on his only appearance for the Rams, a 1-1 draw at Oldham in a Third Division North game. Nearly three years later, without another first-team opportunity, Tate dropped into non-League football.

Other notable 'one-match wonders' include England Test cricketer **Frank Sugg**, who appeared in Derby County's first FA Cup tie on 8 November 1884, a 7-0 home thrashing from Walsall Town. Five additional members of that under-strength side, Derby's inaugural first-class match, were also destined not to reappear. They were Percy Exham, Leonard Gillett, C.Gorham, D.Maycroft and C.Ward.

In March 1914 manager Jimmy Methven included his son, **Jimmy Methven junior**, in a side heading for relegation that lost 3-1 at Bolton. Ten months later he gave future Rams manager **Stuart McMillan** his only Rams outing in the all-Derbyshire clash with Glossop North End. The game ended 1-1 and was the last against the club from the north-west of the county as they dropped out of the League after World War One.

Another famous name to play but once for Derby is Bloomer. Not Steve, of course, but his brother **Philip Bloomer**, who played at left-back in a 3-1 win over Sheffield Wednesday on 28 September 1895.

Derby County's centre-forward for the FA Cup fifth-round game at Crewe in January 1888 later became Archdeacon of The Sudan. At the time **Revd Llewellyn Henry Gwynne** was curate of St Chad's, on St Chad's Road in Derby, but later travelled to Khartoum. Gwynne remained in Egypt until the Cairo riots of 1946 when the cathedral and his home were looted and King Farouk sent an envoy to express his horror.

One future England international striker never quite made an appearance for Derby County. **Phil Boyer** was substitute when Derby beat Cardiff City 5-1 at Ninian Park on 23 September 1967. These were still early days for substitutions and Derby utilised the option on only ten occasions in the League that season, compared to 43 in 1993-94, which meant that some players never got the chances they would today. Brian Clough sold Boyer to York City in July 1968 and he scored goals wherever he went, 159 in the League, spending time at Bournemouth, Norwich City, Southampton and Manchester City and winning his only England cap against Wales in March 1976.

Eddie Thomas was the first substitute utilised by Brian Clough during his reign at Derby, coming on for Phil Waller in a 1-0 defeat at Crystal Palace on 26 August

Goalkeeper Mark Wallington carried on bravely with a painful injury to help the Rams to a vital win at Ipswich, but never played for the club again.

1967. It was not a good sign, however, for Clough never selected Thomas again, selling him to Orient within days.

Mark Wallington was first-choice goalkeeper for the Rams during two successive promotion seasons but he suffered injuries in both campaigns. The second came on 4 April 1987 in an away game at Ipswich Town. Wallington broke a finger in the second half, bravely carrying on to the end of the game as Derby gained a crucial 2-0 win. He never appeared in the Rams first team again, however, with Eric Steele deputising until the end of the season and Peter Shilton then joining the Rams.

When big **Frank Wignall** scored for

Derby County against Crystal Palace at the Baseball Ground on Saturday 6 November 1971, he was joint leading scorer for the club with five goals from ten starts. By Monday, 8 November he had dropped down to managerless, bottom of Division Three club Mansfield Town, signing for £8,000. Derby went on to lift the League championship at the end of the season while Wignall's new club were relegated to Division Four.

World War Two certainly curtailed the careers of many professional footballers and Derby County had their share. Indeed, for two players their Rams careers were expunged completely. **Billy Redfern** was signed from Luton Town to replace Ronnie Dix, sold to Spurs in June 1939. Redfern scored on his debut, a 2-1 home victory over Portsmouth, but played his last League match only three days later in the 1-0 win over Aston Villa at the Baseball Ground on 2 September 1939. Neville Chamberlain was already rehearsing his famous broadcast and by the time the League started up again in 1946, Redfern was almost 36 and long since departed from Derby. **Jim Wilson**, an inside-forward, made his only League appearance for Derby County in the opening match of that ill-fated 1939-40 season, on 26 August, in a 3-0 defeat at Roker Park. He left to join Linfield during the hostilities and continued to live in Northern Ireland into the 1990s.

Other unlucky footballers for whom the war effectively ended their playing careers with the Rams were **Ralph Hann**, **Wilf Walsh** and **Albert Wilson** (all one post-war game each), **Dave McCulloch**, who played wartime soccer at Derby but moved to Leicester City in July 1946, **Les Bailey**, **Tom Hinchcliffe** and Rams legend **Jack Barker**. Finally there was **Verdun Jones**, signed from Aston Villa, who appeared twice in 1937-38 but moved on to Southend United more than ten years later in May 1948 without another League outing. A case of a player who bore the name of a World War One battle whose career was decimated by the second conflict.

The following season the Rams suffered yet another Cup upset at home, this time to Lancashire Combination club New Brighton. But at the end of 1956-57 they were confirmed as Third Division North champions. Here is the staff pictured with the Northern Section championship shield. Back row (left to right): Harry Storer (manager), Martin McDonnell, Albert Mays, Ken Oliver, Terry Webster, Roy Martin, Glyn Davies, Ray Young, Ralph Hann (trainer). Front: Jack Parry, Tommy Powell, Gordon Brown, Ray Straw, Reg Ryan, Dennis Woodhead, Alan Crowshaw. Full-back Geoff Barrowcliffe is missing.

Happy Returns in a Sensational Cup Defeat

THE mid-1950s was a hard time for Derby County supporters. After years as one of the leading clubs in the country the Rams had gone crashing down from the First Division to the Second and then almost straight through to taste Third Division football for the first time in their history. Indeed, they were now only associate members of the Football League and when the competition proper got under way for the FA Cup in 1955-56, Derby County went in at the first round for the first time since the Cup's format had been rejigged in 1925. The Rams had begun that first season of life in Division Three North with some style, hammering neighbours Mansfield Town 4-0 on the opening day of the season — when a Saturday evening crowd of 24,159 saw the Stags beaten — and then winning 5-2 at Southport three days later. And although there were a few slip-ups on the way, by the time the first round of the Cup came around in late November, the Rams were handily placed in the table.

The first-round draw sent Derby to Northern League Crook Town, who created something of a shock by holding the Rams 2-2. On the following Wednesday afternoon, however, goals from Ray Straw (2), Jack Parry (2) and Jesse Pye completed the job and set up an intriguing second-round tie against Midland League club Boston United at the Baseball Ground.

In all other circumstances, the visit of Boston would have been nothing more than mildly interesting — new opponents from the lower reaches of the game — but what was different about this Boston side was that it contained no less than six former Derby players, ranging from experienced men like former Cup winner Reg Harrison and veteran goalkeeper Ray Middleton, who was Boston's player-manager, to one-game Rams like Geoff Hazledine and 34-year-old Dave Miller, albeit that Miller's sole appearance had been at centre-forward between all-time greats Raich Carter and Billy Steel in September 1947. In fact, he was a reserve-team defender in his time at the Baseball Ground

Making up the ex-Rams half-dozen were Geoff Hazledine's brother Don, who had scored six goals in 28 appearances for the Rams, and Ray Wilkins (26), the Gresley-born centre-forward who had the useful striking record of 11 goals in 30 first-team games in a declining Derby side.

The Hazledine brothers were both Derby-born. Inside-right Don (26) had played most of his games during the disastrous 1952-53 season, when the Rams finished bottom of the First Division. Outside-left Geoff, who celebrated his 23rd birthday shortly after his return to the Baseball Ground, made his only senior appearance in a goalless draw at Oldham in February 1954, as the Rams struggled against another relegation.

In terms of years and senior games, Harrison (32) and Middleton (35) were by far the most experienced. Harrison had replaced the injured Sammy Crooks at outside-right to gain his Cup winners' medal against Charlton Athletic in 1946 and altogether had scored 59 goals in 281 first-team games for the Rams before his transfer to Boston in July 1955.

Middleton had made 210 League appearances in Chesterfield's goal before joining the Rams in June 1951. A former England 'B' player, he had been a regular for three seasons at the Baseball Ground, clocking up 116 League appearances before his move to Boston's York Street ground in April 1954.

Boston were also doing well in the Midland League and on the Saturday before they visited Derby they beat Mansfield Town Reserves 2-0. It was, though, only Mansfield's second string and that should have put this contest into perspective. After all, the Rams had thrashed the Stags' first team at the start of the season. And Derby were also coming into the Cup game with a 6-2 home win over Darlington only seven days earlier, when Jack Parry scored a hat-trick and centre-forward Tommy Todd, signed from Crewe for £750 the previous month, hit two goals.

The stage was set, then, for an interesting game but one which the Rams would surely win. Certainly none of the 23,757 crowd could have imagined, even in their wildest dream, what was about to follow as they settled down on a misty early winter's afternoon.

Indeed, had Todd been a little sharper in the opening moments of the game, the Rams might have taken an early lead and dealt a psychological blow from which the non-Leaguers might never have recovered. But when Tommy Powell sent through a great through-pass, Todd faltered and Middleton, nursing a shoulder injury, was able to race out and boot the ball clear.

Thereafter, Boston prospered and the Rams foundered. The Lincolnshire side took the lead after 26 minutes when Wilkins turned in a Harrison shot that flew across the face of the goal. Seven minutes later it was 2-0 when Geoff Hazledine hammered the ball home after Rams goalkeeper Terry Webster had allowed a Howlett shot to slip from his grasp.

Seven minutes before half-time, former Wolves and England inside-forward Jesse Pye pulled a goal back from the penalty spot after a Boston defender had handled, but within three minutes Boston had restored their two-goal advantage when Johnny Birbeck capitalised on a misunderstanding between Webster and Rams centre-half Martin McDonnell and shot home from Howlett's centre.

Shortly afterwards McDonnell injured his knee in trying to stop Birbeck and when the teams re-emerged for the second half, McDonnell was on his way to the Derbyshire Royal Infirmary and took no further part in the game.

In those days before substitutes were permitted, the Rams were now down to ten men with Republic of Ireland inside-forward or wing-half Reg Ryan, the Derby skipper, dropping into the middle to fill the gap left by McDonnell's injury.

Boston were now in rampant mood. Reg Harrison said later: "I've never known

a half-time dressing-room like it. Nobody sat down. We just wanted to get back after them."

And get back after them they did. In the 67th minute, Geoff Hazledine scored his second goal after a good solo run by Wilkins. Three minutes later, Harrison started a move, Wilkins got the ball over and there was the younger Hazledine brother waiting to head home to complete a memorable hat-trick. The sixth and final goal came when Wilkins dribbled the ball away from the advancing Webster before sidefooting it into the net in the 78th minute.

The crowd were stunned into silence and when the scoreline 'Derby County 1 Boston United 6' began to chatter out of teleprinters in newspaper offices all over the country, almost every sports sub-editor must have assumed that it was the wrong way around.

Reg Harrison poked his head around the Derby dressing-room door to offer his commiserations but Rams manager Harry Storer, never known for accepting any defeat with particularly good grace, told him: "You can bugger off for a start!" But later Storer and trainer Ralph Hann sat down with Harrison and asked him about the talent available in the Midland League.

Harrison also admitted that the game had gone exactly to plan. "Not long before the Cup game I'd played against Derby in a testimonial match and noticed that their half-backs didn't push up but that the inside-forwards did. It left a big gap in the middle of the field so our trainer at Boston said, 'Let's just push the ball into the gap and run.' We did — and it worked!"

In truth, Derby had played appallingly with only outside-left Tommy Powell emerging with any credit. In the *Derby Evening Telegraph*, Wilf Shaw summed it up: "You don't win Cup ties if your defenders don't tackle and your forwards lack the spirit of aggression."

He also paid tribute to Boston: "They had no time for kick and rush or unnecessary vigour. Just a good ration of football ability which was allied to 100 per cent effort."

How the Derby Evening Telegraph reported one of the most astonishing FA Cup results in the history of the competition.

On the same day, ironically, Derby's neighbours Burton Albion, then of the Birmingham League, earned a fine goalless draw at Third Division North club Halifax Town and were to win the replay at Lloyds Ground, Burton.

Boston, meanwhile, looked forward to a third-round trip to Tottenham Hotspur and at White Hart Lane, in early January, their Cup dream perished 4-0.

By then, the Rams were concentrating on the League. That season they finished runners-up to Grimsby Town — and did not go up because the old Northern and Southern Sections had only one promotion place each — but did gain promotion 12 months later. Even then there was a Cup shock when Lancashire Combination side New Brighton, a

Derby County: Webster; Barrowcliffe, Upton, Mays, McDonnell, Ryan, Cresswell, Parry, Todd, Pye, Powell.
Boston United: Middleton; Robinson, Snade, D.Hazledine, Miller, Lowder, Harrison, G.Hazledine, Wilkins, Birbeck, Howlett.
Referee: Mr E.T.Jennings (Stourbridge)
Attendance: 23,767.

former League club, won 3-1 at the Baseball Ground in the second round.

Nothing, though, could compare with the sensational defeat by Boston when six former Rams enjoyed a dream return to the Baseball Ground.

Rams centre-forward George Darwin rounds Tommy Younger, the Liverpool goalkeeper who suffered a bad injury in the incident.

Darwin's Winner Topples the League Leaders

WHEN Derby County returned to the Second Division in 1957, after two years in the Third Division North, they made a dreadful start to the season. Away defeats at Fulham and Bristol Rovers saw them concede seven goals before Barnsley hammered the Rams 4-1 at the Baseball Ground in the Rams' first home game since lifting the Northern Section championship in such style.

Clearly, the team which had got them back was not good enough to keep them there and Reg Ryan, the Irish international who had proved such an inspirational skipper in the promotion drive, later summed it up: "We had too many old legs in the side."

Rams manager Harry Storer had already made one key new signing, though, when in May 1957 he brought Mansfield Town's tricky little inside-forward George Darwin to the Baseball Ground, for £4,000 plus reserve defender Keith Savin.

Having given the side which had won promotion its chance, Storer began to make changes and introduced Darwin for the return game against Bristol Rovers at the Baseball Ground. The Rams collected their first points of the season on that Wednesday evening with a 2-1 win, and Darwin marked his Rams debut with a goal in front of a crowd of more than 20,000.

There followed a defeat at West Ham, already installed as one of the favourites for promotion, a draw at Lincoln and then successive home wins over Sheffield United and Lincoln before another defeat, this time at Blackburn Rovers, also promotion favourites. Then a home draw with Ipswich and defeats at Notts County (where Magpies centre-half Peter Russell was sent off for striking Rams winger Dennis Woodhead) and Cardiff left the Rams in the bottom three and facing top-of-the-table Liverpool at the Baseball Ground on 19 October 1957.

Liverpool, under the managership of their former player Phil Taylor, had finished third in each of the previous two seasons. Only the top two went up in those days — there were no play-offs, of course — and now the Reds were desperate to maintain their early-season promotion challenge.

Taylor had made some key signings after taking over as manager from Don Welsh, and one of them was Scottish international goalkeeper Tommy Younger, signed from Hibernian for £9,000 in June 1956. The Reds arrived at Derby confident of taking both points, but they would go home empty-handed and Younger would have particularly unhappy memories of his first visit to the Baseball Ground, especially his first meeting with the diminutive George Darwin.

The Rams had centre-half Martin McDonnell back after the ex-paratrooper had missed three games because of a groin injury, while Liverpool were at full-strength with Scottish international Billy Liddell back after a thigh strain and England Under-23 winger Alan A'Court recovered from influenza.

Liddell won the toss and the Rams kicked off towards the Normanton End and immediately belied their lowly position with some good football. Barrowcliffe gave A'Court no room whatsoever and Ryan went close to opening the scoring on two occasions.

In the 24th minute Derby took a deserved lead when Jimmy Melia conceded a free-kick and Barrowcliffe placed the ball at the far upright where Tommy Powell challenged Younger. The Liverpool goalkeeper missed the ball which fell to Dennis Woodhead and the former Sheffield Wednesday outside-left moved smartly to score his first goal of the season.

Four minutes before half-time came the incident which settled the course of the match. Woodhead won possession on the left and sent Darwin streaking towards goal. Younger dived at his feet but Darwin retained the ball and rounded the now prostrate Liverpool goalkeeper to see an opening goal yawning ahead of him. It was a golden opportunity to make the score 2-0, but Darwin, probably surprised that he still had the ball after Younger's fearsome challenge, shot hurriedly and the ball rolled past the outside of the left-hand post.

Younger, meanwhile, was still lying injured and after the Liverpool trainer and a posse of St John Ambulance men had attended to him he was placed on a stretcher and carried off, apparently suffering from a back injury. The goalkeeper was well enough to walk down the players' tunnel but Liverpool, with Moran in goal, Liddell now at full-back and with only ten men in those days before substitutes were allowed, were a team in disarray.

Younger had damaged his sciatic nerve but when the second half began he was fit

Younger is helped from the field by the Liverpool trainer and a St John Ambulance man.

enough to resume at centre-forward, at least bringing Liverpool back to a full complement of players, although the makeshift leader of the attack was still limping heavily and was providing little more than nuisance value.

Not surprisingly the Rams were now well on top and Darwin was having a remarkable game, tearing the Liverpool defence to shreds. Yet just when the Rams should have been hammering home their advantage, they appeared to relax and Liverpool came back. It was fortunate for Derby that the Reds' best chance fell to Younger. He tried a shot, fell in doing so and had to be helped back to the dressing-room.

Still the Rams should have had more but in the 66th minute it was Liverpool who scored to level matters. Barrowcliffe and McDonnell both made mistakes and allowed Tony Rowley to equalise. First Barrowcliffe saw a sloppy back-pass intercepted by Melia, then McDonnell got

in the way of goalkeeper Terry Webster as Wheeler shot. The Rams' 'keeper was unsighted, and the ball cannoned off him to Rowley, who only had to tap it over the line.

Most of the 22,631 crowd were now complaining that the Rams had thrown away a glorious chance to beat the Second Division leaders but with the minutes ticking away Darwin raced clear, only to be cynically hacked down by White a yard outside the Liverpool penalty area. Today White would have been sent off; nearly 40 years ago he escaped with a finger-wagging from the referee.

Five minutes from time, however, Darwin at last restored the Rams' lead. Ryan and Parry combined to send Darwin clear and the centre-forward beat Moran with a fine shot.

Almost immediately, Younger reappeared to take over in goal again, allowing Liverpool to throw everything forward but it was in vain and that night Black-

63

Stand-in goalkeeper Ronnie Moran is beaten by Darwin's late goal which gave Derby County a surprise victory and knocked Liverpool off the top of the Second Division.

burn Rovers took over the leadership of the Second Division.

Liverpool did not go up that season — indeed, they had to wait for the appointment of Bill Shankly as their manager before returning to the top flight — while the Rams recovered from their bad start to the season to finish 16th.

Little George Darwin ended the season with ten goals from 29 League games. The following season he scored 11 goals in 31 League games and in doing so provided Rams fans with some rare moments of real entertainment as he scampered over the Baseball Ground mud, turning visiting defences inside out. Alas, he never touched the same heights again and when his wife eventually found it hard to settle in the Derby area, he asked for a transfer and in October 1960 joined Rotherham United for £5,000 after netting 33 goals in 97 senior games for the Rams.

Jack Parry – the Rams Court Jester

JOHN 'Jack' Parry was a Derby County professional for 19 years. His skill crossed generations, from Raich Carter to Kevin Hector, and he adapted magnificently to changes in the way that football was played. He began as a utility forward, continued as a goalscoring inside-forward, converted to an attacking wing-half and, then, when systems such as 4-2-4 and 4-3-3 became commonplace, he became a 'link man' or 'midfield dynamo'. But his value to the club was far more than the effort and skill he produced on the pitch. He became a captain, a comedian and an inspiration.

Born in July 1931, Jack Parry was one of a well-known Derby family that specialised in sport. His younger brothers, Ray and Cyril, both played League football, and two other brothers, Reg and Glyn, had spells with League clubs. Ray Parry played 544 League games for Bolton, Blackpool and Bury, while Cyril notched up a dozen for Notts County. In fact, Ray was capped for England at virtually every level — England Schoolboys, England Youth, England Under-23s, the Football League and the full international side. Only Terry Venables has been more comprehensive in representative honours, having been capped for England Amateur XI too.

Jack Parry first attracted the attention of Derby County when he played for Derby Boys immediately after the war. He signed amateur forms in 1947 and turned professional on his 17th birthday, in July 1948. The following April, still only 17, he made his First Division debut as a deputy for Billy Steel, and scored in the 2-2 draw at home to Aston Villa. The forward line that day was Harrison, Morris, Stamps, Parry and Broome.

Jack Parry then faced the problem of learning his trade in a declining team. He was the club's leading scorer in the First Division season of 1951-52 — 11 in 28 games — but his value to the club wasn't fully appreciated until they had slumped to the Third Division North. Then, in

A young Jack Parry at the start of a long career with the Rams, pictured in the team which lost 2-1 to Manchester United at Old Trafford in October 1951. It was Parry's 14th League game for Derby and he went on to play in 483. Back row (left to right) are Ken Oliver, Bert Mozley, Ray Middleton, Geoff Barrowcliffe, Colin Bell and Steve McLachlan. Front: Reg Harrison, Johnny Morris, Jack Stamps, Jack Parry and Hugh McLaren. In contrast to Parry, McLachlan spent 15 years at the Baseball Ground – albeit seven were in wartime – and played in only 58 League games.

1955-56, he was a brilliant goalscoring foil for Jesse Pye and Alf Ackerman. His first-time shooting was breathtaking and his goals included a hat-trick against Darlington. Before the home match against Grimsby Town, on 10 March 1956, Jack Parry had scored 27 goals in 36 League and Cup games. Unfortunately, he was injured that day in a controversial collision with Ray de Gruchy, the Grimsby full-back. As somebody once put it, Jack Parry's back collided with de Gruchy's boot. That season Grimsby Town were the one club promoted to the Second Division, and Derby County finished second.

Parry's back injury troubled him for some time, but he scored seven goals in 18 games during the following season when the Rams won the Third Division North championship. The signing of Gordon Brown created added competition for the inside-forward positions, but Parry was an automatic choice in the Second Division. He continued to score consistently, notching 27 League goals in the next two seasons. When he topped the team's scorers in 1958-59 it was his third time, something that even players like John O'Hare didn't manage. His goals included the second hat-trick of his career, against Grimsby Town in February 1959.

In whatever division he played, Jack Parry retained his First Division hallmark. Like Geoff Barrowcliffe and Ray Young, he had been reared in the company of class players of the late 1940s, and was therefore very comfortable on the ball and had a precision quality to his passing. At the turn of the decade, Jack Parry embarked on a new role as a wing-half.

Away from the pitch, footballers spend a lot of time waiting for kick-off time, so a character and joker can be much

Jack Parry, scorer of well over a century of League goals for the Rams and whose tally of League appearances was a club record until Kevin Hector overtook it.

appreciated. Jack Parry was certainly one of those. Teammates tell legendary stories about comments that livened up training and away trips. Jack Parry took the mickey out of goalkeeper Reg Matthews, teasing him about his smoking, throwing cobs across the dining-room table to test Matthews' reflexes. One day, during a game, Matthews went into the back of the net to fish out an old cap just before a corner-kick came across. It was the first time the goalkeeper had worn the cap for ages. Jackie Parry apparently took one look at him and said to everyone in the penalty area: 'Here's Albert Tatlock come to join us.'

One of the club's young players came from a family that bred budgerigars. "Do any of your kids want a budgie for Christmas?" he asked Jack Parry. "No thanks," came the replay, "We're having turkey this year."

Another time, during pre-season training, the players were out jogging alongside the road when a Mini driver stopped to ask directions.

'There's only room for me and the Boss,' Parry said.

Footballers are very quick to catch on to some minor aspect of their colleagues' personality, and, in return, in the mid-1960s, Jack Parry suffered jokes about his age. Whenever the players saw an old man struggling along the pavement they would shout down the bus, 'There's Jackie Parry.'

His first ever-present season was 1962-63, when football was seriously disrupted by the great freeze. Derby County didn't play a League game for nine weeks, and faced a tremendous fixture-congestion in the run-in. Derby were also favourites to go down to the Third Division, but Jack Parry led a spirited fight against relegation. The skipper played 20 games in 12 weeks, and covered the pitch with incredible energy and inspiration, feeding and prompting forwards like Bill Curry, Barrie Hutchinson and Ray Swallow. After the last home game of the season, a 4-0 win against Portsmouth, Parry slumped faint

and exhausted in the dressing-room. He had done his job magnificently. The team eventually avoided relegation by five points.

He continued to set a fine example by keeping himself fit and healthy, and, for a short time in the 1964-65 season, it looked as though he might fulfil his ambition of leading the club back to the First Division. He was ever-present again, and, late in the season, in February, he scored two goals in 11 minutes in a home game against Swindon Town. They were both typically fierce first-time, right-footed long-range shots. He was in his 34th year at that time, and had now scored over 100 League goals for the club, one of only seven Rams players to have reached that landmark. His 500th League and Cup game was at Northampton in April 1965, when the Derby County chairman, Harry Payne, presented him with a gold watch and the Northampton club gave him the match ball. When asked to say a few words, Parry said he was

> Jack Parry might have made one more appearance for the Rams. In May 1967, just after Tim Ward was sacked, the directors selected the team and asked Parry to play against Plymouth Argyle at the Baseball Ground. It had been 18 months since his last appearance. He declined.

speechless. This earned hoots of derision from the other players.

Sadly, he couldn't keep going for ever in his arduous midfield role. The last of his 483 League appearances — 517 in League and Cup games — was as substitute at Ipswich Town on 23 October 1965, jut a few weeks after he had played against his brother Ray in a game at Bury. He stayed with Derby Council until the end of the following season, taking up a role as mentor to the Reserves, most of whom were 15 years his junior, and then he moved to Boston United.

Rams manager Tim Ward and secretary Cyril Annable check through ticket applications for the FA Cup tie against Manchester United at the Baseball Ground in January 1966.

Those Old Football Specials

ONE of our family heirlooms is a battered leather suitcase which obtains *Derby Evening Telegraph Football Specials* from the mid-1960s. The newspapers are now a paler shade of green, and there are gaps where I have cut out pictures for a scrapbook, but they still tell the story of a fading part of Derby County's history.

I've heard supporters say that very little of note happened between 1962 and 1967, when my father, Tim Ward, managed the club. In the light of what followed, they are probably correct. However, the contents of the suitcase suggest that those five Second Division seasons were eventful enough.

We must have kept these newspapers because my father wrote a weekly page-three column ('Tim Ward Writes'). Some Sundays he borrowed my typewriter and

Eddie Thomas signs for the Rams, watched by manager Tim Ward who later said that the signing of Thomas worked against the manager when a parsimonious board expected regular good signings for next to nothing. Ward used his weekly column in the *Football Special* to vent his feelings after being sacked in May 1967.

tapped out a few hundred words in readiness for a meeting with sports editor George Edwards the following day. Other times, he would start thinking about it on Monday morning when he arrived at work. He received £3 for each article. He later said he didn't do it for the money and he didn't really enjoy doing it.

His columns, like those of Bill Shankly that appeared on page five of the same paper, stayed clear of controversy as much as possible. He was positive in defeat and confident in success, and gave little hint of the frustrations of his job or the humour he developed to cope with them. His main frustration, I suppose, was being alienated from the financial side of the club, and a scarcity of money to spend on players. His money signings were rare: Mick Cullen,

John McCann and Bobby Ferguson in 1962-63; Gordon Hughes and Alan Durban in 1963-64; Eddie Thomas in 1964-65; Billy Hodgson and Derek Draper in 1965-66; and Kevin Hector in 1966-67.

Not surprisingly, Tim Ward's column didn't contain stories about directors excluding him from board meetings until financial business had been discussed. Or about how directors sometimes bothered him for more tickets just before a match. Or about how they might phone his hotel room the night before the match to say they had a room with an en suite bathroom. And he couldn't show his disappointment when Fred Walters, a man for whom he had great respect, had to relinquish the chairmanship to Harry Payne under a new rule which rotated the chair every two years. Harry Payne soon provoked further annoyance by smoking a pipe and fogging the atmosphere on the team coach.

After hearing persistent comments about what was one player's true position, Tim got his own back on one director in a curious way. He asked two midfield players, Jack Parry and Mick Hopkinson, to swap shirts before a match. "It's just a superstition," he told the players. "Play the same way." Later, after the vital 3-1 win, the director came up to Tim and said, "That's what made the difference, he was much better in that position."

Tim did not dare write anything about referees in his column either. For instance, there was a trip to Cardiff when he came back furious after having been reported for entering a referee's dressing-room after the match. The Rams had lost the match 2-1 and couldn't blame the referee for the defeat. However, Alan Durban pointed out that the referee was a Cardiff man, even though the programme showed him to be from Birmingham. When Tim went along to the referee's room, he found it full of people wearing blue and white scarves. He stood outside the room and asked where the referee was from. It turned out that the referee had moved to Birmingham a few weeks before.

It all added to the stress. A football

manager was never out of the limelight. Tim would later joke about the man who came to install central-heating in our bungalow. He spent hours telling Tim how to pick a team and then made a mess of the new heating system.

Even without the aid of *Football Specials* I have a few strong personal memories of incidents on the pitch in the 1960s. I can picture Billy Hodgson getting two hands to a clearance from Carlisle goalkeeper Joe Dean before sidefooting the ball into the empty net and running off as happy as Norman Wisdom when the referee actually gave a goal. I remember seeing a last-minute goal by John Bowers at Bolton and then watching it again on television the next day — a rare event for Derby in those days.

I carry vivid images of players' movements: Frank Upton drilling passes that could pin a winger to the boundary wall; Phil Waller jumping for he ball with his forearm raised; Eddie Thomas and his leggy run, barrel chest and supreme touch with either foot; Kevin Hector scampering, twinkling past defenders and flashing in a shot …

But the *Football Specials* tell other stories too.

I became intrigued by the reserve team's struggles to stay clear of the Central League re-election zone. As I thumbed through the newspapers, I was astonished at the standard of the opposition in the Central League. In 1964-65, for instance, a young Rams Reserves, fielding up to seven teenagers, regularly faced internationals: Dave Hollins and Ollie Burton of Newcastle United one week, Len Allchurch of Sheffield United the next, Alex Parke of Everton, and so on. If it wasn't internationals, it was promising youngsters like Madeley and Greenhoff of Leeds United, Birchenall of Sheffield United, or 18-year-old Tony Brown, who scored four in the first half of one game at West Brom.

At Anfield, on 3 September 1966, Rams Reserves faced top-of-the-table Liverpool Reserves, who had scored 16 goals in their first four games. Judging by the report

('Reserves Reel Under Attack'), the game started dramatically: 'Liverpool did not intend to relax on their goal scoring. within the first minute they had attacked six times, brought five brilliant saves out of Boulton and scored with the sixth. Peplow put across from the right a curling shot, which Boulton could only parry and McDougall easily netted.'

That Liverpool team included Ronnie Moran, Ian Ross, Roy Evans, Doug Livermore and Ted McDougall. (The previous season a strong Liverpool side, including Peter Thomson, had been beaten 1-0 at the Baseball Ground). Besides Colin Boulton, who went on to win two League championship medals in the 1970s, the Derby team included veteran Jack Parry and an assortment of youngsters. Tony Rhodes later played with Halifax and Southport, Mick Jones and Jon Nixon for Notts County and Peterborough, and Phil Boyer with York City, Bournemouth, Norwich City, Southampton, Manchester City and England.

The Reserves also played an interesting game at Leeds on 22 October 1966 ('Leeds run riot against Reserves'). An own-goal set Leeds on the way to an 8-0 win. Peter Lorimer scored four, and Bobby Collins, Terry Cooper, Terry Hibbitt and Rod Belfitt also played. Colin Boulton's injured thumb stopped him keeping goal that day at Leeds, but he was considered fit enough to be substitute. Yes, Boulton was rated that highly as an outfield player.

Some of Tim Ward's signings stand the test of time, particularly Peter Daniel, Colin Boulton, Eddie Thomas, Alan Durban, Phil Boyer and Kevin Hector. One other deserves mention. Perhaps his best signing was Gordon Guthrie, who was offered a full-time post in the mid-1960s and who, in the years since, as trainer and physiotherapist, has received accolades from a succession of widely differing managers.

What else did I learn from skimming through the *Football Specials* of the 1960s? Well, there was the tension of reliving the promotion campaign of 1964-65, which looked exceedingly promising at half-time during the match against Bolton Wanderers on 20 March 1965. The Rams played magnificently in the first half and went in 2-0 up. Then, in the second half, they conceded three. The winning goal that day was scored by young Francis Lee.

Lee's wasn't the only *Football Special* name to be later linked with the club. Nearby at Burton Albion, Peter Taylor was rebuilding with the help of players like Les Green, Richie Barker and Tony Parry, although another Albion youngster, Ian Hutchinson, was to slip away to Chelsea via Cambridge. One of the saddest events of the 1960s concerned the former Rams player Ralph Hunt, who was fatally injured in a car crash returning from watching a cup match at Peterborough on 9 December 1964. Hunt died a week later without regaining consciousness.

The 1965-66 season started badly for the Rams. Southampton were the visitors for the first match of the season. They scored twice in the first five minutes, and then, after 15 minutes, when Geoff Barrowcliffe was injured, another little piece of history was created — Derby County's first substitution: 'Barrowcliffe went off the field and walked round the touch-line with trainer Ralph Hann, who waved to the directors' box. Manager Tim Ward went down to the trainers' bench and, after a brief consultation, Saxton went on . . . After a few minutes Webster switched to right-back and Parry to right-half, enabling Saxton to go to left-half.'

The introduction of the young Bobby Saxton was a sign of two things: the transition to youth which saw Saxton, John Richardson, Peter Daniel and Colin Boulton take over from Ray Young, Geoff Barrowcliffe, Bobby Ferguson and Reg Matthews; and the new era of substitutes (for injured players only at first).

Looking back through the *Football Specials*, it is apparent just how many games had finished 'ten against eleven'. In October 1963, for instance, the Rams lost successive home matches that were affected by injuries. Jack Parry pulled a muscle early in the game against Preston North End and Bill Curry dislocated a shoulder against Sunderland.

When all is said and done, Tim Ward didn't succeed in taking the Rams up to the First Division, and that was what the supporters had every right to expect during his five-year spell as manager. At the end of the 1966-67 season, his contract wasn't renewed. He was quite relieved in some ways, suffering the stress of working hard without the resources that were later to be provided for Brian Clough and Peter Taylor. "I would have loved to have done for Derby County what Cloughie did." Tim Ward said years later. "He was able to dictate. He was in a better position. than I was."

I cannot leave the *Football Specials* without reference to my favourite passage, taken from an issue in April 1968. George Edwards mentioned rumours that the Rams were interested in signing Bournemouth goalkeeper Roger Jones. This was an incredibly prescient remark, because Derby County did indeed sign Jones . . .just over 12 years later.

The Rams in 1958, their days of playing on Christmas Day just ended. Back row (left to right): Harry Storer (manager), Mike Smith, Albert Mays, Frank Upton, Ken Oxford, Terry Adlington, Tommy Powell, Roy Martin, Gordon Brown, Ralph Hann (trainer). Middle: Geoff Barrowcliffe, Johnny Hannigan, Reg Ryan, Ralph Hunt, Ben Clark, Roy Womack, Ray Young. Front: Brian Daykin, Dennis Woodhead, John Bowers, Glyn Davies, George Darwin.

Christmas Crackers for the Rams

COME 25 December each year, Britain is well and truly shut down. Only vital emergency and maintenance services are at work and the only traffic to be seen on usually busy roads is transporting families to their relatives for the turkey and Christmas pud. Hard to imagine, then, tens of thousands of soccer fans descending on their local grounds to watch their side. But just over 30 years ago, that was not just a familiar sight — it was an integral part of the Yuletide season.

Indeed, until 1957 there was a full programme of League football played on Christmas Day, in addition to the still traditional Boxing Day matches we enjoy today. Those festive doubles usually took the form of a home and away fixture with the same club and they often produced bizarrely contrasting results over those 48 hours.

Of course, travelling supporters were not so numerous, so the lack of public transport and no mass car ownership was no great inconvenience. And in those days when the Football League fixtures were worked out by a clerk at League head-quarters rather than by today's computerised system, clubs were usually, but not always, paired with a relatively local opponent.

Derby County did not play on Christmas Day until 1894, although some clubs played on 25 December the year before, and for the first 11 seasons of the Football League the Rams had a regular home fixture with Bolton Wanderers on Boxing Day. This ended only when the Trotters were relegated in 1899.

The first Christmas Day opponents were Sheffield United, the Rams running out 4-1 winners at Bramall Lane in front of 3,000 spectators. West Bromwich Albion were the first Yuletide guests at the Baseball Ground in 1896, when a Steve Bloomer hat-trick helped give County a splendid 8-1 triumph.

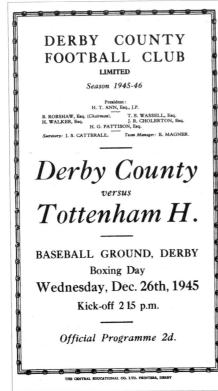

Programme from a 'wartime' Christmas game against Spurs at the Baseball Ground in 1945. The Rams won 5-2 at White Hart Lane on Christmas Day and completed the double – 2-0 – at home on Boxing Day before 30,823 spectators. Although the war in Europe had ended seven months earlier, the League proper did not resume until August 1946.

DERBY COUNTY FOOTBALL CLUB
LIMITED

Season 1945-46

President :
H. T. ANN, Esq., J.P.

B. ROBSHAW, Esq. (Chairman).   T. E. WASSELL, Esq.
H. WALKER, Esq.   J. R. CHOLERTON, Esq.
H. G. PATTISON, Esq.

Secretary: J. S. CATTERALL.   Team Manager: E. MAGNER.

Derby County

versus

Tottenham H.

BASEBALL GROUND, DERBY
Boxing Day
Wednesday, Dec. 26th, 1945
Kick-off 2.15 p.m.

Official Programme 2d.

THE CENTRAL EDUCATIONAL CO. LTD. PRINTERS, DERBY

On Christmas Day 1909, Barnsley were beaten at the Baseball Ground only for Derby to lose 5-1 at Oakwell three days later.

From 1912, the return fixture on Boxing Day became a standard and Derby played on Christmas Day in most subsequent years.

When George Thornewell scored ag-

Derby County's playing staff in 1928, the year in which the Baseball Ground attendance record broken was over Christmas. Back row (left to right): Barclay, Bowers, Scott, Wilkes, Collins, Prince, Smith, Carr. Second row: Enos Bromage (trainer), Ruddy, Cooke, Cooper, Hampton, Bacon, Stephenson, Davison, McDougall. Seated: W.S.Cooper (secretary), Crooks, Malloch, McIntyre, Whitehouse, George Jobey (manager), Bedford, Ramage, Nicholas, J.C.Robson, H.Whiteman (coach). Front: Fereday, Hope, Robinson, Jessop, Barker, Mann, W.Robson, White.

ainst Bradford City on 25 December 1920, he ended a goal drought of more than 720 minutes stretching back eight matches and over two months to the Rams' previous goal, also by Thornewell at home to Arsenal. Despite seven defeats in those barren games, a season's best attendance of 23,820 interrupted their family day to watch the return on Boxing Day when the

Rams and Bradford City drew 1-1. Best Yuletide result for Derby came in 1922 when Crystal Palace were thrashed 6-0, Jimmy Moore scoring the first five goals. Next day the return in South London finished 2-2!

A year later Derby travelled to Nelson on Christmas Day, losing 2-1 to the Lancastrians, but Harry Storer made it one in the eye for the visitors on Boxing Day when he scored four times as the Rams ran out 6-0 winners.

Attendances, although not spectacular, were steadily improving and on Boxing Day 1928 the Baseball Ground record was broken as 30,651 saw Derby lose 2-1 at home to team of the 1920s, Huddersfield Town.

Derby's League attendance record was also twice bettered in 1930s Christmas games: First when 32,320 watched Manchester City tumble to goals from Jack Bowers (two) and Peter Ramage (two) in a 4-1 home win on Christmas Day 1933; then, a year and a day later when 35,260 saw the Rams avenge a 5-1 thrashing at Molineux, beating Wolves 2-0 at the Baseball Ground.

Either side of the war there were topsy-turvy results with Everton. Post-Christmas Eve hangovers were suggested as the reason for the Rams' 7-0 defeat at Goodison Park on Christmas Day 1936. Yet three days later a Dai Astley hat-trick gave Derby a 3-1 win.

In 1946, during the first post-war League season, Derby tumbled to a 4-1 defeat on Merseyside. On Boxing Day, however, with Peter Doherty recalled for his farewell game, the Rams banished the memory of the previous day by trouncing Everton 5-1, the Irish star netting twice.

As the Rams' decline set in during the early 1950s, voices of disquiet began to be heard about having to play and travel on Christmas Day. The 1956 festive fixture with Scunthorpe & Lindsay United, as they were then known, turned out to be the last League match played at the Baseball Ground on Christmas Day.

Derby were lying second in the Third Division North following their 4-0 victory, but it took them until the 54th minute to break down the Iron. An injury to key defender Brownsword kept Scunthorpe's 'top tackler' off the field for a few minutes, during which time outside-left Dennis Woodhead ran riot scoring the first two, with Reg Ryan (64 minutes) and a Geoff Barrowcliffe penalty in the last seconds completing the job. Next day at the Old Show Ground, Derby did the double with a 4-1 victory. Ray Straw, on his way to a club record-equalling 37 League goals that season, scored twice.

On New Year's Eve 1956, Cardiff City proposed that Christmas Day games should be stopped because of travel difficulties and 'a conviction that the public do not want them'. Cardiff were angry that they had endured fog and snow and had to dig out their team coach in order to fulfil a Boxing Day fixture against Manchester United at Old Trafford. They put a proposal to the Football League meeting in March, backed by many clubs, and this signalled the death-knell for Christmas Day games.

The following season, 1957-58, Derby County played their last Christmas Day match. They went down 2-1 at Ashton Gate, in what the *Derby Evening Telegraph* described as a 'below par' performance against a similarly lacklustre Bristol City side. England forward John Atyeo put City ahead on 24 minutes following a goalmouth mêlée. Tommy Powell set up Ryan for the equaliser after 36 minutes, but Atyeo restored Bristol's lead just after the hour. Jack Parry was denied another leveller when controversially ruled offside and the Rams trudged off, having missed Christmas lunch for the final time (if one doesn't count training sessions to prepare for Boxing Day games, of course). Twenty-four hours later, Derby crushed Bristol City 5-2 in front of 25,630 at the Baseball Ground.

A handful of clubs continued to play on 25 December in 1958, but in 1959 the last two Christmas Day games in England were scheduled. Accrington Stanley were due to play Chesterfield, but with both sides making first-round FA Cup exits they brought the game forward to second-round day, leaving Blackburn Rovers striker Derek Dougan to score the last festive goal as his side defeated Blackpool 1-0 and the curtain fell on what was for many supporters a pleasant occasion.

In Scotland, where New Year's celebrations have traditionally been more revered, Christmas Day games continued, when the 25th fell on a Saturday, until 1971. And who knows, perhaps in these days of television-controlled football fixture lists, with Sky Sports and ITV ensuring a disjointed League programme and matches staged on hitherto unfamiliar days, we may once again be presented with a decent excuse to get out of the house on Christmas Day when the relatives arrive!

Derby County Matches on Christmas Day: The full list 1894-1957:

1894 Sheffield United 1 Derby County 4
1896 Derby County 8 West Bromwich Albion 1
1897 Derby County 1 Notts County 2
1899 Derby County 3 Liverpool 2
1900 Liverpool 0 Derby County 0
1901 Derby County 3 Wolverhampton Wanderers 1
1903 Derby County 2 Liverpool 0
1905 Derby County 1 Manchester City 2
1906 Sheffield Wednesday 1 Derby County 1

1907 Derby County 4 Grimsby Town 0
1908 Wolverhampton Wanderers 1 Derby County 1
1909 Derby County 2 Barnsley 1
1911 Derby County 2 Grimsby Town 1
1912 Derby County 1 West Bromwich Albion 2
1913 Derby County 0 Aston Villa 2
1914 Nottingham Forest 2 Derby County 2
1919 Derby County 2 Arsenal 1
1920 Bradford City 2 Derby County 2
1922 Derby County 6 Crystal Palace 0
1923 Nelson 2 Derby County 1
1924 Oldham Athletic 0 Derby County 1
1925 Port Vale 0 Derby County 1
1926 Bolton Wanderers 3 Derby County 1
1928 Huddersfield Town 0 Derby County 0
1929 Leeds United 2 Derby County 1
1930 Blackburn Rovers 1 Derby County 0
1933 Derby County 4 Manchester City 1
1934 Wolverhampton Wanderers 5 Derby County 1
1935 Portsmouth 3 Derby County 0
1936 Everton 7 Derby County 0
1946 Everton 4 Derby County 1
1947 Blackburn Rovers 3 Derby County 4
1948 Arsenal 3 Derby County 3
1950 Derby County 1 Tottenham Hotspur 1
1951 Huddersfield Town 1 Derby County 1
1953 Bury 4 Derby County 0
1954 West Ham Utd 1 Derby County 0
1956 Derby County 4 Scunthorpe & Lindsey United 0
1957 Bristol City 2 Derby County 1

Rams goalkeeper Ken Oxford dives at the ball as skipper Glyn Davies and a Huddersfield Town forward tangle at the Baseball Ground in December 1958. Despite having centre-half Ray Young limping on the right wing for much of the match with a heavily bandaged thigh – there were no substitutes allowed in those days – Derby won 3-1 with goals from George Darwin, Tommy Powell and a Dave Cargill penalty. That season the Rams finished seventh in the Second Division, their highest placing since being promoted in 1957, until they won the championship under Brian Clough in 1969.

The Rams first-team squad in the summer of 1965, picturing 12 of the players who helped do the double over Coventry City the previous autumn. Standing (left to right): Bobby Saxton, Phil Waller, Eddie Thomas, Reg Matthews, Colin Boulton, Ray Young, Ron Webster, Mick Hopkinson. Seated: Alan Durban, Gordon Hughes, Bobby Ferguson, Geoff Barrowcliffe, Jack Parry, Billy Hodgson, John Bowers. On ground: John Richardson, Nigel Cleevely. After Bowers was injured in the first match against Coventry, Cleevely took his place and scored on his debut, but in the summer the Rams signed Hodgson from Sheffield United to fill the problem outside-left position.

John Bowers' Finest Hour – Then Tragedy Struck

JOHN Bowers bore a famous football name. His father, also John but always known as Jack, had led Derby County's forward line so fearlessly in the 1930s, when he achieved the remarkable scoring return of 183 goals in only 220 League and Cup games for the Rams before being transferred to Leicester City in November 1936.

Bowers senior played three times for England, broke the Rams' individual scoring record for a season — both for League goals and League Cup goals — and netted 16 hat-tricks in his Derby career. In August 1943 he returned to the Baseball Ground as assistant trainer and was then appointed physiotherapist. And in

February 1957 his son John also signed for the Rams.

Young John was never going to be as good as his illustrious father. Indeed, he was never even going to be the same kind of footballer. Where Jack Bowers led the line, hurtling in head first amid a forest of legs and flying boots to steer the ball home, John was a player who preferred the wider open spaces of the wings.

When he signed for Derby he continued in his full-time profession as an advertising representative with the *Derby Evening Telegraph*, working out of their old town centre office in Albert Street. And after making his League debut for the Rams at Huddersfield in November 1959, on his 20th birthday, he remained a part-time professional, working five days a week and training on Tuesday and Thursday evenings.

When Harry Storer was the Rams manager, John Bowers managed only the barest handful of matches each season. But under Tim Ward, he began to establish himself on the left wing towards the end of the 1963-64 season, playing in the last 12 games of that campaign, and he was in from the start of 1964-65. The Rams won the first game of the season 3-2 at Crystal Palace and Bowers scored one of their goals. And he netted twice in a 4-1 win at Leyton Orient on the first Saturday of September.

At last it looked as though the speedy winger was in for an extended run in the Rams first team and the visit of high-flying Coventry City on 9 September 1964 was just the stage consolidate that position.

Bowers did that all right, marking a night of high drama at the Baseball Ground with yet another goal. But then tragedy struck.

Under Jimmy Hill, Coventry City were undergoing the first stages of their so-called 'Sky Blue Revolution'. Hill had taken a modest club with a mediocre team, and with the touch of a genius married skilful marketing to a passionate approach to the game and brought about a huge increase in support for a now successful Coventry team. In 1963-64, Coventry won the Third Division championship with some of the biggest crowds in the club's history regularly packing Highfield Road. They began the following season by winning their first five games and stormed to the top of the Second Division watched by crowds well in excess of 30,000.

Thus, when Coventry visited the Baseball Ground for their sixth game, they brought thousands of fans with them and swelled the gate to 32,803, the biggest attendance for a League game at Derby since the 33,330 who saw the visit of Grimsby in March 1956, for the top of the table clash in the Third Division North.

On a balmy autumn evening, the Rams soon demonstrated that they would not be daunted by the Coventry bandwagon and after 14 minutes it was John Bowers who scored the most glorious of goals to put Derby into the lead.

Out on the left flank, Bowers pushed the ball to Ian Buxton, the Derbyshire cricketer, and then raced for the return. Centre-forward Buxton tricked George Curtis, the Coventry centre-half, and then Bowers took the return pass at great pace, fought off two challenges in a run across the face of the Coventry goal and cracked a magnificent shot out of Wesson's reach. The Baseball Ground erupted in a wall of noise not experienced for many years — and after tonight not to be repeated until after the arrival of Brian Clough some years later.

It should have been John Bowers finest hour. Alas, four minutes later he suffered an injury which would keep him out of the game for several months. Challenging for the ball, he fell heavily, 'turned' his ankle and was carried from the field.

The Rams were now down to ten men — no substitutes were allowed in League games then — and it was Coventry's turn to pour forward. But the Derby defence proved more than equal to anything that the Sky Blues could throw at them. In goal, Reg Matthews was magnificent and at full-back Geoff Barrowcliffe steadied things down. Centre-half Ray Young was also so composed and in midfield Alan Durban, withdrawn from his usual attacking role after the injury to Bowers, held the ball up well. Instead of being overwhelmed, the Rams were playing their way out of trouble.

After 38 minutes Bowers returned, but with his ankle heavily bandaged he was no more than a limping passenger on the left wing. Still, though, the Rams looked dangerous and Durban whipped in a great shot which Wesson saved brilliantly.

Then, in the 71st minute, Eddie Thomas, signed from Swansea Town for £6,000 only two weeks earlier, kept up his record of scoring in every game by making it 2-0. Thomas ran on to a good pass from Durban, with whom he was to form such a fine striking partnership, and clipped the ball into the net despite a heavy challenge from behind and the sight of Wesson rushing towards him.

If the noise which greeted Bowers' goal had been remarkable, then that which followed Thomas' strike was deafening in the extreme, settling, as it did, the result with the Rams still depleted.

With a minute to go, Coventry scored through Smith, whose cross-shot was turned in by Jack Parry, but the game was won and Derby fans poured out into the narrow streets around the Baseball Ground, buzzing with what they seen.

John Bowers was out of the first team for ten weeks, and then managed only one appearance before returning for the last 15 games of the season. But after that injury he was never the same player and in May 1966 was transferred to Notts County where he ended his career.

On the Saturday following the defeat of Coventry, his place was taken by Nigel Cleevely, who scored on his debut in a 4-4 draw against Charlton at the Baseball Ground, after the Rams had trailed 3-0 at one stage. The following Wednesday, Derby went to Highfield Road and beat Coventry again, this time 2-0 with goals from Durban and Thomas before a crowd of 38,278.

At the end of the season the Rams finished ninth, one place above Coventry on goal-average. The Sky Blues had to wait until 1967 for promotion to Division One. That year, Brian Clough arrived as the Rams' manager and such nights of passion and intensity became almost the norm at the Baseball Ground again.

Tony Rhodes clears the ball against Stoke City at the Baseball Ground in August 1969 as Alan Durban closes in. A crowd of 36,170 saw this goalless draw, the Rams' fifth game back in Division One. There still appears to be some work to do on the Ley Stand, which was built in the summer, and the original floodlights are still in situ, although qualification for European football would eventually demand better illumination for televised night games.

August 1969 – and a New Dawn Shines

THE date 9 August 1969 was an important one in Derby. The first man had set foot on the moon less than three weeks earlier, the Manson murders had taken place only the day before, and in Ulster, the call for troops to patrol Londonderry and Belfast was about to be realised.

But in Derby there could only be one topic that would dominate the news. Derby County were back in Division One of the Football League.

Sixteen years had passed since the Rams lost 1-0 at home to Preston North End in April 1953 and struggling times, relegation to the Third Division North and years of mid-table mediocrity in Division Two had followed.

Now, all that seemed forgotten as Derby County prepared for the visit of Burnley after a summer break following the glorious Second Division championship season.

The summer of '69 had produced a heatwave, a new stand at the Baseball Ground, transfer rumours and, hard to believe now, disquiet amongst supporters that Brian Clough's team would not be up to the job in the top flight.

The *Derby Evening Telegraph* produced a special 'Rams back in the First Division' issue on 6 August and sports editor George Edwards expressed doubts about Les Green's 'lack of inches', Ron Webster 'horribly ill at ease whenever wingers take the ball inside him', Dave Mackay — 'will he be too slow?' — and John Robson's 'lack of experience'. Even Kevin Hector and Roy McFarland did not escape criticism!

The squad was certainly the smallest in the First Division and throughout July the Rams were reportedly chasing Hull City striker Ken Wagstaff. Indeed, this story was so important that the two main *Derby Evening Telegraph* headlines on 21 July were: 'Walk On Moon' and 'Blow For Rams — Hull Keep Wagstaff'.

Clough, in an interview with Edwards, stated that the players he wanted had not become available but he could have 'easily spent £150,000 if necessary'.

When asked about the forthcoming 1969-70 season, he said: "Obviously I'd like to see us playing great attacking football and beating teams like Liverpool and Leeds, but you have to be realistic. We aren't good enough to risk that sort of approach."

Was Clough being unusually cautious? Or was he talking tongue-in-cheek? Whatever, Liverpool and Leeds both had four goals put past them at Derby in the exciting season to follow.

Basically, though, the feeling was that Derby would finish about 15th or 16th. Anything more would be a bonus.

To mark the return to top-flight status a new east stand had sprung up above the old Popular Side terracing over the long hot summer and work was just about complete for the Burnley game. The contractors had two problems — lack of time and difficult access. Leys Malleable

Castings had agreed to make some land available but the design had to be altered considerably to cantilever the stand over part of the factory.

Derby ordered the building of the Ley Stand, as it surely will always be remembered, as late as 31 March, with work beginning in May. When major work was complete at the end of July, it was the shortest time such a job had been done by the contractors.

From the day the new stand was given the go-ahead, season ticket applications had flooded in, many fans enclosing blank cheques. The club decided to issue tickets on a two-season basis at £25, and even this was almost over-subscribed.

It is difficult today to convey the feverish, heady atmosphere of those days at the Baseball Ground, almost impossible for those who didn't live through it. But the town was gripped in a seemingly ever upward spiral of change and the biggest attendances the old ground ever saw.

It is a fair indication of how much football costs as entertainment now when looking at Derby County's prices for that 1969-70 pre-decimalisation season. Adult admission for the Pop Side was 5s (25p) with Normanton and Osmaston Ends 6s (30p). Relatively cheap football to attract the fans in an era where the price of a Pop Side season ticket was 50p cheaper than a Hotpoint electric kettle!

Park-and-ride schemes, unheard of in Derby, were set up in August at Victory Road and Moor Lane, and special buses were laid on from all areas of dense support such as Burton, Heanor and Alfreton.

On the opening day, a 13-year-old boy was reported waiting four hours before the kick-off, foregoing lunch to get a good position. The *Derby Evening Telegraph* quoted a 15-year-old Burnley fan who had hitch-hiked from Blackburn in the early hours: "I didn't even known where Derby was, so I set off early." All the turnstiles were open by 1pm due to the masses of people outside. Halcyon, innocent days.

As for the match itself, Burnley came for

a point and got one. Behind their solid defence goalkeeper Peter Mellor, making his League debut, was kept very busy on a slippery surface due to heavy rain. Hinton tested the young 'keeper early on with a long-range effort and Hector was inches wide right on half-time. Derby were by no means outclassed and were well on top but just couldn't find a way through with both O'Hare and Durban coming closest in the second half.

After 81 minutes it looked as if the Rams would start this historic season with a defeat when McFarland handled a shot from Les Latcham. Frank Casper stepped up to take the penalty, but Green became the hero of the day, diving to his left to make a superb save. Mellor was forced to leave the field after a collision with O'Hare, but with only two minutes left Derby couldn't test substitute goalkeeper Latcham.

The match was watched by 29,459 spectators and heralded an unbeaten run of 11 games in the First Division (making 22 in all with the 1968-69 run in) and a great first season back: Derby finishing fourth, there were famous victories over Tottenham, Manchester United, Liverpool, Everton and a controversially weakened Leeds at home, a never to-be-bettered average home attendance of 35,924 (helped by a record crowd of 41,826 to see the visit of Spurs), and the Rams were denied European soccer only by a controversial ban for administrative irregularities.

There has never been a season like it in the Rams' 110-year history.

Incredibly, the opening game back in Division One against Burnley was the Rams lowest League attendance of the season. The 29,459 crowd was the only home gate below 30,000 in a campaign when 754,407 attended League games at the Baseball Ground and with League and FA Cup ties the season's total at home rose to 924,868.

When the Rams returned to the First Division in 1969, they recorded some memorable victories before huge attendances. Here, John Fitzpatrick

of Manchester United puts through his own goal to help Derby to a 2-0 win in front of a crowd of 40,724.

Alan Durban celebrates, Alex Stepney looks back in anguish and the Rams have scored again in the 1970 Watney Cup Final against Manchester United at the Baseball Ground.

Sponsored Triumphs for the Rams

THE early 1970s were great times at the Baseball Ground as Derby County played host to some of the most exciting football in front of capacity crowds in the major League and Cup competitions. Sponsorship in football was in its infancy in those days and companies looking to get involved had to be content with small-scale tournaments. But even these low-key competitions were fiercely contested and well supported, unlike today's so called 'Mickey Mouse' cups. Derby County were good enough to land two pieces of silverware within two years to complement their League championship successes in a similar period.

The summer of 1970 had been a

scorcher and on 1 August it was a sweltering day. Die-hard Derby County supporters had been hoping that they would be travelling across Europe to watch their side in the coming months but the ban from European soccer due to financial irregularities had put paid to that. Instead they found themselves invited to join in with the first Watney Cup, in the era of the Party Seven and Red Barrel beer which was anathema to real ale drinkers.

Eight teams competed in the competition and the Rams opening game was at Craven Cottage. Derby tried a 4-2-4 system using Frank Wignall as an extra striker and it almost backfired as Fulham led 3-1 before Derby brought on John McGovern and reverted to 4-3-3. The Rams levelled, taking the tie to extra-time which they dominated, winning 5-3 in front of 18,501 spectators.

The competition used an experimental offside law but Sheffield United were difficult to break down in the semi-final and it took a brilliant solo goal from McGovern to settle the game. The attendance was 25,322, an impressive figure for what was, in a way, a pre-season friendly.

The Final, however, brought Manchester United to the Baseball Ground and on 8 August 1970 there were 32,049 present to see a quite brilliant Rams show as Derby cut United apart again and again. Goals from McFarland, Hinton, Durban and Mackay gave the Rams a 4-1 win with George Best replying for United.

It could have been eight or nine and the Rams did a lap of honour with the imposing shield, presented by Sir Stanley Rous. Some players later remarked that the euphoria of that hot afternoon contributed to a season of disappointment in 1970-71 as the start of a new campaign felt as flat as the crates of ale left behind by the sponsors. Derby finished ninth, but there was another trophy for the cabinet and the framework of the championship side was in place.

The 1971-72 season will forever be remembered as the one that gave Derby County their first League championship. But that wasn't the sole success of the campaign. The Texaco Cup had been devised to provide a competitive contest between the First Division sides of England and Scotland and invitations went out to clubs that had missed out on European qualification. Brian Clough decided to use the competition to try out some of his reserve players, themselves in the process of lifting the Central League championship trophy.

Dundee United were the first to be eliminated, losing 6-2 at the Baseball Ground in front of 20,059 on 15 September. The Rams went down 3-2 at Tannerdice in the second leg, but had done more than enough to proceed. Stoke were beaten 4-3 on aggregate with young Steve Powell making his debut in the home leg, and on 24 November the Rams met Newcastle in the semi-final.

A John O'Hare goal settled a close encounter and a fortnight later Derby won 3-2 on Tyneside with goals from John McGovern, Colin Todd and Jim Walker in front of 37,000 Geordies.

In the Final, Derby were to meet Airdrieonians in a strange, protracted affair. The away leg was goalless on 26 January 1972, but it was to be three months before 25,102 could attend the Baseball Ground for the return. The match, which had earlier been postponed, came when Derby had only one League game left, against Liverpool, which they had to win if they were to stand any chance of lifting the title, so their minds were elsewhere as they struggled to find their rhythm.

It proved a bad-tempered evening and Colin Boulton was fortunate not to be sent off as he punched Airdrie forward Drew Jarvie, but referee Jack Taylor was content to have a quiet word. The club later fined the goalkeeper after watching television evidence. Eventually the Rams won 2-1 with goals from a Hinton penalty and Roger Davies, then yet to appear in a League game.

Five days hence from their Texaco Cup win, Derby defeated Liverpool on a 89

Kevin Hector watches as his header is tipped over the bar during the 1972 Texaco Cup Final second leg at the Baseball Ground.

Roger Davies heads home Barry Butlin's centre to score the Rams' second against Airdrie.

memorable May evening and were crowned League champions shortly afterwards, but the Rams excursions into these additional competitions had been useful and produced success. After all, Brian Clough didn't enter any competition he had no intention of winning.

At The Right Club, At The Wrong Time

WHEN Derby County won their second League championship in 1974-75 and stood at the very pinnacle of British football, a young full-back was just starting out at the Baseball Ground. He was 18 years old and trying to force his way into the Central League side of the club he had joined from school. The Irish lad was to become a star in his own right at Derby, but the glittering success his older clubmates were celebrating was soon to evaporate, the glory days had reached their zenith and the Derby County for which Langan was to turn in so many great performances in the late 1970s was a declining power. The attacking right full-back, however, would not have been out of place in those championship sides. Indeed he would have graced them. In short, he arrived at the right club at the wrong time.

Langan was born in Dublin on 15 February 1957 and signed professional forms for Rams manager Dave Mackay in February 1975 after joining Derby from school in 1973, coming over to England with Don O'Riordan, with whom he represented the Republic of Ireland youth team. Langan made steady progress in the Reserves, often playing in midfield as well as at full-back. His first senior recognition came when Mackay named him in first-team squads in September 1976. Langan didn't make it into the side but the manager showed faith in considering him for what were still glamour games at a time when Derby frequently staged English soccer's Match of the Day.

Storm clouds were brewing, however, and within weeks Mackay was sacked and Langan had to wait five months before he made his debut. Derby had slumped to the wrong end of the table and a relegation struggle hit the club for the first time since the mid-1960s. New manager Colin Murphy was under constant threat of dismissal, but by far his best decision at Derby was to introduce Langan at right-back for the visit of Leeds United on 12 February 1977.

In an era where it had become common for Derby to pay big transfer fees, Langan was only the fifth home-grown player to be introduced to League football since 1967. And, Steve Powell excepted, they had made less than ten appearances between them. Although the Rams went down 1-0 that day to Leeds, the young full-back was an instant success with his superb tackling and darting attacking forays upfield as the crowd made him an overnight favourite.

That afternoon saw the first of 91 consecutive appearances and, coupled with the signing of Gerry Daly from Manchester United shortly afterwards, Langan's arrival signalled a turnaround for the Rams as they rose from bottom of Division One on 5 March, to 15th in May, losing only two of their last 17 League games and reaching the FA Cup sixth round. His versatility was also on show when, in May 1977, with Derby desperate for a point at Highbury, the seemingly inexhaustible Langan, wearing the number-nine shirt in midfield, marked fellow Dubliner Liam Brady out of the game as the Rams gained a vital point from a goalless draw.

In the close season Murphy may have thought that he had turned the corner, but six games into 1977-78 he was replaced by Tommy Docherty and for Derby County only struggle lay ahead. Throughout the Doc's tempestuous time at the Baseball Ground, Langan remained a fixture amid constant comings and goings. He was the club's only ever-present in 1977-78, continuing to surge up from the back, taking players on and setting up many a goal with his accurate centres. It was rare refreshment in those days to hear the whole ground applauding his endeavours at the end of a length-of-the-field charge. Langan gained deserved international recognition in April 1978 and was voted Derby's Player of the Year at the end of that season.

Over the following two troubled campaigns, Langan remained the Rams' most consistent performer, forming a successful partnership with Steve Buckley as two attacking full backs. Surprisingly, he was often neglected by the Republic of Ireland, winning only four of his 25 caps during his time at the Baseball Ground. In the summer of 1979, Colin Addison arrived to replace Docherty as manager

and Derby slumped into further relegation mire.

Langan became unsettled, and although his form on the pitch remained as reliable as ever, he became involved in a bust-up with Addison when the Irishman refused to travel with the team to an FA Cup tie at Bristol City. He turned up after travelling down by train but was promptly sent home, fined two weeks' wages and told that if he wanted to leave, he should put in a written request which he duly did. Bruce Rioch was also fined after taking Langan's side and allegedly 'using foul and abusive language' to the manager.

Apparently the cause of Langan's frustration was that he believed Addison had refused to inform him of offers from other clubs, but the result was that he was dropped for two games. Langan appeared to put this behind him, performing superbly during the fightback that spring, his crosses creating goals for newly-signed strikers Biley and Swindlehurst.

But Derby had left themselves too much to do and relegation came in May 1980, their 11-year stay in the top flight over. The upturn in form in the last third of the 1979-80 season led to a genuine belief that Derby would bounce straight back up with the same side, Rams supporters' hearts sank on 28 June 1980 when, with the new season only weeks away, news broke that Derby had sold David Langan to Birmingham City for £350,000, a Blues' club record.

He had settled his differences with Addison by then and signed a new contract with Derby, but it was inevitable that a First Division club would want to utilise Langan's talents, and it was a major blow to Derby's 'We'll be back in '81' hopes.

Langan admitted it was a wrench to leave after seven years but Derby's worsening bank balance meant the sale had to go through. The full-back had played in 155 out of 160 games since his Rams debut, scoring only one goal — a long-range effort against Arsenal in September 1979 — but creating many more.

David Langan in determined mood, sending a colleague goalwards with another well-measured pass.

He became a great favourite at St Andrew's, and later at Oxford, where he overcame serious injury problems to help United to the old First Division and to League Cup Final victory at Wembley.

In Derby, David Langan is remembered as the overlapping full-back who could surely have graced the Rams' best teams, without doubt a genuine star in a declining side. When Langan moved on he left a massive hole at right-back, an area that has caused Derby problems ever since and his position has never been effectively filled.

Peter Taylor looks apprehensive, Brian Clough downright gloomy. Brighton chairman Mike Bamber (between the two) has just announced that Clough has agreed to stay as manager of the Goldstone club. But Clough desperately wanted to return to the big time and was soon manager of Leeds United. That turned out to be a disaster – although Clough pocketed a small fortune in compensation – while Taylor remained manager of Brighton. Eventually the two joined up again at Nottingham Forest and scaled even greater heights than they had at the Baseball Ground.

Peter Taylor – Star-spotter to the Great Escape

PETER Taylor was born in Nottingham in 1928 and was on Forest's books as an amateur goalkeeper before signing for Coventry in May 1946. Nine years later, after only 90 appearances for City, he joined Middlesbrough, becoming first-choice 'keeper for four seasons at Ayresome Park, but more significantly striking up a great friendship with 'Boro's dynamic goalscoring legend-in-the-making, Brian Clough.

Taylor retired in 1961 and was managing Burton Albion when Clough asked him to become his assistant at Hartlepools United in 1965. Together they were an instant success and when Derby County offered Clough a £5,000 a-year manager's position in May 1967, the young, brash northerner insisted that Taylor accompany him as his assistant (at half his salary).

The next six-and-a-half years, of course, were gloriously triumphant and well documented, but the character of Taylor is worthy of closer scrutiny. It was commonly thought that Taylor's role was one of 'star-spotter' whilst Clough was the motivating factor. Taylor always contested this generalisation saying that it did 'an injustice to both of us'.

The assistant manager was, however, frequently absent from Rams matches, scouting for other players and endeavouring to improve the wealth of talent which he and Clough had gathered at the Baseball Ground. Roy McFarland has said: "Peter's great strength was as a number two with Clough more comfortable handling the press and being the front man."

Rams goalkeeper Colin Boulton said: "Cloughie knocked you down and Peter built you back up again. It was like bad cop, good cop. Cloughie would rant and rage in the dressing-room, then he would storm out and Peter would come over, put his arm around you and say, 'He doesn't mean it. He knows you're a good player.' Maybe it was all stage-managed. Maybe it was just instinctive. But it worked."

After their traumatic departure from the Baseball Ground, they went to manage Brighton. Clough was then tempted by Leeds United, but Taylor stayed at the Goldstone Ground. Clough's time at Elland Road was short and far from sweet, but the two men joined up again to lead Nottingham Forest to European glory before falling out to the extent that they did not speak to each other.

When they were together, Taylor — inevitably — seemed overshadowed by his more demonstrative partner, but he came out of the shadows during his second spell at Derby in the early 1980s. It was certainly another eventful time, but now the circumstances were much different. After sharing in further success,

Happy days at the Baseball Ground. Peter Taylor and Brian Clough greet Frank Wignall who had just been signed from Wolves to help in the Rams' run-in towards the Second Division championship in 1969. It was just the start as Clough and Taylor conquered the First Division and gave Rams fans some glorious nights of European football to remember.

both domestic and European, with Clough at Nottingham Forest, Taylor announced his retirement from the game in May 1982. He said he was exhausted.

It came as a surprise therefore when he was persuaded to take on one of the most difficult jobs in football only six months later. It is impossible to overstate the enormity of the task which confronted Taylor in keeping Derby in the Second Division in 1982-83, or to exaggerate the turmoil the club suffered at that time.

On the day he took over from John Newman, the Rams were firmly rooted to the foot of the division with only one win and eight points from 13 games. Even as late as January they still propped up the table with 15 points from 21 matches.

Taylor had a long-established reputation for gags and one-liners, and he arrived back at the Baseball Ground with a stream of quotes, many of which achieved local immortality. "Managing Derby is a doddle", was accompanied by "My missus could keep this lot up".

What influence Mrs Taylor had on proceedings is not known but a tremendous job was done in 1982-83 as Derby rallied to finish 13th, achieved a remarkable 15-match unbeaten run, snatched points from difficult away games backed by a huge travelling contingent renewed in hope and spirit, and reached the FA Cup fifth round and on the way

Six months into retirement after leaving Forest, Peter Taylor is introduced to a Baseball Ground press conference as the new manager of ailing Derby County in November 1982. He was persuaded back into the game by new chairman Mike Watterson, the Chesterfield-based snooker millionaire (seated next to Taylor). Beside him is Stuart Webb, the Rams' former secretary who had returned to the club, and director Fred Fern.

knocking out Clough's Forest with a patched-up side in the third round!

The fifth-round exit also saw the last attendance of over 30,000 at the Baseball Ground, and the highest crowd at Derby for five years, as 33,022 packed in to see a late Norman Whiteside goal end the Rams' brave efforts to topple eventual Cup winners Manchester United.

During what became known as Derby's 'Great Escape' season, Taylor had shown great acumen in bringing in the right players. Despite deep financial problems he brought Roy McFarland, along with Mick Jones, back from Bradford City as his assistant (at a cost of £65,000 in fines for poaching — con-

Mick Brolly (left) is congratulated by Bobby Davison and Kevin Wilson after scoring in the 2-0 win over Bolton Wanderers at Burnden Park in March 1983 as the 'Great Escape' under Peter Taylor gathered momentum.

troversy was never far away). Archie Gemmill also returned to provide a massive midfield boost as the Rams' engine room, and his best signing was Bobby Davison from Halifax Town, a new fans' favourite and one who would go on to join the Derby goalscoring greats with more than a century of goals.

Bobby Davison, signed by Taylor from Halifax Town for £80,000, in action in the home draw with Barnsley in April 1983. Davison was Taylor's first – and best – cash signing in his time as Derby manager. The player went on to prove the Rams' most consistent scorer for long after Taylor had left the Baseball Ground for good.

Paul Futcher was another Taylor coup, arriving from Oldham Athletic for £115,000. "He's good enough for England" was Taylor's quip. Amazingly, a decade later Futcher was still playing and in September 1994 turned out for Grimsby Town against the Rams at the Baseball Ground.

Steve Cherry was restored to keep goal and played superbly, and a series of loan deals helped to transform the team in a remarkable turnabout, Derby losing only three times in the 21 games of the second half of the season.

In the 1983 close season, optimism was high and promotion predicted on the strength of the upturn in form since Taylor's appointment. Not for the last time, the bookmakers installed Derby County as promotion favourites and season ticket sales were good. The manager once again produced some cracking quotes — "Just watch us go!" and "You will not believe the players I will be bringing in".

What did come in was Bobby Campbell, a big centre-forward who McFarland had known from his Bradford City days and who proved a sad failure, and an ageing and apparently unfit John Robertson, a player Taylor and Clough had revitalised at Forest but who was to prove a big disappointment at Derby.

The signing was a controversial one, nonetheless, and it signalled the end of Taylor's friendship with Clough. Appar-

Kevin Wilson scores in the 2-0 home win over Burnley at the end of April 1983. The Rams' immediate relegation worries looked almost over as Taylor's remarkable turnaround of the club's playing fortunes continued. Two away defeats followed, however, leaving a cliff-hanging last day of the season.

The strain begins to show on the final day of the 1982-83 season. Assistant manager Roy McFarland shouts instructions and Peter Taylor can hardly bear to watch. The Rams beat Fulham in a controversial game and managed to finish 13th, a massive achievement after relegation had seemed a certainty only a few weeks earlier.

ently the deal had been struck while Clough was on holiday.

Derby made an awful start to 1983-84, the 5-0 defeat at Chelsea signalling the arrival of a campaign of disaster. In early October, after Barnsley had won 2-0 at the Baseball Ground, the manager proclaimed "Give me nine games — if I've not turned it round by then you can write me off for all time, string me up and call me a fake."

Eight defeats in the opening 12 matches still failed to dampen Taylor's optimism and it was from this period that the famous "top six by Christmas" remark came. Another of his elaborate quotes was, "I won't pack it in. They will have to shoot me to get rid of me."

Apart from a five-game unbeaten stretch in November-December, the League programme was a harrowing one for club and supporter alike. Yet First Division Norwich City were knocked out of the FA Cup in front of a near 26,000 crowd as

like scoring once Plymouth had taken an early lead. Taylor amazed the crowd as the end grew nearer by withdrawing leading scorer Bobby Davison and bringing on 37-year-old defender Dave Watson and, at the final whistle, laid into Archie Gemmill, saying "I'm sorry Archie you're finished. Your legs have gone".

This to the man who had played his heart out for Derby County over the last two seasons and before and who had done more than most in the unhappy campaign.

Derby supporters could be forgiven for thinking that their manager was cracking up and following two heavy defeats in the League, the Rams, now cleared by the High Court to continue trading, parted company with Taylor for the last time, with relegation to Division Three a near-certainty.

Peter Taylor went back into retirement after 16 hectic months in a very difficult job. He reflected on things, saying, "We were in the cart because I bought badly in the summer. I did not stick to my principles of building a side. My first priority has always been to get it right at the back and I neglected that.

The prospect of having Robbo in the side blinded me".

Looking back now, that time can be examined with a broader perspective. It would have proved a stiff task for any manager and although Taylor lost his way badly in the relegation season, nothing can ever undermine the tremendous achievement he pulled off during the 'Great Escape' of 1982-83.

His rift with Clough, sadly, was never healed. The dispute had worsened with the publication of Taylor's book *With Clough by Taylor* and when Taylor died in Majorca on 4 October 1990, the management pair who had created the finest football teams the East Midlands has ever seen had not spoken to each other in years. Clough attended the funeral of his old friend and colleague, though, and one can only guess at what thoughts, what memories, what regrets crossed his mind on that autumn day.

Derby reached the quarter-final. Everyone was full of confidence that Third Division Plymouth Argyle would be no obstacle to a semi-final place, and following their fortunate goalless draw at Home Park (with 9,000 Rams followers making the trip) it seemed that Derby would prosper at the Baseball Ground. It was not to be and sadly everything came crashing around Taylor's head that night.

Financially Derby were facing their darkest hour with High Court appearances and winding-up petitions, and on the pitch the team never looked

Kevin Hector signs for Derby County in September 1966, watched by manager Tim Ward and members of the Rams board of directors.

Kevin Hector – King of the Baseball Ground

AT 3.25pm on Saturday, 24 September 1966, Huddersfield Town centre-half John Coddington was chaperoning the ball towards his goalkeeper. A young man, barely an adult, wearing white shirt and black shorts, sprinted from somewhere outside the normal range of Coddington's vision. The newcomer stretched his legs either side of the centre-half and flicked the ball into the net with his right foot. Spectators were shocked at first. They hadn't seen a Derby County player do anything so quick for years. They couldn't believe their eyes. It had to be the new signing from Bradford Park Avenue. It had to be Kevin Hector.

Comparisons were immediate. The 21-year-old Hector was the most exciting thing since Carter and Doherty. Older spectators talked of Steve Bloomer, or even Jimmy Moore, who had combined individualism with goalscoring 40 years

Hector heads a goal against Chelsea at the Baseball Ground in February 1970, the Rams' first season back in the top flight.

Manchester United's Ian Ure gets in a tackle on Hector at the Baseball Ground in October 1969. A goal from Hector and an own-goal by John Fitzpatrick gave the Rams victory in front of a 40,724 crowd.

before. Everyone agreed that Kevin Hector was something special for an ordinary Second Division team. Here was a star at the perfect time. England had won the World Cup, interest in football was growing, and Derby County were back in the entertainment business, offering excitement and a promise of what might come.

Perhaps it helped that his surname was that of a Greek God, a hero of Troy. Derby County supporters referred to Kevin Hector simply as 'the King'. Behind the scenes he became 'Zak', a nickname that derived from the fictional Zak Bishop, hero of a new soap opera called *United*. There was a big difference between Zak Bishop and Kevin Hector. The *United* series was short-lived, but Kevin Hector's playing days with Derby went on to May 1982. In two spells, he played more games than any other Derby County player in history and only Steve Bloomer has scored more League and Cup goals for the club. Hector won a Second Division championship medal, two League championship medals and winners' medals for the Texaco Cup, Watney Cup and FA Charity Shield. His two England

caps as a substitute, and two appearances for the Football League, were scant reward for his brilliant career.

Born in Leeds in November 1944, Kevin Hector continued to live in Leeds while he played for his first professional club, Bradford Park Avenue. His prolific goalscoring — 113 goals in 176 League games — helped Park Avenue to remain a middle-of-the-table Fourth Division club. When Hector left, Bradford signed Peter Deakin from Peterborough United but, really, Hector was irreplaceable. Bradford slumped to re-election positions in successive seasons and were voted out of the Football League in 1970.

While many managers doubted whether Hector could score goals at a higher level, Derby County chief scout Sammy Crooks was convinced. Hector was signed by Tim Ward, then the Rams' manager, for £34,000. It seemed a lot at the time but proved an exceptionally cheap deal. For Brian Clough and Peter Taylor, arriving at Derby in the summer of 1967, the presence of Hector was one of the attractions of the job. Earlier that year Clough had told Ward that he had signed one of the two best players in the Fourth Division. The other was Roy McFarland.

Hector was an incredibly resilient, consistent striker who reached double figures in goals in 11 consecutive seasons. He played under Tim Ward, Brian Clough, Dave Mackay and Colin Murphy, before Tommy Docherty unloaded him prematurely — and in unhappy circumstances — to Vancouver Whitecaps. When he returned to England, he played with Burton Albion before another new Rams manager, Colin Addison, signed him back in October 1980. Hector played for Derby County for two more seasons, as a Second Division midfielder.

Only 5ft 8in, and less than 11st, Kevin Hector demonstrated that size is not essential to success in soccer. What mattered was his speed, control and eternal good balance. Gerald Mortimer of the *Derby Evening Telegraph* once observed that the newspaper's files contained stacks of photographs of Kevin Hector but there

Champions! Hector lifts the League championship trophy after the presentation at the Baseball Ground on a Sunday in May 1972.

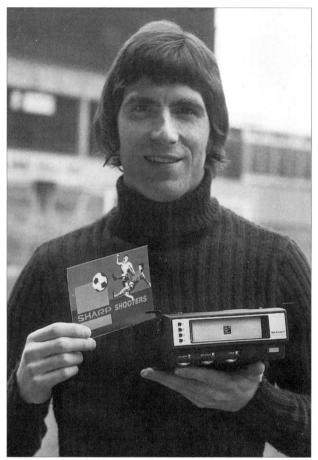

Kevin Hector with his 'Sharpshooter of the Fifth Round' trophy after his hat-trick against QPR in the 1972-73 FA Cup.

wasn't one where he was off-balance.

He was two-footed and exceptionally good in the air, frequently beating bigger men to crosses from the likes of Alan Hinton. His secret lay in timing his run, attacking the ball and jumping a few feet ahead of his marker. England supporters still recall that moment towards the end of a vital World Cup qualifying game in October 1973, that frustrating game which saw England 'massacre' Poland 1-1. Sir Alf Ramsey, never the best tactician with substitutes, had somehow forgotten that Kevin Hector was on the bench until reminded by one of his players. With his country desperate for a goal that would send England through, Kevin Hector came on for the last two minutes…and he nearly did it. Hector merely repeated what he had done so many times for Derby County, sneaking through a packed penalty area to meet a corner, flashing a header past the goalkeeper — in this case Jan Tomaszewski, Brian Clough's favourite 'clown' — only for the ball to be scrambled away from the goal-line. One of these days, when we watch that Hector header again on television, the ball will go in and England will go through to the 1974 World Cup finals.

Perhaps Kevin Hector's greatest talent was his ability to ride tackles. He was quick, he had pace and, as David Miller once wrote about him, he 'could wriggle through keyholes'. Despite rough treatment from defenders, he somehow escaped serious injury. Under Clough and Mackay he rarely missed game, forming superb partnerships with John O'Hare, Roger Davies, Francis Lee, Charlie George and many others. (In fact, a good quiz

Back at the Baseball Ground in 1981, this time directing operations in a deeper role. Hector's 'second' career as a Derby player was short and came at a time when the club's fortunes were far removed from those of his first, long, spell. But they ensured that he topped the list of Rams appearances and his 201 goals put him second only to Steve Bloomer in the club's overall list of scorers.

question is to name 20 striking partners for Kevin Hector. Don't forget Barry Butlin but no points are lost for not remembering Derek Hales!)

His allure can be judged by one small incident from a Boxing Day game against Wolverhampton Wanderers in his first season at the Baseball Ground. The crowd — just under 30,000 — were disappointed as the Rams went 3-0 down to a Wolves team heading for the First Division. As the final whistle approached, spectators streamed out of the ground prematurely. They walked around the pitch in droves. Then, suddenly, they stood still, scores of them, and swivelled in unions to watch the game again. Just because the ball had gone near Kevin Hector.

The supporters' special relationship with Kevin Hector remained throughout his career, even when Derby County became champions, even when Kevin Hector was just one great player in a great side. He would always be 'The King' because his signing was the first tangible evidence that the club's directors suddenly wanted Derby County to improve and become a great side again. Hector was the first signal that it was about to happen. And it did.

The first signs came in 1968-69 when the Rams romped the Second Division. The partnership of Hector and O'Hare was in place, Hinton was supplying crosses, and there was a confidence that was a joy to watch. Hector scored in the first four rounds of the League Cup that season, including the only goal of the thrilling fourth-round replay against Everton.

No post-war player has scored more goals for Derby County, and there is no record of the number of other goals he made with runs to the by-line or by being fouled for a free-kick or penalty. Altogether he scored 201 in first-class games for the club. How do you choose the best or the most valuable? There was the goal in Italy in 1973 that almost set up the chance of a European Cup Final. There was one at Wembley that heralded an FA Charity Shield win against West Ham United in 1975. And his five against Finn Harps (seven over two legs) was an astonishing performance in the 1976-77 UEFA Cup competition.

The easiest way to summarise his effect on the Derby public is to remind ourselves that adulation began on 24 September 1966, when he slipped in to score past Huddersfield's John Oldfield, and was still there on 15 May 1982, when he scored past Watford's Steve Sherwood in a 3-2 win that ensured safety for Derby County and, afterwards, he faced the ordeal of a pitch invasion that ripped the shirt from his back. In between his name had been chanted several hundred times a season: 'Hector, Hector, Hector . . .'

Rams chairman W.H.Bendle Moore meets the Duke of York, later to become King George VI, at Maine Road in 1934, before a Rams match against Manchester City. Bendle Moore was a major figure on the Derby County board in the inter-war years.

Money, Money, Money.

DERBY County's finances have been as unpredictable as events on the field. Perhaps it all started with an incident in the late 1880s when the assistant secretary went abroad with ticket takings, changed his name and became court tailor to King Alphonso of Spain.

Derby County was formed in 1884 as an offshoot of Derbyshire Cricket Club, and the cricket club benefited by £586 in the first six years. But the 1888-89 accounts were severely criticised by the auditors: 'They have been kept in a very loose and unsatisfactory manner. Many of the books and papers have been either lost or destroyed, but the ticket account enclosed represents the known deficiency of the late assistant honorary secretary, making a total deficiency by S.Richardson on the issue of tickets for the two seasons of £194 10s 3.'

Not surprisingly, the cricket and football clubs split in 1891, and the football club was soon dependent on money from sources other than at the gate. The £1,000 proceeds from a Drill Hall bazaar were particularly appreciated in 1894.

Two years later, on 14 August 1896, Derby County Football Club became a limited company. The club's objectives included 'to promote the practice and play of football, cricket, baseball, lacrosse, lawn tennis, hockey, bowls, bicycle and tricycle riding, running, jumping, the physical training and development of the human frame.'

The nominal capital was £5,000, divided into 5,000 shares at £1 apiece. Only 1,508 shares were taken up, and only four of the 195 shareholders had a significant number. W.M.Jervis the president, who leased the Baseball Ground and sub-let it to the club, had the most shares (150). Arthur Brown and Arthur Wilson each had 50, and a Repton plumber, John Wroughton, had 40.

The company thrived in its early years. Most football clubs experienced financial pressures around the turn of the century, but Derby County's financial reserves were boosted by successful FA Cup runs and three appearances in the Final. When the Football League introduced a maximum-wage rule in 1901, Derby County were one of the few clubs wanting to pay the likes of Steve Bloomer more than the stipulated £4 per week maximum.

Then the club nearly went under in 1907, when a loss of £632 coincided with relegation to the Second Division. In July, a public meeting was held at the Guildhall to consider the parlous state of the club. The board estimated that receipts of £250 per home game were necessary for

survival, and yet the previous season's home games had averaged just over £180. Mr W.T.Morley, the chairman, addressed the meeting. "Is the club worth continuing, or is it not?" he asked.

The crisis was temporarily averted when an extra 730 shares were taken up, predominantly by the new president, Major Winterbottom, who bought 200, and solicitor Robert Chambers, who purchased a hundred. By 1911, however, the club owed £710 to the bank, and things continued to slide. The promotion season of 1912-13 brought a £750 loss, and, when the £1,500 signing of Jimmy Moore failed to save relegation the following season, almost £5,000 was owed to the bank. Horace Barnes was sold to Manchester City for a record £2,500 and the directors dispensed with the services of trainer Arthur Latham in 1915.

When the club closed down in 1916, some pundits warned that Rams fans might start supporting those clubs with the courage to keep going during the war. Some of these fears proved justified when Derby County were resurrected. On 17 February 1919, a public meeting was convened at the Guildhall by the Mayor, Alderman W.B.Robotham, 'to save Derby County Football Club from a very real threat of extinction.'

W.T.Morley, the club's chairman, pointed out that the club still owed the bank £1,300; he wanted to clear the arrears and have £2,000 reserve. Another important force on the board, Bendle Moore, emphasised the seriousness of the plight by saying that the directors wouldn't carry on unless at least £3,000 could be raised. Otherwise Derby would have to 'sell their players to meet their liabilities and then pass out'.

The club survived, thanks to a subscription fund, the formation of a Working Men's Committee to encourage workers to take up shares, and the benevolence of Sir Gordon Ley, who became president and agreed to forgo Baseball Ground rent that he was owed by the club.

The first season after the war brought a

Members of the Rams board when the club won the FA Cup in 1946. From left to right are H.Walker, T.E.Wassall, O.J.Jackson (president), Ben Robshaw (chairman) and J.R.Cholerton. Robshaw, along with secretary Jack Catterall, was suspended *sine die* by the Football Association after yet more financial irregularities were uncovered at the Baseball Ground. Jackson had already served a suspension and for Robshaw this was a second suspension. He had earlier been banned along with manager George Jobey and several other directors.

profit of £529, but then came three loss-making seasons that determined the destiny of the company. Hereafter, the name of Derby County would be forever linked with a hefty bank overdraft.

It was again a relegation season that began the financial decline. In 1920-21, big money was spent on Storer, Rance and Paterson, but the Rams went down to the Second Division. By 1923 the bank was owed £8,410 and the following season the Rams missed promotion to the First Division by a single goal. In September 1924, a special resolution increased the limit of the authorised capital to £20,000 and a clause limiting borrowing powers was deleted.

The company bought the Baseball Ground in 1924 and provided money for manager George Jobey to spend on players. A loss of £6,349 in the promotion season (1925-26) increased the bank overdraft to £18,750, a sum that was 'secured by personal guarantee of the directors, jointly and severally'.

For the next 13 seasons, Derby County were one of the top teams in Division One but the overdraft crept higher and higher — to £28,491 in 1938 — because money was poured into ground improvements, the signing of international-class players, a field at Burley Lane (Quarndon) and club houses, the first being 70 Leacroft Road. Bendle Moore was the chairman during this period of sustained success, and Oswald 'Ossie' Jackson was an astute

financial advisor. Jackson showed a gambler's instinct and a love of sport. He had begun work at Clemson's boot-and-shoe business and then made a success of Jackson and Davis. Later, he was chairman of Ford and Weston and a major figure behind Bennett's ironmongery and Eaton's the jeweller. A greyhound and racing enthusiast, his racing colours matched those of Derby County — black and white.

In 1941 a bombshell hit the club. A joint FA-Football League commission sat at Derby and discovered irregularities in the club's books. It transpired that between 1925 and 1938 bonuses and 'under-the-counter' payments had been concealed by procedures like paying the manager for journeys he didn't make and inventing extra groundsmen in the books. The outcome was *sine die* suspensions for manager George Jobey, four directors (Moore, Pattison, Ann and Robshaw) and two former directors (Green and Jackson).

In fact, the suspensions were all lifted before the end of the war, and the commission's chairman, Mr A.Brooke-Hirst, helped dispel rumours with a clear statement: 'There was nothing in the charges against the club which reflected on the honesty or integrity of the directors of the club. Nor was there anything in the charges which suggested, or even hinted that the directors had benefited personally by anything which had been done.' Nevertheless, a stable period of rule was over. There were only 11 different directors between 1925 and 1938. (Compare this with 25 between 1971 and 1984.)

During the war years the club were grateful for the yeoman service of Ben Robshaw and Gilbert Dickenson, who acted as honorary secretary. Then came the FA Cup success of 1946 and a buoyant post-war period, but the club paid a price because another joint commission investigated the books for 1945-46, when a small, inexperienced staff had been overworked. It was alleged that the club had failed to apply the PAYE system to players' wages and benefits, thereby withholding £2,710 from the Inland Revenue. In November 1949 chairman Ben Robshaw and former secretary Jack Catterall were suspended *sine die*.

These disruptions might have defeated a weaker club, but Derby County retained their continuity. Oswald Jackson was back as president and chairman, and Cyril Annable had returned from RAFVR wartime service to take over as secretary in June 1946. Annable held the post for 22 years.

A decline in playing fortunes in the 1950s was compounded by a national decline in attendances. the directors tightened the reins and steered a slow course to financial stability. They also reacted curiously to the removal of the maximum wage in 1961, determined to cut costs in the face of the omnipresent bank overdraft, which now grew towards £50,000. There was familiar talk of outsiders loaning the club money for investment, but one possible candidate, Sam Ramsden, was too old to satisfy the requirements of the 1948 Companies Act.

In 1964, the board passed a resolution to rotate the chairmanship. Fred Walters thus ended his five-year period as chairman, and the club entered a volatile era which saw ten different chairmen in the next 20 years.

Chairmen came and went in the late 1960s. The club briefly entered the Second Division promotion pack under Harry Payne, spent a record club fee on Kevin Hector under Sam Longson, won promotion to the First Division under Sydney Bradley, and then spent another record fee on Colin Todd with Sam

Chairman Sam Longson presided over the record purchase of Kevin Hector, although manager Tim Ward had a hard job in persuading him that Derby should pay such a big fee. Longson will be better remembered as the man who brought Brian Clough to the Baseball Ground – and as the man who effectively fired-him..

Longson in charge again (after a boardroom battle had resulted in three directors resigning).

As ever, there was a price to pay. Cyril Annable's successors as secretary — first 21-year-old Malcolm Bramley, then reluctant stand-in Alan Collard — had barely coped, and the books were investigated once more. A joint commission concluded that there had been 'gross negligence' in the administration of the club, for which the members of the board had to take some responsibility. The club were fined £10,000 and banned from European competition for the 1970-71 season.

By the summer of 1971 the ground had a new stand but debts of £76,161 were also in place. The club attempted to issue the remaining 13,852 shares at £2 per £1 share.

Then came the most glorious period in the Rams history — League champions in 1971-72 and again in 1974-75.

Elation and optimism are evident in chairman Sam Longson's 1975 report to the shareholders: 'Football is going through a very difficult and transitional period at present with many important issues within the game being discussed — television, increased prices, hooliganism, freedom of contract for players — and many clubs at present are feeling the pinch. We at Derby can say that we have not felt the pinch as much as other clubs.'

In the next nine years seven chairmen and seven managers tried to cope with unforeseen financial difficulties. The bank overdraft doubled — £50,000 to £100,000 — in the two years following the second championship. After Tommy Docherty had managed a transit camp for players, 'bank interest' became a significant factor in the club's balance-sheet. Like other clubs, Derby County were searching for more income from outside the game. The supporter's club had always been a great source of help — they even provided the £5,150 fee to sign Gordon Brown in January 1957 — and the club shop and other commercial activities were to be expanded. Sponsorship was also necessary. The first deal came in 1977 when Saab provided £100,000 worth of vehicles. In the years to come, major sponsors would include Patrick, Bass, Sportsweek, BPCC, Maxwell and Auto Windscreens.

The 1979-80 season was one of the most significant in the club's financial history. New manager Colin Addison invested heavily in players — Emery (£100,000), Osgood (£150,000), Barry Powell (£350,000), Biley (£350,000), Davies (£40,000) and, after hours with the bank manager, Dave Swindlehurst £410,000). Sadly, the team were relegated to the Second Division, and, even more unfortunately, the playing decline once more coincided with financial problems that affected the whole of football: the retain-and-transfer system had been replaced by freedom of contract; the Sports and Safety Act demanded ground improvements; and the nation's economic recession and alternative attractions helped continue the decline in attendances.

Wage bills of football clubs increased by 45 per cent in the two seasons following 'freedom of contract'. Whereas Rams stars of 1969 had been earning £40 or £45 per week, eight club employees were earning ten times that in 1980, and one was in the £45,000 to £50,000 a year bracket. Chairman Richard Moore and the management team did much to redress the balance by selling high-wage players, but only at Second Division prices.

In January 1982 an attempt was made to float 60,000 £10 shares. The Kirkland family had been a dominant force until then — largely through shares acquired by Jack Kirkland between August 1972 and May 1973 — but now John Kirkland hoped that this new issue would widen the power base. 'There were people who were indeed set against making the issue a public one of voting shares,' said John Kirkland in March 1982 in an exclusive interview with Neil Hallam of the *Derby Trader*. 'They said, as though it was totally undesirable, that we'd end up having to hold annual meetings at the Baseball Ground. Frankly that would suit my idea of democracy just fine.'

The share issue met with a poor response, and every week the directors searched for new ways of reducing the deficit. A bad start to the 1982-83 season brought more radical change. Mike Watterson, a millionaire snooker promoter, was the new chairman. Peter Taylor took over as manager. And several new directors joined the board.

The club incurred some unfortunate expenses — a £10,000 fine for inducing Roy McFarland to leave Bradford City and become Taylor's assistant, plus £55,000 compensation to the Yorkshire club. Then, early in 1983, supporters of Leeds United and Chelsea inflicted £40,000 worth of damage to the Baseball Ground within eight days. The season ended (78 seconds early) with a pitch invasion during the game against Fulham. Costly mesh fencing was installed around the pitch.

Mike Watterson, like so many directors, underestimated the effect of football on his life. He resigned in July 1983 and John Kirkland took over to steer the club through their most difficult season yet. First, there was frantic rallying to pay players on occasions when the bank failed to honour wage cheques. Then, on 3 February 1984, the Inland Revenue issued a winding-up petition. The bank immediately froze the club's account,

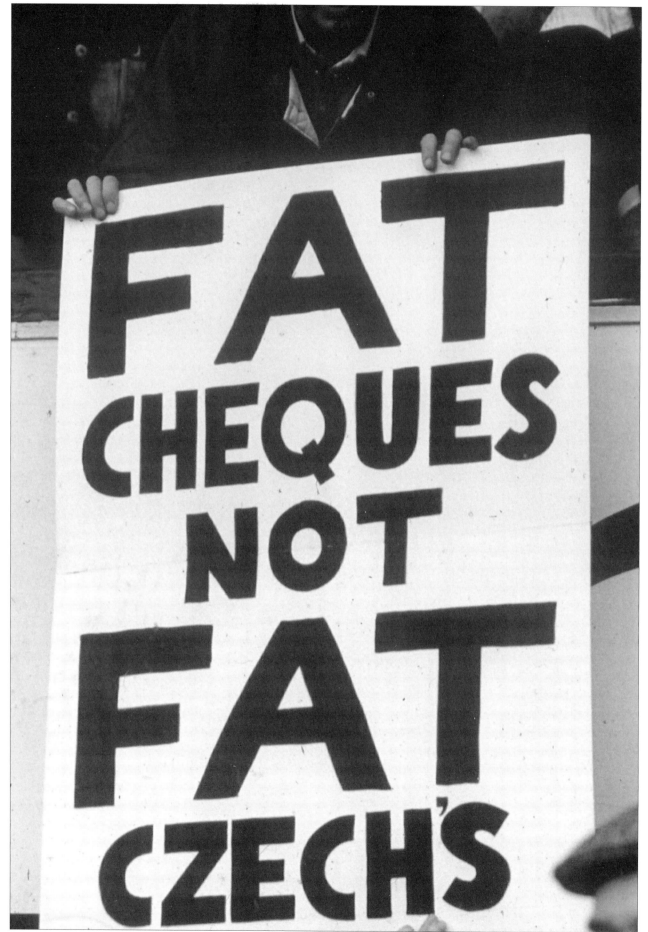

Derby fans express their displeasure in Robert Maxwell's sudden disinterest in the club which resulted in a total ban on transfers. Only later, after Maxwell's controversial death, did it become obvious why the apparent millionaire publisher could not produce cash to help Derby County.

which was embarrassing because Telford United's share of FA Cup fourth-round receipts was lodged there.

The club had debts of £1.5 million, and among the preferential creditors were the Inland Revenue (£132,000), Customs and Excise (£78,000), Derby City Council (£58,000) and National Westminster Bank (£750,000). Chief executive Stuart Webb negotiated several potential rescue packages, and the local councils were approached without success. Eventually, Robert Maxwell, millionaire publisher and Oxford United chairman, emerged as a likely backer.

Early offers of 70p in the pound failed to satisfy Justice Mervyn Davies in the High Court and it was only after a series of adjournments that a rescue plan was approved. The ground would be sold (to Maxwell) for £300,000 and the bank would accept a loss. Four new directors joined the board. The club ended the season still in business . . .but relegated to the Third Division.

With Ian Maxwell as chairman, and Arthur Cox as manager, the club entered a period of expansion which saw a rapid rise from the Third Division to the First. At that point, in 1987, Robert Maxwell controversially moved from Oxford United to take over as chairman at Derby. Over the next three years, the chairman made the sort of calculations that many of his predecessors had also made, in this case, 'We need 20,000 gates, and we're not quite getting them.'

The club's first £1 million transfer took place in 1988 when Dean Saunders arrived and the wage bill continued to rise. In 1990 Derby County had 12 employees who earned over £50,000 per annum, including three £100,000-plus men. That was the year that Robert Maxwell announced that he was looking for a buyer for Derby County. With typical modesty, he summed up his role in the club's history in the 1990 report: 'If it were not for the Maxwell family and certain members of the board of directors including Stuart Webb, Derby County would have been relegated in March 1984 to the dustbin of history from whence there is no return.'

It took all season to find a buyer. Then the sales of Mark Wright and Dean Saunders — the money going into Maxwell's coffers — financed the transition to a local consortium. Soon afterwards, in 1991-92, local newspaper millionaire Lionel Pickering introduced massive additional funding, lending Derby between £10 and £12 million to spend on players.

Over the years directors have been pilloried from all directions: supporters expect new players and success; players expect suitable rewards; managers have sometimes grown frustrated at a lack of understanding of playing matters. However, the club has survived. As the company's centenary approaches, we are reminded of W.T.Morley's words of 1907: 'Is the club worth continuing, or is it not?'

So far, there has always been somebody around to answer 'Yes'.

Bobby Davison raises his arms in triumph after scoring the goal which ensured Second Division survival for another season. But the victory over Fulham was tainted by serious crowd disorder.

The Missing 78 Seconds

I T WAS a troubled season for Derby County — only two wins in their first 22 League games and some major spots of bother, particularly in January, when games with Leeds United and Chelsea triggered serious crowd disturbances on successive Saturdays, albeit all by rival fans. By the last Saturday of the season, however, the club had rallied. A run of 15 unbeaten League games had pulled them on to the fringe of the relegation zone in Division Two. A win in the last game of the season, at home to Fulham, would ensure safety.

Fulham had their own interests. Malcolm Macdonald's young team had been in the top three for most of the season. A recent bad run had created

The match against Fulham is over. Or is it? The crowd, who have spilled on to the pitch, obviously think so but there is still over a minute to play according to referee Ray Chadwick.

anxiety, but a win at Derby would guarantee promotion to Division One at Leicester City's expense.

After 75 minutes' play Derby County's Bobby Davison volleyed the first goal of the game. A small pitch invasion by celebrating fans was soon contained, but the crowd gathered round the edge of pitch, about five or six deep. The pitch became smaller.

Robert Wilson, a Fulham midfield player, was kicked by a spectator while the ball was in play. The touch-lines were no longer visible. The referee, Ray Chadwick from Darwen, did his best under the circumstances. Then, when he blew his whistle for offside, the fans, thinking the game was over, swarmed on to the pitch to celebrate Derby's 1-0 win.

Referee Chadwick's watch showed 78 seconds still to play, but the teams had to leave the field. A second Fulham player, Jeff Hopkins, was assaulted in the process. He was too shocked to continue. The referee did not take the players back on to the pitch.

Fulham manager Malcolm Macdonald felt his team deserved a replay. He argued that it wasn't Fulham's fault that the crowd had invaded, cut the game by 78 seconds and interfered with some of the later minutes. Others felt that Derby had deserved to win, looked well on top and the chances of Fulham scoring two goals in the last 78 seconds were minimal. One national newspaper asked readers to recall all those games where away teams had scored two in the last 78 seconds after being one down.

The Football League ruled that the result should stand. Fulham appealed to the Football Association, but with no joy. The only tangible outcome was that Derby County were forced to spend money to improve the security of their ground. They erected perimeter fencing, which stayed a permanent fixture for almost six years.

Derby County skipper Mark Wright beats Sheffield Wednesday's Carlton Palmer to a high ball at the Baseball Ground.

Mark Wright's Derby days – Best of his Career

WHEN Derby County signed Mark Wright from Southampton in August 1987, the £760,000 fee paid by Arthur Cox shattered the club record, which had stood since Dave Swindlehurst joined the Rams in April 1980. It proved money well spent as Wright played a massively important role in keeping Derby afloat during that difficult first season back in Division One.

Born in Dorchester-on-Thames on 1 August 1963, Wright had signed professional for Oxford United in 1980, on his 17th birthday. He made his League debut just over a year later and, following only ten further first-team appearances, joined Southampton in March 1982 for £80,000, as a makeweight in a complicated transaction involving another future Ram, Trevor Hebberd, who, along with George Lawrence, went to Oxford while Keith Cassells and Wright journeyed to The Dell.

Wright had five good years on the south coast, becoming the Saints' regular centre-half in 1982-83, the season he won England Under-21 honours, and progressed to the full international side on 2 May 1984, against Wales at Wrexham.

Wright won 16 England caps with Southampton but missed the 1986 World Cup finals in Mexico after breaking a leg in an FA Cup semi-final against Liverpool.

When he arrived at the Baseball Ground, however, Wright brought with him the reputation of being something of a hothead. At Southampton he had several disagreements with their managers, including a one-month suspension for speaking to the press about the internal strife at The Dell and a much-publicised after-match fracas with Lawrie McMenemy. Indeed, Wright was sent off on three occasions whilst with Derby but it is generally acknowledged that the player matured considerably under Cox.

One sending off may have been a turning point. After Norwich midfielder Trevor Putney had fouled Wright's close friend Ted McMinn, the Rams defender raced half the length of the pitch to administer revenge upon the Norwich player. Cox, while critical, had appointed Wright team captain shortly prior to this incident and this gave him extra responsibility which he had failed to exercise. From here on it was this same responsibility upon which he thrived.

Classy and elegant with plenty of time on the ball and supremely dominant in the air in either penalty area, Wright soon became a firm favourite with the Rams supporters who judged him, quite correctly, as the best centre-half since Roy McFarland.

This opinion was not initially shared by England manager Bobby Robson, who inexplicably preferred Arsenal's Tony Adams, at that time a much inferior footballer to Wright. It was a situation that was not forgotten by Rams followers who gave Adams a torrid time whenever he played at the Baseball Ground.

For the Rams, Wright formed a good partnership with the steady Rob Hindmarch as Derby won many away points in finishing fifth in the old First

Division 1988-89. Yet the Rams captain again found himself in the international wilderness where he was to remain for almost two years and 16 matches after Robson brought his 'attitude' into question following England's poor showing in the 1988 European Championships. Wright's hour, however, was to come.

As Robert Maxwell tightened the screws on the club and Derby's fortunes began to wane, Mark Wright performed superbly and consistently. The Rams just about stayed up in 1989-90 and as the goals dried up Wright was essential in the scrap for points in the second half of the season. And he also weighed in with six vital goals during the campaign.

He was chosen for the World Cup squad, but was not the manager's first-choice centre-half. Bobby Robson said he was unsure of Wright's fitness and with Terry Butcher, who had played under Robson at Ipswich Town, a fixture in the England side, it was difficult to see where Wright could fit in. But a disappointing opening draw with the Republic of Ireland showed up the English style as technically poor, causing Robson to rethink his tactics.

Wright was finally brought in to play as a continental-style sweeper and he proved a resounding success, showing the skill and poise which everyone at Derby saw every week. In the next game, against Egypt, the Rams centre-half towered above the opposing defence to score the only goal of the match. Those in the Derby area watching the game on live television leaped up in joy and the town was awash that night with cries of "Ooh, Mark Wright!" in celebration of the first Rams player to score for England for almost 40 years (the last was Jack Lee in his only international appearance, against Northern Ireland in Belfast in October 1950).

Wright played in all the subsequent games of the competition, sustaining a nasty head injury during the quarter-final thriller against Cameroon, but bravely, and typically, he insisted in carrying on, head bandaged. The Rams' skipper picked

Mark Wright battles for the ball with Carlisle United's Keith Walwyn in October 1990.

up a fourth-place medal and won critical acclaim and new admirers alike as one of the true stars of Italia '90.

Almost 12 months later, Wright was honoured in being chosen to captain his country when England met the USSR at Wembley in May 1991. Altogether he won 24 of his 43 caps during his time at the Baseball Ground but the post-World Cup season of 1990-91 was to prove Wright's last as a Derby player. Maxwell put the club up for sale. No incoming transfers were permitted and poor results compounded this frustrating time for all at the Baseball Ground.

Wright continued to perform well, but he was fighting a losing battle as Derby withered on the vine. On 16 April 1991, on the eve of a match at Old Trafford that the Rams, realistically, just had to win to avoid relegation, Maxwell made his ridiculous and lengthy statement giving his views on the club and also announcing that Wright, along with Dean Saunders, would be sold at the end of the season.

The supporters were bemused and it was a difficult situation for the players, who seemingly had no choice in the matter. On the following Saturday relegation became a reality as Derby lost in Manchester for the second time in four days, this time at Maine Road.

In July 1991, Mark Wright signed for Liverpool for £2.3 million and captained them to FA Cup success in 1992, but his three years at Anfield have not proved

happy ones for the player. He has once again lost his England place, been plagued by injuries and fallen out with the management. Liverpool spent millions on two central defenders early in the 1994-95 season and Wright's future on Merseyside looked bleak, fuelling wishful rumours in the Midlands that he might return to Derby County.

In August 1994, Wright was poised to return to the Rams on loan at the same time as Steve Hodge, then languishing in Leeds' reserve side, who came to bolster the midfield. Unfortunately the Wright deal fell through, the Liverpool man apparently sustaining an injury in training, Hodge's loan spell then being increased after his significant contribution coincided with the Rams' much-improved performances.

Although Mark Wright left Derby in sad circumstances, with relegation and crippling financial constraints dogging the club, he retained great memories of his time at the Baseball Ground. Popular with the supporters, Wright was twice voted Player of the Year in his four seasons with the Rams. He has also publicly expressed his debt to Arthur Cox, and player and supporter alike can look back fondly at his association at Derby where he tempered his aggression to harness his talent, resurrected his international pedigree to the highest stage in the world and, quite simply, played the best football of his career.

Rob Hindmarch connects with a free-kick to score against Sheffield United in the FA Cup.

Great Cup Games – and the Rams are on the Way Back

ARTHUR COX spent the first of his nine seasons at Derby County halting a slide which had seen the Rams drop from League champions to Division Three and near extinction in nine years. Now, at the start of 1985-86, Cox's new side was beginning to take shape.

The previous season had seen Geraint Williams, Gary Micklewhite and Trevor Christie join the club and the trio were supplemented in the summer by new captures Ross MacLaren, Jeff Chandler and goalkeeper Mark Wallington.

As the season progressed, it became more and more significant that Cox had put together a side that could battle on opposing turf, winning many more away points than the Rams had been used to for years.

Indeed, from 31 August to 22 February, Derby were unbeaten away from home in the League, and in League and Cup games they put together a 15-match run without defeat on their travels.

In the autumn, two League Cup performances against First Division Leicester City seemed to prove a turning point. A Ross MacLaren penalty and a Jeff

Chandler goal gave Derby a 2-0 lead from the home leg, and at Filbert Street a 1-1 draw was flattering to the Foxes. Derby outplayed their opponents, leading through Bobby Davison's first-half chip shot, and could have scored five or six.

Nottingham Forest ended the Rams hopes in the competition with a 2-1 win at the Baseball Ground, but Cox knew his team need not fear loftier opposition.

The FA Cup run began against Crewe Alexandra in November. The tie saw the Rams debut of John Gregory, signed from Queen's Park Rangers for £100,000 to orchestrate play from midfield. Crewe, including future superstar David Platt, were brushed aside 5-1 with goals from a Chandler penalty and Davison and Christie (two each).

Rams supporters were certainly not used to FA Cup games before January. Indeed, since the Football League was founded this was only the fourth season Derby had been involved at this early stage.

The second round saw recent opponents in the competition return in the guise of Telford United. In 1984, Derby had struggled to beat the non-League outfit 3-2, but this time there was to be no repetition. The Rams stroked the ball around magnificently to hammer the Shropshire lads 6-1. Gregory opened the scoring on 31 minutes and Derby were regretting several missed opportunities when McKenna equalised on half-time.

After the break, however, the Rams took control with Jeff Chandler hitting a hat-trick and Gary Micklewhite netting twice. Derby might have scored ten but were denied by many fine saves from Telford goalkeeper Kevin Charlton, who, two years later, played a few games for Scarborough following a gap of more than 10 years since his last League appearance for Hereford United.

The third round draw sent Derby to Kent for a tie at Gillingham. By now the severe winter had set in causing many postponements.

On a bone-hard pitch at the Priestfield Stadium, Derby were without Bobby

Bobby Davison (far right) dives to convert Chandler's cross into Derby's second goal against Lincoln City in November 1985. It was Davison's 12th of the season.

Gary Micklewhite (second left) steers the ball past Judge for the Rams' third goal in the 7-0 thrashing of Lincoln.

Davison, injured during an abandoned game at Newport on New Year's Day. Andy Garner stepped in and put the Rams ahead after 19 minutes with good close control before turning and hitting his shot inside the post. Gillingham pressed hard, eventually equalising after 69 minutes through Robinson, and Derby battled well in defence to take the tie back to the Baseball Ground, where six inches of snow on top of a sheet of ice was enough to see the replay postponed until Monday, 13 January when heavy rain was this time the order of the night.

Arthur Cox had been honoured as Third Division Manager of the Month and his side needed extra-time in a classic Cup tie battle to see off Gillingham. Christie put Derby in front seven minutes after the interval and it looked as if Wallington's great form in goal would keep it at 1-0.

However, with three minutes to play Robinson headed the leveller. Thirteen minutes into the first period of extra-time, Garner scored at the second attempt and Christie rattled in a third after Graham Harbey's shot had hit the bar. Chandler had been substituted in both games, snuffed out completely by Gills right-back Mel Sage, who Cox signed seven months later.

The fourth-round journey to Bramall Lane was made by 9,700 Rams supporters, the club's largest away following for ten years. Davison was still injured and, due to the bad weather, the Rams had played little soccer since the previous round.

A fixture pile-up was beginning to look worrying; on 6 February, Derby had played the least number of games in the Football League and had 22 to squeeze in the 12 weeks remaining.

Cox stuck with Garner up front as his other option, emerging Reserves hot-shot Phil Gee, was Cup tied having played, and scored, for Gresley Rovers against Friar Lane Old Boys in the competition's initial qualifying round in August 1985!

The date of 26 February proved a tremendous afternoon for Derby County. Victory over a Sheffield United side seventh in Division Two was a great result. Skipper Rob Hindmarch poked in the only goal of the game and performed heroically as did Wallington in goal, Paul Blades, Steve Buckley and Ross MacLaren in an excellent defensive display.

Out of the hat came a draw against the tougher half of Sheffield for the sixth round, although a full house at the Baseball Ground would have to wait for the match as the blizzards continued. Four times the match was postponed before referee Neil Midgley allowed it to proceed on 5 March.

It was a tremendous contest between a Rams side on the up-and-up, and a top six

side from the First Division. Davison returned for Derby after only one practice game, but he was involved all evening. Eight weeks since his last first-team game, Bobby took only 23 minutes to put Derby one up, running on to Gregory's perfect through-ball to stroke his shot past Martin Hodge.

Wednesday were level on 34 minutes when Christie put past his own goalkeeper as he tried to clear, but Derby had much the better of a game memorable for Hodge's great saves and controversial injury. Falling badly as he and Davison went up for a cross, Hodge was tumbled over by the Rams striker as he chased a later through-ball. Davison angered Wednesday's supporters and players alike, although his booking seemed harsh given the conditions.

Ending at 1-1, Derby had missed their best chance of progress. In the tunnel Arthur Cox and Hodge were involved in a flare-up. According to the Wednesday 'keeper: "He said 'You deserve an academy award for acting' — so I flew off the handle."

Up at Hillsborough for the replay, two Carl Shutt goals, one in each half, sent Derby out of the FA Cup for another season, but leaving them to clinch promotion in a nail-biting run-in which included eight games in both March and April, and four in May.

The Cup ties, however, 12 in major competitions, had proved this Derby side had the ability to compete at higher levels. They also boosted season ticket sales for next season and raised £350,000 in revenue. A total of 117,772 saw Derby's seven FA Cup games in 1985-86 in contrast to only 7,431 the previous season, and after seasons of turmoil and decline 1985-86 is remembered with universal fondness as the season Derby County were on the way back.

Kerry Dixon celebrates his second goal for Chelsea in the remarkable game at the Baseball Ground in December 1990 which produced ten goals.

Home and Away Under Arthur Cox

ARTHUR COX created Derby County's most successful ever away teams, once equalling and twice breaking the club record for away wins in one season. However, the club's home results and performances, once so reliable, became more unpredictable during the same period, confidence undoubtedly suffering and eventually resulting in the club's record number of home defeats in 1992-93.

Cox built his battling sides, first around players like Rob Hindmarch, Ross MacLaren and John Gregory when 1985-86 saw a record haul of 38 away points (this takes into account converting the old two points for a win system). With Bobby Davison and Phil Gee plundering breakaway goals and his defence holding tight, Cox's Rams set another record in 1986-87 as Second Division champions with 11 away victories.

Things got tougher in the old First Division, but travelling triumphs became increasingly as likely as home wins over the next six years. Once again Cox's side, although struggling to score many goals,

121

This time Gary Micklewhite is on target for the Rams against Chelsea.

Tottenham's Gary Lineker dives for the ball at the Baseball Ground in January 1991.

Manager Arthur Cox makes his point to Jason Kavanagh. Cox was well-known for his vociferous instructions during matches,

were difficult to beat. For instance, in 1989-90 Derby avoided relegation from the top-flight by two places and only three points, yet only three clubs, champions Liverpool (37), runners-up Aston Villa (38), and fourth-placed Arsenal (38) conceded fewer goals than the Rams 40. And only 19 of these were in away games, a figure bettered only by Villa and eighth-placed Wimbledon.

The 1990-91 season was a different story, however, as Derby crashed to the bottom of the table, winning only five times all season and avoiding defeat only three times on their travels.

Following relegation in 1991, both records aforementioned were smashed as Derby recorded a new club record of 12 away wins and a remarkable 41 points were gathered at opponents' grounds. This time it was Simon Coleman and Andy Comyn who provided the defensive backbone and 34 away goals were scored, with the temporary return of Bobby Davison on loan being a bonus.

In 1992-93, Cox's last full season, the Rams set a club record, winning seven

consecutive League matches away from home, but also sadly suffered ten home defeats during the campaign.

The support away from home for Derby County has held up remarkably well as home attendances gradually dwindled in comparison. Derby were consistently better supported on their travels during the 1980s than in the 1970s when there were League championships to be won.

The traditional catchment area of support grew enormously from those days, encompassing a thriving London branch of supporters producing a monthly magazine, *Capital Ram*, and pockets of support in areas such as the West Midlands, Greater Manchester and Cheshire and further afield to Scandinavia.

Derby were generally a poor away side for most of the pre-Clough seasons, relying on a solid home record, as did many clubs.

In 75 seasons before Arthur Cox was appointed manager, the Rams won eight or more away games a season on only ten occasions. In Cox's nine seasons in charge

Martin Taylor celebrates after the FA Cup victory over Bolton Wanderers in February 1993.

Mark Pembridge scores from the penalty spot against Swindon Town at the Baseball Ground in March 1993.

they did this on five occasions, a fine effort. In all Derby were unbeaten in 57 per cent of League away games under the Cox regime. At home the Rams won less than half their games, losing more than one game in four at the Baseball Ground, 29 per cent of their matches.

Here is the complete breakdown of that era's home and away League games.

	P	W	D	L	F	A	Pts	P	W	D	L	F	A	Pts
1984-85	23	14	7	2	40	20	49	23	5	6	12	25	34	21
1985-86	23	13	7	3	45	20	46	23	10	8	5	35	21	38
1986-87	21	14	6	1	42	18	48	21	11	3	7	22	20	36
1987-88	20	6	7	7	18	17	25	20	4	6	10	17	28	18
1988-89	19	9	3	7	23	18	30	19	8	4	7	17	20	28
1989-90	19	9	1	9	29	21	28	19	4	6	9	14	19	18
1990-91	19	3	8	8	25	36	17	19	2	1	16	12	39	7
1991-92	23	11	4	8	35	24	37	23	12	5	6	34	27	41
1992-93	23	11	2	10	40	33	35	23	8	7	8	28	24	31
1993-94	2	2	0	0	6	0	6	5	0	2	3	2	11	2
TOTAL	192	92	45	55	303	207	321	195	64	48	83	206	243	240

Marco Gabbiadini scores for the Rams against Leicester City at the Baseball Ground at the end of 1993.

Cox Era Over and Heartbreak at Wembley

THE 1993-94 season was one of the most important and eventful in the long and colourful history of Derby County Football Club. Following the massive investment made by Lionel Pickering during 1991-92, the club had failed to win promotion by a whisker and lost out in the Play-offs to sixth-placed Blackburn Rovers. Players had come to the club for huge fees in the form of Marco Gabbiadini from Crystal Palace (£1.2 million) Paul Kitson from Leicester City (valued at £1.3 million) Tommy Johnson from Notts County (£1.3 million) and Paul Simpson from Oxford United (£500,000.) During the next few months this was topped up with the signings of Mark Pembridge (Luton Town, £1.25 million), Darren Wassall (Nottm Forest, £600,000)

Derby's Craig Short gets the ball ahead of Nottingham Forest's Robert Rosario at the City Ground in August 1993.

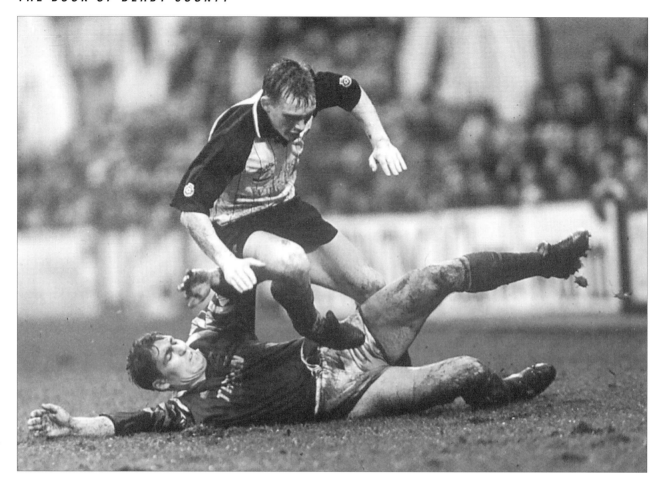

and after the season was under way, the monumental £2.5 million which Arthur Cox lavished upon Notts County centre-half Craig Short and the addition of Martin Kuhl (from Portsmouth, £800,000). All in all, a team had been assembled which was expected to win promotion to the FA Premier League. The bookmakers certainly thought so and supporters accepted it as something of a certainty. It proved to be very different.

In 1992-93, the Rams stuttered from one home defeat to another, despite some stunning away form. Never did they show any great consistency and they fell away badly, missing the Play-offs by ten points, and automatic promotion by 22. Never once were Derby in the top six. Pressure had grown upon Cox with most journalists eager to bandy about the term '12 million pound misfits'. Financially, too, things were worsening with the local media revealing weekly losses on a grand scale and doubts about whether Derby could afford to hang on to the club's young stars.

August 1993 saw a new season begin

Mark Pembridge takes flight over Birmingham City's Steve McGavin at the Baseball Ground in February 1994.

with almost the same side which had finished the old one. Ted McMinn had departed for Birmingham City for £250,000 and full-back Mark Patterson, strangely never popular with Arthur Cox, was allowed to join Peter Shilton's Plymouth Argyle. Central defender Andy Comyn also moved to the Devon club and the only outlay by Derby was £750,000 on Nottingham Forest's full-back Gary Charles, who had played for England.

Season ticket sales had rallied as ever and optimism was high as Cox's side hammered Sunderland 5-0 in the season's opening game at the Baseball Ground. A crowd of 18,072 watched the one-sided match, with some home fans were locked out as the ground reduced capacity — now only 20,000 — meant that many areas had filled to the new safety limits. Everyone, though, inside and out, must have wondered if Cox' side had gelled at last.

Cox moved into the transfer market again to secure Sheffield Wednesday's

THE BOOK OF DERBY COUNTY

utility player John Harkes for £800,000. An international for the USA, Harkes was best known to Rams supporters for his spectacular 30-yard goal in a League Cup replay at Derby in December 1990. Harkes replaced Paul Simpson for a tough away match at newly-relegated Nottingham Forest, where the Rams acquitted themselves well, a Micky Forsyth goal earning a point.

Derby rediscovered their old habit of flattering to deceive as the season progressed. Home wins over Bristol City and Peterborough followed, but there were alarming away reverses at Middlesbrough and Birmingham City (both lost 3-0) and Notts County (4-1), the latter in a new stadium the home fans mockingly claimed was built with the Johnson/Short transfer money.

Cox was under even more pressure now and the town was awash with speculation about when, rather than if, there would be a change in management. Comments made by Lionel Pickering seemed to fuel rumours as the club's owner publicly expressed his exasperation as to some of his manager's tactics. Add to this stories of unrest within the team and morale was at a generally low ebb all round.

On Saturday, 2 October Derby had no fixture. They were to play West Bromwich Albion on the Sunday, televised live on the Central Match. That evening word broke that Cox had resigned, stating that he could no longer continue managing the club with his severe back injury. It transpired that he hadn't been at the ground for weeks, had been conducting team talks by telephone and he would accept a substantial severance. Roy McFarland was to succeed Cox, with a brief succinctly defined by Lionel Pickering at the time. "This is a golden opportunity for Roy, but he's under no illusions. We want promotion this season."

If Albion thought all the turmoil would have an adverse effect on Derby they were mistaken. The players produced a display of tremendous attacking football to win a great game by 5-3.

McFarland's tactics and selection proved

less rigid than his predecessor and the mood lightened at the Baseball Ground. Paul Simpson, often a scapegoat under Cox, was given an extended run and Derby won five of their first six League games under McFarland including a 3-1 triumph over Crystal Palace — one of the best Derby performances of the season — and two much-needed away wins at Bolton and second-placed Charlton.

Disappointingly, the Rams made an exit from the Coca-Cola League Cup, losing 1-0 at home to Spurs, but a bigger shock was a 4-0 live TV thrashing at the Baseball Ground, courtesy of Steve Bull and Wolves. The defence was run ragged by the 'Tipton Terrier' who hit a hat-trick, and doubts grew as goals were leaked at an alarming rate, despite the efforts of goalkeeper Martin Taylor, performing weekly heroics, often to keep the score down. The defeat by Wolves was even more disappointing, considering that a victory would have taken Derby County to the top of the table.

November was a bad month for Derby, who lost at Oxford after missing a stack of easy chances to lead, and 3-1 at home to Southend, outplayed after an early Simpson goal. A draw at Molineux was a creditable result after the home mauling a month earlier, but Derby really should have won. Gabbiadini twice gave the Rams the lead with two great goals, but on 45 and 90 minutes, sloppy defending and sheer bad luck gave Wolves a draw.

A defeat at Roker Park, the only goal following a needless Martin Kuhl back pass, meant that Derby needed something unusual — a good Christmas return. Three wins out of four provided just that. Paul Kitson scored the only goal at Barnsley but picked up an injury. This paved the way for the return to the side of out-of-favour Tommy Johnson.

During the previous campaign, Johnson had been widely pilloried after a string of missed chances but now, playing mostly in his more natural position down the middle, he was to prove a revelation, building up a popular following with supporters as the goals flowed.

129

Paul Kitson scores in the 2-0 win over Charlton Athletic at Derby in April 1994.

On Boxing Day, rivals Leicester were beaten 3-2 in a thriller. Derby led 2-0 at half-time, the Foxes pulled level, then Johnson ran through to clinch a winner. The Rams lost by the odd goal in three at Stoke on New Year's Day, then pulverised bogey team Tranmere Rovers 4-0 on 3 January with a Gabbiadini hat-trick.

The next weekend saw an early FA Cup exit at Premiership club Oldham, but that was perhaps no bad thing as the Rams could concentrate on promotion alone. A last-kick winner by Johnson defeated Portsmouth, but two defeats followed, at

Luton and home to Watford. Craig Short was sent off at Oldham after a fracas with Darren Beckford, so would miss the trip to League leaders Crystal Palace. Simon Coleman had departed from the Rams Reserves to Premier action with Sheffield Wednesday and McFarland had brought in former Everton and Wales captain Kevin Ratcliffe 'on trial'.

Gordon Cowans, however, was to be McFarland's first cash signing and a master-stroke. The 35-year-old former England midfield star had cost £75,000 from Aston Villa, two years after Derby had chased him when he played a major role in Blackburn's promotion. It was a controversial and interesting week at Derby, and it proved to be a turning point in the season.

On the Friday before the Palace match, Paul Kitson was quoted in the *Today* newspaper. In a lengthy interview, what came out appeared to be a major broadside at the club, management and in particular strike partner Marco Gabbiadini, Kitson said there was 'no discipline in the side' since McFarland took over, and pledged his admiration for the previous manager. The piece was billed as a 'Come and buy me' plea to Premiership clubs and was received with open hostility by McFarland and supporters. Coming on the heels of a local article by Darren Wassall arguing that there should still be room for a Cox return, it undermined McFarland's position of authority, despite Kitson's claim that the newspaper took his remarks out of context. The events of the next day were therefore doubly satisfactory.

The Rams took the field at Selhurst Park without Kitson, who had been dropped from the 13. Wassall, too, missed the match (and the next 18) with a hernia injury. Cowans made an excellent debut, Ratcliffe came in and Paul Williams, switched to central defence, was magnificent. He looked completely at home and was to remain Derby's outstanding performer right to the end of the season, despite an initial degree of personal indifference to his new role. Derby played Palace off the park, leading through Charles' first goal for the club and denied a deserved win only by a 30-yard wonder goal in injury time by Dean Gordon.

Apology accepted and fine administered, Kitson returned the next week to some initial jeers but played well in the 2-0 win over FA Cup heroes Bolton. Then followed a great fight back to win at Watford 4-3. Derby led 1-0, then they trailed 3-2 before turning a deficit round for the first time in the season, with two

late strikes from Johnson and Gabbiadini. At last the side looked to have some mettle and, with Cowans leading by example, some composure.

A worrying home defeat by Middlesbrough and a draw at the Baseball Ground against a Birmingham side which had lost 11 away matches on the trot highlighted the strange nature of the division as Derby stumbled up to fourth, despite dropping five points in two games. Three more draws followed and the Rams were always on the fringe of the top three, but often dropping down to sixth as the season drew to a climax.

March ended with a further fitness problem for Kuhl and with Simpson and Harkes back in the side, the latter following injury, and a victory at The Hawthorns completed the double over West Bromwich. The now usual thrashing at Tranmere was a blip as Barnsley were beaten at Derby. Gabbiadini was dropped after the defeat at Prenton Park, giving a fast pairing of Johnson and Kitson in attack who linked up superbly.

On 5 April, Easter Tuesday, Derby went to Filbert Street. In a first half of high drama the Rams stormed into a 2-0 lead after 12 minutes, only to be rocked by an Ivan Roberts hat-trick inside half-an-hour as Leicester exposed Derby's defensive frailties at set pieces. Former Leicester player Kitson then scored his second and Derby's third to give a 3-3 interval score. The second half was inevitably an anticlimax, although Kitson was denied a hat-trick, Leicester goalkeeper Poole producing a magnificent save.

Four days later Derby tore a disappointing Stoke apart 4-2 at the Baseball Ground with superb performances from both Williams and Kitson. And when the Rams produced a fine performance to beat Charlton one week later, a Play-off place looked certain and even automatic promotion not yet ruled out.

On the Wednesday, however, Derby could not finish off Notts County, who took a late lead only for a disastrous own-goal by Dijkstra to give the Rams a last-second draw. A late Kitson goal achieved another 1-1 scoreline at Grimsby, setting up the home match with Nottingham Forest. Derby began well but following a soft goal given away from a free-kick, were never in it. Charles gifted his former club the points with a bizarre near own-goal (although Stone claimed it) and a miserable night meant that Forest were all but promoted, whilst Derby needed other teams to suffer poor results to help them to ensure a Play-off place.

Wolves and Notts County duly obliged with these and Derby nervously beat Oxford 2-1 to all but mathematically book a place in the end-of-season promotion lottery. Kitson picked up an injury and was left out of the 4-3 defeat at Southend in the final League match, when Williams and Charles were also rested, contributing to a disjointed Rams line-up.

The final League table saw Derby in sixth position on 71 points, five more than 1992-93 and paired with third-placed Millwall, over two legs, the first at home. Shane Nicholson would not be involved in the Play-offs. The Rams left-back did himself no favours when he was arrested and charged with affray, following an incident in Albert Street in the week before the home leg. McFarland promptly dropped him from the squad.

Derby completely dominated the Baseball Ground match against the Lions, winning with goals by Cowans and Johnson, although they ought to have had five. Millwall came to defend and were a poor side. For Derby, Gabbiadini, recalled for the injured Kitson, had his best game for three months. Forsyth, missing since late January, returned well in place of Nicholson, his greater experience proving invaluable. Derby, therefore, had a two-goal lead to take to the New Den. Would it prove enough? Would the new stadium prove intimidating? The answer was yes to both questions, although the margin and manner could hardly have been imagined. It was with trepidation that most of the 2,000 Derby contingent made

their way to what was to become a notorious Millwall game. Lion's manager Mick McCarthy was quoted in the Press trying to stir things up, blasting Derby for their 'lap of honour' after the first leg. He need not have bothered, Derby scored only ten minutes into the hostile atmosphere of the match. Pembridge put Johnson clear, he whipped over a cross-cum-shot and Gabbiadini delightedly slid the ball past Casey Keller.

A dream start became ecstasy minutes later as Johnson raced into the Millwall half before powering a shot into Keller's left-hand corner. The South Londoners now needed five goals and many of their followers couldn't take any more, spilling on to the pitch and causing a hold-up of 20 minutes. Derby fans were marooned in the temporary safety of the upper tier but were already wondering just how they would get out in one piece.

Play resumed and just before half-time Millwall were completely out of the game, Pat Van Den Hauwe touching a harmless ball past his goalkeeper to give Derby a 3-0 lead. A second pitch invasion followed, during which Martin Taylor was punched and kicked to the ground and Paul Williams assaulted, in quite awful scenes. Some 32 minutes were lost in all, Millwall scored a late goal, the referee overturned a penalty and Keller was lucky not to be dismissed for handling Johnson's goal-bound chip out of his area. Referee Brian Hill gave a tremendous display, but a great Rams performance was soured by football's lowest mentality.

Outside afterwards Derby cars were wrecked, including the BBC Radio Derby vehicle, and Rams fans were trapped in the coach park until after 11pm as police battled with gangs of Millwall lunatics. The Premiership, meanwhile, breathed a sigh of relief at the result.

It wasn't over then, however, Millwall chairman Reg Burr launched an outrageous attack on Williams, who along with Gary Charles, Derby's other black player, had been substituted by McFarland, who feared for their safety. Burr said "Mr Williams is an unpleasant

Rams players run for cover at The New Den in the Play-off semi-final.

player who incites trouble and over three matches this season has behaved badly." Gordon Taylor, secretary of the PFA, insisted upon a full apology for the quite unfounded comments, hugely insulting to a player who had performed quite magnificently week in week out for over three months.

Millwall faced disciplinary action in the summer (although the resulting FA punishment was negligible), and their club, from chairman and manager down, emerged without any credit whatsoever from the situation. Derby, however, had conducted themselves impeccably and were rewarded with a Wembley Play-off Final against Leicester on 30 May.

The ten-day interval before the Final seemed lengthy, but Wembley fever certainly gripped Derby as fans queued for up to six hours in pouring rain for the best seats. Some 36,000 tickets were sold by each club and Derby were the favourites in many eyes, especially in view of their superb win at the New Den. McFarland announced that the match was bigger than an FA Cup Final and he was

right. The club's very financial future was probably at stake.

The Rams' Wembley performance went according to plan in every aspect but the final score. Derby dominated from the start and it was no surprise when Johnson ran out to a superb ball from Simpson and held off two defenders before slotting it past Gavin Ward. All looked well and the Rams could have added to this lead but with four minutes of the first half remaining, Martin Taylor went for a cross, only to be impeded by Iwan Roberts. Steve Walsh put the ball into the Rams' net and referee Roger Milford, in his last game, let the goal stand.

It was a setback but Derby were once again the superior side in the second half. Johnson, was on the receiving end of some rough tackling but the pressure looked to have paid off when Harkes rushed through on to a Cowans pass to place the ball past Ward, only to see it roll wide. Three minutes later, in the 87th of the match, came the unthinkable. Former Rams player Ian Ormondroyd got his head to a rare Leicester cross, Taylor

133

Tommy Johnson flies over Leicester's Simon Grayson at Wembley in the Play-off Final.

produced a brilliant save, but Walsh was first to the ball to stab home a winner and break Derby's hearts. Players and supporters were stunned. So was Brian Little, the Leicester boss, who conceded that Derby had played the better football.

The result, however, had knocked the spirit out of Derby County and the city itself. Financially, the future had to be faced — failure to gain Premiership status and all the spin-offs associated with it was a devastating blow. The immediate speculation was that several players would

have to be sold and McFarland's future considered. Paul Kitson, who played only the last three minutes at Wembley, was again linked with top clubs. Paul Williams had a clause in his contract enabling him to depart if promotion was not achieved. Craig Short, Mark Pembridge and Tommy Johnson would also surely be Premiership targets. Had Derby finally missed their best shot? Lionel Pickering showed his frustration clearly enough in series of interviews with national newspapers, but the emerging position appeared to be that

McFarland would continue as manager but would have to raise some £3.5 million from transfers to pay off the season's debt.

The close season proved quiet, as season tickets again, and inevitably with Derby County supporters, sold well. Martyn Chalk was sold to Stockport County for £40,000 and Richard Goulooze returned to Holland for £70,000.

In addition to Martin Kuhl and reserve goalkeeper Steve Sutton, Welsh international midfielder Mark Pembridge went on the transfer list. He accompanied his request with some scathing comments about the club and his personal ambitions, all of which won him few friends in a crowd which had been more than patient with someone who had so far proved a disappointing signing with too many indifferent performances.

Reflecting on the turbulence of the previous campaign, Derby County looked to 1994-95 with confidence and with a general feeling that Roy McFarland had done enough to suggest that watching the Rams would be entertaining again and that, if he could keep his best players, Derby could challenge once more for promotion. Alas, early-season results in 1994-95 suggested the opposite and when results did improve, Paul Kitson was involved in a controversial on-off transfer saga involving Premiership high-flyers Newcastle United as open warfare broke out between club owner Lionel Pickering and chairman Brian Fearn, in scenes, as ever at Derby County, of high drama. Kitson was eventually sold for £2,250,000 after initially turning down personal terms with Magpies' boss Kevin Keegan.

It's all over. Martin Taylor and Mark Pembridge look forlornly at the Leicester celebrations. For Rams fans it was a devastating moment.

Attendance Facts

The most people to watch Derby County in any match is 120,000.

This was the official attendance in the European Cup Round Two (second leg) game against **Real Madrid** on **5 Nov 1975** in the Santiago Bernabéu Stadium. The Rams lost 5-1 (6-5 agg).

Apart from the 1946 FA Cup Final (see below), Derby County have appeared in one match where over 80,000 were present: **80,407** v Birmingham City at Maine Road Manchester (FA Cup semi-final replay). This is a record for a midweek game between two Football League clubs outside an FA Cup Final.

Over 70,000: six (three FA Cup; two European; one Play-off Final).

Over 60,000: 15 (eight League; six FA Cup; one European).

Over 50,000: 53 (43 League; eight FA Cup; one League Cup; one Charity Shield).

During the 'boom' years following World War Two, there were 31 League attendances between 50,000 and 70,000 in the period 1946-50. In season 1948-49, a total of 1,534,575 spectators watched the 42 League games. That is an average of 36,537, the most in any one season.

HIGHEST

Football League:
69,007 v Arsenal (a), 30 Mar 1934, Division One (lost 1-0).

FA Cup:
98,215 v Charlton Athletic (at Wembley Stadium), 27 Apr 1946, Final (won 4-1).

League Cup:
57,393 v Manchester United (a), 19 Nov 1969, Fifth Round (lost 1-0).

LOWEST

Football League:
500 v Grimsby Town (h), 22 Apr 1903, Division One (drew 2-2).

FA Cup:
1,500 v Walsall Town (h), 8 Nov 1884, Round One (lost 7-0).

League Cup:
1,611 v Hartlepool United (a), 4 Sep 1985, Round One (lost 2-0).

PROGRESSIVE HOME ATTENDANCE RECORDS
ALL-TIME
COUNTY GROUND

1,500 v Walsall Town	8 Nov1884	FA Cup
2,000 v Birmingham St G	24 Oct1885	FA Cup
5,000 v Aston Villa	14 Nov1885	FA Cup
10,000 v Everton	18 Jan1890	FA Cup
15,000 v Sheffield Wed	30 Jan1893	FA Cup
15,500 v Blackburn Rovers	24 Feb1894	FA Cup

12,000 spectators watched the FA Cup Final replay between Blackburn Rovers and West Bromwich Albion on 10 Apr 1886 which broke the ground record.

BASEBALL GROUND

10,000 v Sunderland	14 Sep1895	League
10,000 v Sheffield Wed	28 Sep1895	League
10,000 v Stoke	12 Oct1895	League
12,000 v Bolton Wanderers	26 Dec1895	League
20,000 v Aston Villa	1 Feb1896	FA Cup
20,000 v Sunderland	1 Jan1901	League
20,000 v Newcastle United	26 Dec1901	League
25,000 v West Bromwich A	27 Dec1902	League
25,481 v Wolverhampton W	29 Jan1921	FA Cup
27,873 v Newcastle United	2 Feb1924	FA Cup
30,557 v Bolton Wanderers	27 Dec1926	League
30,651 v Huddersfield T	26 Dec1928	League
30,825 v Blackburn Rovers	23 Jan1932	FA Cup
34,218 v Sunderland	4 Mar1933	FA Cup
37,727 v Wolverhampton W	27 Jan1934	FA Cup
37,830 v Nottingham Forest	25 Jan1936	FA Cup
38,063 v Northampton Town	11 Feb1950	FA Cup
41,826 v Tottenham Hotspur	20 Sep1969	League

LEAGUE
COUNTY GROUND

3,000 v West Bromwich Albion	15 Sep1888
5,000 v Preston North End	29 Sep1888
8,000 v Notts County	19 Sep1891
10,000 v Preston North End	5 Dec1891
10,500 v Bolton Wanderers	26 Dec1893

BASEBALL GROUND

10,000 v Sunderland	14 Sep1895
10,000 v Sheffield Wednesday	28 Sep1895
10,000 v Stoke	12 Oct1895
12,000 v Bolton Wanderers	26 Dec1895
15,000 v Aston Villa	8 Feb1896
19,500 v Bolton Wanderers	26 Dec1896
20,000 v Sunderland	1 Jan1901
20,000 v Newcastle United	26 Dec1901
25,000 v West Bromwich Albion	27 Dec1902
25,381 v Leicester City	6 Dec1924
26,370 v Oldham Athletic	26 Dec1924
26,724 v Sheffield Wednesday	27 Feb1925
30,557 v Bolton Wanderers	27 Dec1926
30,651 v Huddersfield Town	26 Dec1928
32,320 v Manchester City	25 Dec1933
35,260 v Wolverhampton W	26 Dec1934
35,683 v Everton	27 Dec1938
35,713 v Arsenal	29 Nov1947
35,787 v Manchester United	20 Aug1949
37,652 v Wolverhampton W	8 Oct1949
37,708 v Everton	6 Sep1969
41,826 v Tottenham Hotspur	20 Sep1969

FA CUP
COUNTY GROUND

1,500 v Walsall Town	8 Nov1884

2,000 v Birmingham St George	24 Oct 1885
5,000 v Aston Villa	14 Nov 1885
10,000 v Everton	18 Jan 1885
15,000 v Sheffield Wednesday	30 Jan 1893
15,500 v Blackburn Rovers	24 Feb 1894

BASEBALL GROUND

20,000 v Aston Villa	1 Feb 1896
22,500 v Plymouth Argyle	20 Feb 1909
22,892 v Everton	25 Feb 1911
25,481 v Wolverhampton Wanderers	29 Jan 1921
27,873 v Newcastle United	2 Feb 1924
28,551 v Blackburn Rovers	30 Jan 1929
30,825 v Blackburn Rovers	23 Jan 1932
34,218 v Sunderland	4 Mar 1933
37,727 v Wolverhampton Wanderers	27 Jan 1934
37,830 v Nottingham Forest	25 Jan 1936
38,063 v Northampton Town	11 Feb 1950
41,705 v Sheffield United	24 Jan 1970

LEAGUE CUP
BASEBALL GROUND

11,114 v Barnsley	19 Oct 1960
21,864 v Norwich City	14 Nov 1960
24,827 v Birmingham City	11 Oct 1967
25,079 v Lincoln City	1 Nov 1967
31,904 v Leeds United	17 Jan 1968
34,346 v Chelsea	2 Oct 1968
34,370 v Everton	23 Oct 1968
35,014 v Swindon Town	30 Oct 1968
38,893 v Manchester United	12 Nov 1969

EUROPE
BASEBALL GROUND

27,350 v FK Zeljezničar	13 Sep 1972
38,100 v Benfica	25 Oct 1972

CUP ATTENDANCE RECORDS
ROUND-BY-ROUND
FA CUP

First Round - Highest

41,000 v Aston Villa(a)	7 Jan 1922

Lowest

1,500 v Walsall Town(h)	8 Nov 1884

Second Round - Highest

50,393 v Newcastle United(a)	6 Feb 1924

Lowest

2,000 v Mitchell St George(h)	20 Nov 1886

Third Round - Highest

53,212 v Manchester City(a)	7 Jan 1950

Lowest

2,000 v Owlerton(h)	26 Nov 1887

Fourth Round - Highest

59,700 v Newcastle United(a)	13 Mar 1911
52,736 v Tottenham Hotspur(a)	7 Feb 1973
50,349 v Tottenham Hotspur(a)	10 Mar 1923

Lowest

12,607 v Leyton Orient(a)	4 Mar 1963

Fifth Round - Highest

66,903 v Arsenal(a)	17 Feb 1934
63,077 v Arsenal(a)	29 Feb 1972
62,641 v Manchester City(a)	13 Feb 1931
62,230 v Everton(a)	16 Feb 1935
53,490 v Everton(a)	13 Feb 1971

Lowest

4,000 v Crewe Alexandra(a)	7 Jan 1888

Sixth Round - Highest

76,588 v Aston Villa(a)*	2 Mar 1946
75,118 v Sunderland(a)†	8 Mar 1933
51,385 v Portsmouth(a)‡	26 Feb 1949

Attendance record for Villa Park.
†Attendance record for Roker Park.
‡Attendance record for Fratton Park.

Lowest

26,906 v Plymouth Argyle(h)	14 Mar 1984

Semi-finals (full list - date order)

35,000 v Wolves (Perry Barr)	21 Mar 1896
25,000 v Everton (Victoria Ground)	20 Mar 1897
30,000 v Everton (Molineux)	19 Mar 1898
24,500 v Stoke (Molineux)	18 Mar 1899
33,603 v Sheffield U (The Hawthorns)	15 Mar 1902
17,500 v Sheffield U (Molineux)	20 Mar 1902
15,000 v Sheffield U (City Ground)	27 Mar 1902
40,500 v Millwall (Villa Park)	21 Mar 1903
20,187 v Bolton Wanderers (Molineux)	19 Mar 1904
34,000 v Bristol City (Stamford Bridge)	27 Mar 1909
27,600 v Bristol City (St Andrew's)	31 Mar 1909
50,795 v West Ham U (Stamford Bridge)	24 Mar 1923
51,961 v Manchester City (Leeds Road)	18 Mar 1933
65,000 v Birmingham C (Hillsborough)	23 Mar 1946
80,407 v Birmingham C (Maine Road)	27 Mar 1946
60,000 v Manchester U (Hillsborough)	13 Mar 1948
55,000 v Manchester U (Hillsborough)	3 Apr 1976

Finals (full list - date order)

62,017 v Nottingham F (Crystal Palace)	16 Apr 1898
73,833 v Sheffield U (Crystal Palace)	15 Apr 1899
63,102 v Bury (The Crystal Palace)	18 Apr 1903
98,215 v Charlton Athletic (Wembley)	27 Apr 1946

Apart from those already mentioned, the attendance record for The Den (48,672) still stands after Derby visited in the FA Cup.

LEAGUE CUP

First Round - Highest

21,487 v Chesterfield(h)	14 Aug 1968

Lowest

1,611 v Hartlepool United(a)	4 Sep 1985

Second Round - Highest

38,975 v Sunderland(a)	29 Oct 1973

Lowest

3,596 v Hartlepool United(a)	25 Oct 1982

Third Round - Highest

34,346 v Chelsea(h)	2 Oct 1968

Lowest

8,192 v Reading(a)	20 Oct 1965

Fourth Round - Highest

44,705 v Everton(a)	16 Oct 1968

Lowest

23,196 v Lincoln City(a)*	15 Nov 1967

Attendance record for Sincil Bank.

Fifth Round - Highest

57,393 v Manchester United(a)	19 Nov 1969

Lowest

23,631 v Darlington(h)	29 Nov 1967

Semi-finals (full list)

31,904 v Leeds United(h)	17 Jan 1968
29,367 v Leeds United(a)	7 Feb 1968

The Rams have helped break the attendance records on several League grounds including Villa Park, Fratton Park, Roker Park and Sincil Bank. In February 1937 a record crowd of 48,672 packed The Den to see Millwall, then in the Third Division South, score a sensational 2-1 fifth-round FA Cup defeat over Derby, who finished that season in fourth place in Division One. Here, goalkeeper Ken Scattergood sees the ball escape him as the Lions attack.

BY COMPETITION

Football League

Division One - Highest

69,007 v Arsenal(a)	30 Mar 1934	

Lowest

500 v Grimsby Town(h)	22 Apr 1903	

Division Two - Highest

59,448 v Manchester United(a)	29 Nov 1924	

Lowest

500 v Glossop North End(a)	5 Sep 1914	

Division Three North - Highest

33,330 v Grimsby Town(h)	10 Mar 1956	

Lowest

3,937 v Gateshead(a)	15 Dec 1956	

Division Three - Highest

21,036 v Rotherham United(h)	9 May 1986	

Lowest

3,032 v Orient(a)	4 May 1985	

Play-offs - Highest

73,671 v Leicester City (Wembley)	30 May 1994	

Lowest

16,470 v Millwall(a)	18 May 1994	

FA Cup - Highest

98,215 v Charlton Athletic(Wembley)	27 Apr 1946	

Lowest

1,500 v Walsall Town(h)	8 Nov 1884	

League Cup - Highest

57,393 v Manchester United(a)	19 Nov 1969	

Lowest

1,611 v Hartlepool United(a)	4 Sep 1985	

European Competition - Highest

120,000 v Real Madrid(a)	5 Nov 1975	

Lowest

2,217 v Finn Harps(a)	29 Sep 1976	

DIMINISHING ATTENDANCE RECORDS

COUNTY GROUND

1,500 v Walsall Town	8 Nov 1884	FA Cup
1,500 v Wolverhampton W	12 Jan 1888	League
1,500 v Accrington	15 Feb 1890	League
750 v Darwen	2 Dec 1893	League

BASEBALL GROUND

10,000 v Sunderland	14 Sep 1895	League
8,000 v Bury	19 Oct 1895	League
6,000 v Burnley	9 Nov 1895	League
4,000 v Preston North End	4 Mar 1895	League
4,000 v Liverpool	12 Apr 1898	League
3,000 v Nottingham Forest	20 Apr 1899	League
3,000 v Preston North End	4 Apr 1900	League
2,000 v Sunderland	5 Apr 1902	League
500 v Grimsby Town	22 Apr 1903	League

When 15,711 turned up to see Derby County lose 2-1 at home to Hull City on 20 April 1968, they could not have believe that it would be almost 11 years before the Rams played before a lower home League attendance. this was when 15,227 saw a Division One game with Bolton Wanderers which Derby won 3-0 on 21 March 1979. Indeed, following the Hull match Derby County's home League gate did not fall below 20,000 until 24 August 1977 when 19,809 watched a goalless draw with Ipswich Town.

Appearances

Most Appearances
League
Kevin Hector 478/8
Jack Parry 482/1
Geoff Barrowcliffe 475
Steve Bloomer 474
Jimmy Methven 458
Ron Webster 451/4
Roy McFarland 437/5
Sammy Crooks 408
Archie Goodall 380
Tommy Powell 380
Johnny McIntyre 349
Jack Nicholas 347

Archie Goodall, a controversial figure in the Rams' early history but who still made a record number of consecutive appearances for the club.

Archie Gemmill appeared in a record number of European matches for the Rams.

FA Cup
Jimmy Methven 52
Steve Bloomer 50
Archie Goodall 42
Sammy Crooks 37
Jack Nicholas 36
Archie Gemmill 35
Charlie Morris 35
Kevin Hector 34
Chick Musson 34
Roy McFarland 33
Steve Powell 31/1
Colin Todd 30
Ron Webster 30

League Cup
Kevin Hector 42
Roy McFarland 37
Ron Webster 34
Micky Forsyth 33
Alan Durban 30/1
John O'Hare 28/2
Geraint Williams 26/1
Gary Micklewhite 23/2
Steve Powell 24
Alan Hinton 23/1
Mel Sage 22/2
Steve Buckley 21
Archie Gemmill 20
Colin Todd 20

Europe
Archie Gemmill 21
Colin Todd 21
Kevin Hector 20
Colin Boulton 18
David Nish 16
Roy McFarland 15
Bruce Rioch 13
Henry Newton 12
Ron Webster 10/1
Peter Daniel 10

Consecutive Appearances
League
Archie Goodall 151
Steve Buckley 122
Steve Buckley 117
Gary Micklewhite 112
Les Green 107
Dean Saunders 106
Bobby Davison 105
Kevin Hector 105
Jack Nicholas 104

> The 30 matches Colin Todd played in the FA Cup were consecutive. His injury in January 1978 prevented him from overtaking Archie Goodall's record which had stood for 79 years.

FA Cup
Archie Goodall 30
Colin Todd 30
Kevin Hector 24
Colin Boulton 22
Steve Bloomer 20
Archie Gemmill 20
Roy McFarland 20
John McGovern 18
John O'Hare 15
Steve Buckley 14
Ron Webster 11
Steve Bloomer 10(twice)

League Cup
Kevin Hector 36
Roy McFarland 25
Archie Gemmill 19
Ron Webster 18
Les Green 17
Alan Hinton 17
Willie Carlin 14
Alan Durban 14
Reg Matthews 14
John O'Hare 14
Colin Boulton 12
Jack Parry 12
Dean Saunders 12
Gary Micklewhite 11

All Matches

Archie Goodall 167
Colin Boulton 131
Dean Saunders 130
Colin Todd 130
Les Green 129
Steve Buckley 127
Bobby Davison 126
Jack Nicholas 120
Steve Buckley 119
Colin Boulton 115
Kevin Hector 113
Jack Nicholas 109

Steve Buckley had two long spells when he did not miss a game for the Rams and also managed some spectacular goals for the club. Here the full-back is being congratulated by a spectator with Kevin Wilson about to add his own applause after another fine Buckley strike against Rotherham United at the Baseball Ground in April 1982.

Consecutive Scoring in Successive Games

Jack Bowers 7 - 3 Jan to 14 Feb 1931 (17)
Horace Barnes 6 - 1 Sep to 27 Sep 1913 (First 6 matches of season) (7)
Alf Bentley 6 - 6 Nov to 11 Dec 1909
Steve Bloomer 6 - 23 Jan to 6 Mar 1897 (10)
Jack Bowers 6 - 4 Feb to 4 Mar 1933 (11)
Jack Bowers 6 - 26 Aug to 23 Sep 1933 (First 6 matches of season) (10)
Raich Carter 6 - 30 Jan to 23 Mar 1946 (All FA Cup) (9)
John Goodall 6 - 5 Sep to 17 Oct 1891 (First 6 matches of season) (8 goals)
Jimmy Lyons 6 - 6 Jan to 10 Feb 1923
George Stephenson 6 - 19 Nov to 26 Dec 1927 (8)
Ray Straw 6 - 5 Sep to 22 Sep 1956
Eddie Thomas 6 - 29 Aug to 15 Sep 1964 (7)
Tommy Johnson 5 - 30 April to 30 May 1994 (Last 2 League & all 3 Play-off games))
Alf Bentley 5 - 16 Jan to 6 Mar 1909 (First 5 FA Cup games) (8)
Tommy Powell 5 - 7 Jan to 4 Mar 1950 (Every FA Cup tie) (5)
Barry Hutchinson 3 - 11 Oct to 14 Nov 1960 (League Cup) (3)

In the first 19 matches of 1933-34, Jack Bowers scored in 15 (24 goals)
In the 20 matches from 14 Nov 96 to 5 Apr 1897 Steve Bloomer scored in 15 (21 goals)

Most Goals Scored in a Season (League)   (League & Cup)

22 Matches	1890-91	47	1890-91	51
30 Matches	1893-94	73	1896-97	86
34 Matches	1898-99	62	1898-99	76
38 Matches	1907-08	77	1910-11	82
42 Matches	1927-28 & 1936-37	96	1936-37	104
46 Matches	1956-57	111	1955-56	118

Fewest Goals in a Season   (League)

22 Matches	1888-89	41
30 Matches	1894-95	45

34 Matches	1904-05	37
38 Matches	1990-91	37
42 Matches	1920-21	32
46 Matches	1984-85	65

Most Goals Conceded (League)

22 Matches	1890-91	81
30 Matches	1894-95	68
34 Matches	1903-04	60
38 Matches	1990-91	75
42 Matches	1936-37	90
46 Matches	1955-56	55

Fewest Goals Conceded (League)

22 Matches	1889-90	55
30 Matches	1895-96	35
34 Matches	1901-02	41
38 Matches	1911-12	28
42 Matches	1968-69	32
46 Matches	1985-86	41

Former Derby Boys star Peter Newbery scored only two goals for the Rams but the first of them was the club's 4000th League goal in their 2,333rd League game. Newbery's other goal came in the very next match, a Wednesday evening 2-2 home draw with Southampton when he hit a blistering ground shot into the Osmaston End goal.

1000th League Goal
Jimmy Long (second goal) in a 2-1 win v Blackpool (h) 30 Nov 1907
599th League game
2000th League goal
Jimmy Gill (fourth goal) in a 4-4 draw v Huddersfield Town (h) 16 Apr 1927
Took another 623 League games (1222nd League game)
3000th League Goal
Reg Harrison (third goal) in a 5-1 win v Everton (h) 26 Dec 1946
529 (1751)
4000th League Goal
Peter Newbery in a 2-1 defeat v Leyton Orient (h) 10 Sep 1960
582 (2333)
5000th League Goal
Kevin Hector in a 1-0 win v Arsenal (a) 8 Nov 1975
639 (2972)
6000th League Goal
Paul Kitson (second goal) in a 3-3 draw v Leicester City (a), 5 Apr 1994
781 (3753)

League Firsts

First Game 8 Sep 1888 v Bolton Wanderers (a) W 6-3 also first win and first away win
First Defeat 15 Sep 1888 v West Bromwich Albion (h) L 1-2 also first home game
First Home Win 22 Dec 1888 v Notts County W 3-2
First Draw 22 Sep 1888 v Accrington D 1-1

Overall Records in a Season

Most Wins

All: 28 in 1955-56 18 home, 10 away.

Home: 18 in 1955-56 & 1956-57 (3N) 17 in 1948-49 (Div 1), 17 in 1925-26 (Div 2) 14 in 1984-85 (Div 3)

Away: 12 in 1991-92

Fewest Wins 5 - 1920-21 & 1990-91(all matches)

3 - 1920-21 & 1990-91(home)

0 - 1976-77 (away)

Most Draws 19 - 1982-83 (all)

12 - 1920-21 (home)

10 - 1976-77 (away)

Fewest Draws 1 - 1890-91 (all)

1 - 1890-91, 1907-08, 1958-59, 1989-90 (home)

0- 1890-91 (away)

Most Defeats 26 - 1954-55 (all)

10 - 1992-93 (home)

17 - 1954-55 (away)

Fewest Defeats 5 - 1968-69 (all)

1 - 1889-90. 1895-96, 1898-99, 1901-02, 1908-09, 1929-30, 1955-56, 1968-69,1971-72, 1973-74, 1986-87 (home)

4 - 1968-69 (away)

Most Points

2 - Point System	3 - Point System
22 Games - 21 1889-90	38 Games - 58 1988-89
30 Games - 41 1895-96	42 Games 84 1986-87
34 Games - 36 1899-00	46 Games - 84 1985-86
38 Games - 54 1911-12	40 Games - 43 1987-88
42 Games - 63 1968-69	
46 Games - 63 1955-56, 1956-57	

Most Games in a Season

59/3 - Marco Gabbiadini 1992-93

61   - Paul Kitson 1992-93

60   - Mark Pembridge 1992-92

58   - Ross MacLaren, Gary Micklewhite,
        Steve Buckley 1985-86 Micky Forsyth 1992-93

Most Players Used

32 - 1920-21, 1977-78, 1979-80

Fewest Players Used

16 - 19 74-75, 1971-72, 1895-96

Unchanged Team

12 - 1895-96

First Substitute
Bobby Saxton v Southampton (h) 21 Aug 1965

First Substitute to score
Richie Barker v Plymouth Argyle (a) 20 Jan 1968 - Division Two
Roger Davies v Liverpool (h) 24 Jan 1976 - FA Cup
Kevin Wilson v Halifax Town (h) 15 Sep 1982 - FL Cup
Jeff Bourne v Slovan Bratislava 1 Oct 1975 - European Cup
Jeff Bourne v Velez Mostar 27 Nov 1974 - UEFA Cup (2 goals)
Andy Garner v York City (h) 19 Oct 1985 - Division Three (2 goals)

Consecutive Substitute Appearances
6 Andy Garner 5 Sep 87 - 29 Sep 1987

Most Substitute Appearances
In League season (1975-76) Roger Davies 16
All-time Steve Cross 42, Sep 1986 - Sep 1991

First Goal
League
George Bakewell v Bolton Wanderers (a)
8 Sep 1888 (scored twice)

FA Cup
A.Smith v Birmingham St George (h)
24 Oct 1885

League Cup
Ian Buxton v Watford (a) 11 Oct 1960

Roger Davies, the first substitute to score for the Rams in the FA Cup.

Most Goals

All matches		League	
Steve Bloomer	332	Steve Bloomer	293
Kevin Hector	201	Jack Bowers	167
Jack Bowers	183	Kevin Hector	155
Harry Bedford	152	Harry Bedford	142
Jack Stamps	126	Jack Parry	105
Alf Bentley	112	Sammy Crooks	101
Alan Durban	112	Jack Stamps	100
Sammy Crooks	111	Alf Bentley	99
Jack Parry	110	Alan Durban	93
Bobby Davison	106	Bobby Davison	91

FA Cup		League Cup		Europe	
Steve Bloomer	38	Kevin Hector	15	Kevin Hector	16
Jack Stamps	26	Alan Hinton	11	Charlie George	10
Jack Bowers	16	Dean Saunders	10		
Raich Carter	16	Alan Durban	8	**Play-offs**	
Ben Warren	14	John O'Hare	8	Tommy Johnson	4
		Kevin Wilson	8		

Average Home League Attendances

SEASON	AGGREGATE	AVERAGE	HIGHEST	LOWEST
1888-89	32,000	2,909	5,000	1,500
1889-90	39,500	3,591	5,000	1,500
1890-91	38,000	3,455	5,000	2,500
1891-92	71,500	5,500	8,000	3,000
1892-93	89,500	5,967	10,000	2,000
1893-94	83,475	5,565	10,500	700
1894-95	64,750	4,317	8,000	1,500
1895-96	124,000	8,267	15,000	4,000
1896-97	121,500	8,100	19,500	5,000
1897-98	130,700	8,713	15,000	4,000
1898-99	122,500	7,206	10,000	3,000
1899-00	141,000	8,294	15,000	3,000
1900-01	132,000	7,760	18,000	4,000
1901-02	158,000	9,290	20,000	2,000
1902-03	168,500	9,910	25,000	**500**
1903-04	163,500	9,620	22,000	4,000
1904-05	151,500	8,910	15,000	5,000
1905-06	144,500	7,610	15,000	3,000
1906-07	132,000	6,950	10,000	4,000
1907-08	169,500	8,920	18,000	2,000
1908-09	123,000	6,470	12,000	2,000
1909-10	151,000	7,950	15,000	5,000
1910-11	153,500	8,080	20,000	2,000
1911-12	201,000	10,580	18,000	5,000
1912-13	200,000	10,526	20,000	6,000
1913-14	188,500	9,920	12,000	4,000
1914-15	128,000	6,740	14,000	2,000
1919-20	279,711	13,319	21,366	8,000
1920-21	336,221	16,011	23,820	8,000
1921-22	224,803	10,705	22,803	7,000
1922-23	228,200	10,867	22,500	4,000
1923-24	289,559	13,789	21,622	7,000
1924-25	354,987	16,904	26,370	6,465
1925-26	342,599	16,314	26,724	5,824
1926-27	407,285	19,395	30,557	11,830
1927-28	340,906	16,234	26,008	8,323
1928-29	354,178	16,866	30,651	9,319
1929-30	335,517	15,977	30,307	9,102
1930-31	315,835	15,038	24,783	6,613
1931-32	275,971	13,141	25,790	7,765
1932-33	309,408	14,734	26,043	6,465
1933-34	391,996	18,666	32,320	13,416
1934-35	404,288	19,252	35,260	8,336
1935-36	439,579	20,932	30,087	14,494
1936-37	429,972	20,475	30,688	10,802
1937-38	363,041	17,288	33,101	8,035

SEASON	AGGREGATE	AVERAGE	HIGHEST	LOWEST
1938-39	401,115	19,101	35,683	6,697
1946-47	497,870	23,708	31,786	10,994
1947-48	567,927	27,044	35,713	16,277
1948-49	625,741	29,797	34,446	22,888
1949-50	551,934	26,283	37,652	11,147
1950-51	488,446	23,259	32,471	9,129
1951-52	460,935	21,949	28,791	8,582
1952-53	454,304	21,634	31,496	12,844
1953-54	362,967	17,284	28,205	9,382
1954-55	314,265	14,965	20,214	5,987
1955-56	407,200	17,704	33,330	10,794
1956-57	451,017	19,609	29,886	7,655
1957-58	416,424	19,829	25,630	13,549
1958-59	398,798	18,990	24,343	11,796
1959-60	332,119	15,815	26,394	10,440
1960-61	295,978	14,094	21,608	8,841
1961-62	334,529	15,929	27,355	6,739
1962-63	253,925	12,092	24,408	8,673
1963-64	251,562	11,979	20,305	5,934
1964-65	292,225	13,915	32,803	7,457
1965-66	297,004	14,143	27,265	6,810
1966-67	333,205	15,867	28,678	10,545
1967-68	439,177	20,913	28,161	15,711
1968-69	580,841	27,659	34,976	21,737
1969-70	**754,407**	**35,924**	**41,826**	29,451
1970-71	658,702	31,367	36,007	23,521
1971-72	696,153	33,150	39,450	26,738
1972-73	625,026	29,763	38,462	20,347
1973-74	583,545	27,788	36,003	23,348
1974-75	561,094	26,719	36,882	21,197
1975-76	595,355	28,350	36,230	22,488
1976-77	525,175	25,008	32,892	21,312
1977-78	461,842	21,992	33,384	18,189
1978-79	452,654	21,554	30,156	15,935
1979-80	395,228	18,820	27,783	15,381
1980-81	350,320	16,682	20,353	13,846
1981-82	248,381	11,828	16,046	7,518
1982-83	285,616	13,601	21,124	8,075
1983-84	270,029	12,859	18,691	9,711
1984-85	238,752	10,381	16,113	7,943
1985-86	284,893	12,387	21,036	9,571
1986-87	326,786	15,561	21,385	10,768
1987-88	345,621	17,281	26,356	14,214
1988-89	336,464	17,709	25,213	13,758
1989-90	333,233	17,539	24,190	13,694
1990-91	311,222	16,380	21,729	11,680
1991-92	336,907	14,648	22,608	10,559
1992-93	345,738	15,032	21,478	12,166
1993-94	366,934	15,954	19,300	13,370

Debut Goalscorers

A total of 85 players have scored on their debuts, the first was John Knox in the FA Cup game against Aston Unity on 30 October 1886.

The last to score on his debut for the Rams was Richard Goulooze on 29 September 1992 against Barnsley (a) when Derby won 2-1 in the Anglo-Italian Cup.

Twelve players have scored two goals on their debut:

Issac Monks	15 Oct 1887	v Staveley (a)	W 2-1 FA Cup
James Nelson	6 Sep 1890	v Blackburn Rovers (h)	W 8-5 Football League
Fred Bevan	2 Nov 1907	v Gainsborough T (h)	W 5-2 Division Two
Stan Fazackerley	31 Aug 1925	v Clapton Orient (h)	W 3-1 Division Two
Dave McCulloch	22 Oct 1938	v Manchester United (h)	W 5-1 Division One
Jack Stamps	18 Mar 1939	v Charlton Athletic (h)	W 3-1 Division One
Tommy Powell	25 Aug 1948	v Huddersfield Town (h)	W 4-1 Division One
Jock Buchanan	5 Feb 1955	v Port Vale (h)	W 6-1 Division Two
Ian Buxton	21 Nov 1959	v Ipswich Town (h)	W 3-1 Division Two
Des Palmer	19 Aug 1961	v Middlesbrough (a)	W 4-3 Division Two
Frank Sheridan	18 Oct 1980	v Queen's Park R (h)	D 3-3 Division Two
Jeff Chandler	17 Aug 1985	v AFC Bournemouth (h)	W 3-0 Division Three
Dean Saunders	29 Oct 1988	v Wimbledon (h)	W 4-1 Division One

The only Rams player to score a hat-trick on his debut is Ted Garry on 2 September 1907, when Derby beat Lincoln City (h) 4-0 in the opening game of the season.

The youngest player to score on his debut is Tony Reid on 12 November 1980 when Derby beat Chelsea (a) 3-1. He was aged 17 years and 187 days.

The oldest player to score on his debut is Stan Fazackerley on 31 August 1925 against Clapton Orient (h) when he scored twice in Derby's 3-1 win. He was aged 33 years and 301 days. These were the only goals he ever scored for the Rams.

ONE GAME PLAYERS

There have been 87 players who have only played one game for Derby. Six of the players who turned out in the Rams' opening game never played again and there have been five instances where two players in the same line-up never turned out again.

Jack Stamps, one of 12 players to have scored twice on their Derby County debut. The most recent was Dean Saunders, against Wimbledon in October 1988.

Ted Garry, the only man ever to score a hat-trick on his Rams debut.

Hat-Trick Facts

First: Spilsbury, FA Cup 5 Nov 1887 v Ecclesfield (6-0).
First League: Higgins (4), 9 Mar 1889 v Aston Villa (5-2).
First League Cup: O'Hare, 13 Sep 1967 v Hartlepools United.
First European: George, 22 Oct 1975 v Real Madrid (European Cup).
Most in a season: Bowers 5 (three, four-goal games) 1930-31; Bowers 4 (one, four-goal game) 1933-34, all League games.
Most by club in a season: 6 - 1896-97 Bloomer 3 (one, four-goal game), Stevenson 1 (four-goals) in League and Bloomer 2 in FA Cup; 1930-31 Bedford 1, Bowers 5 (three, four-goal games), all League games.
Against same club: Keith Havenhand scored two hat-tricks against the same side (Bristol Rovers) in the same season with the same scoreline (4-1).
Fastest between matches: Kevin Wilson scored two hat-tricks in four days, 1984-85; Jack Bowers scored three hat-tricks in four matches, 1933-34.
Best sequence: Jack Bowers - 14 goals in five games.
Triple hat-tricks in game: Hector (5), George and James, UEFA Cup, 15 Sep 1976 v Finn Harps (12-0).
Double hat-tricks in game: Whitehouse (4) and Bedford, Football League, 19 March 1927 v Sheffield Wednesday (8-0); Crooks and Stockill, Football League, 8 Dec 1934 v West Bromwich Albion (9-3).
Youngest hat-trick player: Andy Garner - 18 years 30 days.
Oldest hat-trick player: Steve Bloomer - 38 years 261 days.

FULL LIST:
SIX IN A MATCH
League: Bloomer.
FIVE IN A MATCH
League: Higgins, McMillan, Moore, Gallacher, Davies.
UEFA Cup: Hector.

FOUR IN A MATCH
League: Bowers 5, Bentley 3, Bedford 2, Storer 2, Ackerman 1, Bloomer 1, Carter 1, Fairclough 1, Higgins 1, Lee 1, Leonard 1, Lyons 1, Whitehouse 1, Rioch 1, Stamps 1, Stephenson 1, Stevenson 1.
FA Cup: Bedford 1, Stamps 1.
League Cup: Hinton 1, Wilson 1.
HAT-TRICKS
League: Bloomer 14, Bowers 10, Bedford 10, Bauchop 5, J.Goodall 5, Hector 5, Bentley 4, Curry 3, Durban 3, Lee 3, Straw 3, Astley 2, Davison 2, Havenhand 2, McMillan 2, Parry 2, Stamps 2, P.Williams 2, Arkesden 1, Barclay 1, Barnes 1, Biley 1, Crooks 1, Fairclough 1, Fordham 1, Gabbiadini 1, Gallacher 1, Garner 1, Garry 1, George 1, Gill 1, Harrison 1, Hodgkinson 1, Hodgson 1, Leonard 1, Moore 1, Morris 1, Morrison 1, Paterson 1, Pye 1, Saunders 1, Simpson 1, Stephenson 1, Stockill 1, Storer 1, Whitehouse 1, Wilson 1.
FA Cup: Bloomer 4, Spilsbury 2, Stamps 2, Astley 1, Bentley 1, Boag 1, Bowers 1, Carter 1, Chandler 1, Davies 1, Davison 1, Durban 1, Gemmill 1, Hector 1, Miller 1, Pembridge 1, Warren 1.
League Cup: Harford 1, O'Hare 1, Saunders 1.
European Cup: George 1.
UEFA Cup: George 1, James 1.
Zenith Data Systems Cup: Saunders 1.

Scottish international Hughie Gallacher, who scored five goals in one game against Blackburn Rovers in December 1934, only a month after signing for the Rams. At the end of that season Gallacher was the club's leading scorer with 23 goals from 27 League games.

A Great Cup Era

During the 6-0 defeat by Bury in the 1903 FA Cup Final, Derby County used three different goalkeepers in the second half, changing them four times. Jack Fryer, who started the game with a groin strain, lasted longest with a 48-minute spell and let in two goals. Charlie Morris took over, conceding one goal in the 56th minute before Fryer replaced the full-back a minute later to have another put past him, Morris taking over again only for the score to be increased again in the 59th minute. Three goals in three minutes. Morris lasted 16 minutes before the final goal went in before Jimmy Methven

replaced the Welshman and managed to last 15 minutes without conceding a goal. In the four rounds prior to the Final they had scored ten and conceded only one.

During the nine seasons between 1896 and 1904 Derby County reached the semi-final stage no less than seven times, being defeated in the Final three times. Their biggest victory was against Barnsley St Peter's winning 8-1, Steve Bloomer scoring a hat-trick. Their full record during that period is thus:
P41 W24 D8 L9 F91 A52

The Rams in 1906, at the end of a great FA Cup era for the club. Back row (left to right): Nicholas, Maskrey, Morris, Arthur Latham (trainer). Middle row: Jimmy Methven (manager), Cleaver, Warren, Hall, Wood, W.S.Moore (secretry). Front row: J.W.Davis, Wood, Long, Richards, G.Davis.

Football League Statistics

Best start to a season
7-0 v Barnsley (h) 2 Sep 1914

Worst start to a season
0-8 v Sunderland (a) 1 Sep 1894

Unbeaten from start of season
1948-49 16 matches no defeats

Consecutive wins from start of season
Five in 1905-06

Worst run from start of season
1899-1900 4 defeats
1920-21 8 matches no wins
1976-77 8 matches no wins
1990-91 9 matches no wins

Best unbeaten runs
22 games from 8 Mar 1969 to 20 Sep 1969
16 games from 17 Oct 1914 to 23 Jan 1915
16 games from 21 Aug 1948 to 6 Nov 1948
15 games from 22 Jan 1983 to 30 Apr 1983

Most consecutive victories
Nine in 1968-69 (last nine games)
Seven in 1933-34
Six in 1911-12 & 1914-15

Consecutive games without victory
20 in 1990-91
14 in 1954-55

Unbeaten home runs
23 games from 5 Oct 1929 to 11 Oct 1930
22 games from 3 Apr 1971 to 1 Apr 1972
　　　　　　(including eight from start)
21 games from 6 Sep 1986 to 15 Aug 1987
20 games from 1 Apr 1933 to 24 Feb 1934

Unbeaten away runs
13 games from 25 Jan 1969 to 13 Sep 1969
13 games from 31 Aug 1985 to 8 Feb 1986
10 games from 29 Aug 1992 to 20 Dec 1992

Consecutive defeats
Eight in 1888-89 & 1987-88

Consecutive draws
Six in 1926-27

Consecutive games scored
All: 27 games from 26 Sep 1964 to 27 Mar 1965
Home: 32 games from 22 Dec 1888 to 17 Oct 1891
Away: 19 games from 3 Oct 1964 to 7 Sep 1965

Consecutive games without scoring
All: 8 games from 30 Oct 1920 to 25 Dec 1920
Home: 4 games from 3 Nov 1906 to 22 Dec 1906

Kevin Hector, most appearances for the Rams and 201 goals into the bargain.

Away: 8 games from 24 Apr 1979 to 13 Oct 1979

Consecutive clean sheets
All: 6 games from 8 Apr 1912 to 22 Apr 1912 (last six)*
Home: 6 games from 22 Mar 1924 to 30 Aug 1924
      6 games from 24 Apr 1963 to 11 Sep 1963
Away: 6 games from 2 Mar 1912 to 14 Sep 1912
*Derby also conceded only one goal in the last 11 League games in 1911-12

Most clean sheets in a season
23 games in 1971-72 (42-match season)
21 games in 1911-12 (38-match season)

Fewest clean sheets in a season
One game in 1890-91 (22-match season)
Three games in 1990-91 (38-match season)
Four games in 1931-32, 1950-51 & 1967-68 (42-match season)

Best end-of-season performance
Most goals: 6-2 v Ipswich Town (a) Division One - 24 Apr 1976
Biggest margin: 5-0 v Bristol City (h) Division Two - 19 Apr 1969

Worst end-of-season performance
0-6 v Brentford (a) Division One - 2 May 1936
2-6 v Burnley (a) Division One - 3 May 1930
Derby finished runners-up in both these seasons

High scoring games

13 goals:	2-11	v Everton (h) FA Cup first round	18 Jan 1890
	8-5	v Blackburn Rovers (h) League	6 Sep 1890
12 goals:	9-3	v West Bromwich Albion (h) Div One	8 Dec 1934
	12-0	v Finn Harps (h) UEFA Cup first round	15 Sep 1976
11 goals:	4-7	v Preston North End (a) Div One	6 Dec 1947
	6-5	v Sunderland (h) Div One	16 Dec 1950
10 goals:	7-3	v Everton (h) Div One	9 Sep 1893
	5-5	v Everton (h) Div One	15 Oct 1898
	7-3	v Stoke City (h) Div Two	24 Oct 1925
	4-6	v Sheffield Wednesday (h) Div One	26 Nov 1927
	6-4	v Aston Villa (a) Div One	15 Nov 1930
	4-6	v Southampton (a) Div Two	1 Apr 1964
	5-5	v Birmingham City (a) Div Two	9 Apr 1966
	8-2	v Tottenham Hotspur (h) Div One	16 Oct 1976
	4-6	v Chelsea (h) Div One	15 Dec 1990

Other close high scoring games

9 goals:	5-4	v Aston Villa (h) League	18 Oct 1890
	4-5	v Notts County (h) Div One	19 Oct 1892
	4-5	v Wolverhampton W (h) Div One	22 Sep 1900
	4-5	v Blackburn Rovers (h) Div One	20 Nov 1926
	5-4	v Grimsby Town (h) Div One	14 Dec 1929
	5-4	v Manchester United (h) Div One	5 Sep 1936
	5-4	v Arsenal (h) Div One	3 Feb 1937
	4-5	v Chester (a) League Cup second round	23 Sep 1964
	5-4	v Darlington (h) League Cup fifth round	29 Nov 1967

Longest unbroken run in top flight
20 seasons from 1926-27 to 1952-53

Longest League season
Nine months   1946-47 - 31 Aug to 31 May
or longer   1962-63 - 18 Aug to 18 May
              1993-94 - 14 Aug to 30 May (includes Play-offs)

First game played on a Sunday
27 Jan 1974 v Coventry City (a) FA Cup fourth round

Current League clubs still to face Derby County in League, FA or League Cup
Barnet, Hereford United, Scarborough, Torquay United and Wycombe Wanderers.

Goalscorers
Thirty or more goals in a season League and Cup

43	- Jack Bowers (1932-33) in 47 games
39	- Jack Bowers (1930-31 in 34 games
37	- Jack Bowers (1933-34) in 41 games
	- Ray Straw (1956-57) in 46 games
32	- Alf Bentley (1908-09) in 40 games
31	- Steve Bloomer (1896-97) in 33 games
	- Alf Bentley (1909-10) in 40 games
	- Harry Bedford (1929-30) in 45 games
30	- Steve Bloomer (1898-99) in 33 games
	- Harry Bedford (1928-29) in 44 games

League only

37	- Jack Bowers (1930-31) in 33 games
	- Ray Straw (1956-57) in 44 games
35	- Jack Bowers (1932-33) in 41 games
34	- Jack Bowers (1933-34) in 37 games
30	- Alf Bentley (1909-10) in 38 games
	- Harry Bedford (1929-30) in 42 games

Most players in double figures in same season

Five in seasons 1927-28 & 1955-56 - League only
Five in seasons 1936-37 & 1948-49 - League & Cup
Five in season 1993-94 - League, Play-offs & Cup

Football League's leading goalscorers

1895-96 - Steve Bloomer - 22 goals
1896-97 - Steve Bloomer - 24 goals
1898-99 - Steve Bloomer - 24 goals
1900-01 - Steve Bloomer - 24 goals
1903-04 - Steve Bloomer - 20 goals
1932-33 - Jack Bowers - 35 goals

Division Three North
1956-57 - Ray Straw - 37 goals

The Rams in 1932-33, when Jack Bowers was the leading scorer in the Football League as Derby finished seventh in the First Division One. Back row (left to right): Cooper, Hann, Nicholas, Kirby, Louis Edwards (trainer), Collin, Barker, Keen. Front row: Crooks, Hutchison, Bowers, Ramage, Duncan.

Cup Statistics

FA CUP

First game
1 Nov 1884 v Walsall Town (h) 0-7

First victory
24 Oct 1885 v Birmingham St George (h) 3-0

Biggest victory
8-1 v Barnsley St Peter's (h) 30 Jan 1897 (round one)

Heaviest defeat
2-11 v Everton (h) 18 Jan 1890 (round one)

Least successful period
For six successive seasons from 1963-64 to 1968-69, Derby were knocked out at their first attempt in the third round.

For ten successive seasons from 1951-52 to 1960-61, Derby did not progress beyond the third round, although for two seasons they competed in the first two rounds.

Beaten by eventual winners (outside the Final)
1894-85 by Aston Villa (round one)
1901-02 by Sheffield United (semi-final second replay)
1912-13 by Aston Villa (round one)
1913-14 by Burnley (round two)
1923-24 by Newcastle United (round two third replay)
1947-48 by Manchester United (semi-final)
1982-83 by Manchester United (round five)

Beaten by non-League opposition
2-3 by Sheffield Wednesday (h) 31 Jan 1891 (round two)
1-6 by Boston United (h) 2 Dec 1955 (round two)
1-3 by New Brighton (h) 8 Dec 1956 (round two)

Longest tie
In 1923-24, in the second round, Derby and Newcastle United shared three 2-2 draws at the Baseball Ground, St James' Park and Burnden Park, Bolton before the Magpies won 5-3 at St James' Park in the third replay. The games were played on 2, 6, 11 and 13 Feb respectively, constituting 420 minutes of football.

FOOTBALL LEAGUE CUP

First game and victory
11 Oct 1960 v Watford (a) 5-2

Biggest victory
7-0 v Southend United (h) 7 Oct 1992

Heaviest defeat
0-5 v Southampton (a) 8 Oct 1974 (round three)
0-5 v West Ham United (a) 1 Nov 1988 (round three)

Least successful period
The Rams have lost in their opening round for three consecutive seasons twice, from 1962-63 to 1964-65 and 1979-80 to 1981-82.

Beaten by eventual winners (outside the Final)
1967-68 by Leeds United (semi-final)
1968-69 by Swindon Town (round five replay)
1990-91 by Sheffield Wednesday (round four replay)
1992-93 by Arsenal (round three replay)

International Facts

In season 1976-77 Derby County had nine current internationalists on their books: Roy McFarland, Colin Todd and Charlie George for England; Bruce Rioch and Archie Gemmill for Scotland; Rod Thomas and Leighton James for Wales; Gerry Daly and Tony Macken for the Republic of Ireland. Plus Kevin Hector and David Nish, both capped earlier whilst with the Rams. They earned a total of 30 caps between them in that season, Archie Gemmill the most with nine.

During September of that season Derby had an unchanged side against Liverpool (h) and Norwich City (a) with nine internationals in the team: David Nish, Roy McFarland, Colin Todd, Charlie George and Kevin Hector for England; Bruce Rioch and Archie Gemmill for Scotland; Rod Thomas and Leighton James for Wales. Only Graham Moseley in goal and Henry Newton were uncapped. The Liverpool side were also abundant with internationalists, only David Johnson (capped in 1980) was uncapped, making 19 of the 22 players internationals. Derby lost 3-2 as Liverpool went on to take the League Championship.

In 1977-78 Derby played 16 internationalists although only 18 caps were won during the season: Roy McFarland, David Nish, Colin Todd, Kevin Hector, Charlie George, Jeff Blockley and Gordon Hill for England; Archie Gemmill, Don Masson and Bruce Rioch for Scotland; Rod Thomas and Leighton James for Wales; David Langan, Gerry Daly, Tony Macken and Gerry Ryan for the Republic of Ireland.

The most players the Rams have supplied for any one team is three, on seven occasions. Six times for England and once for the Republic of Ireland.

ENGLAND
Steve Bloomer, John Goodall and George Kinsey against Wales, 16 Mar 1896 (Bloomer scored five times).
Tommy Cooper, Jack Bowers and Sammy Crooks against Scotland, 14 Apr 1934.
Jack Barker, Sammy Crooks and Errington Keen against Wales, 17 Oct 1936.
Roy McFarland, David Nish and Colin Todd against Wales, 11 May 1974 and against Northern Ireland, 15 May 1974.
Roy McFarland, Colin Todd and Charlie George against the Republic of Ireland, 8 Sep 1976.

REPUBLIC OF IRELAND
Gerry Daly, David Langan and Gerry Ryan against Turkey, 5 Apr 1978.

The most internationals playing in the same match while with the Rams is four, on three occasions.

Scotland v Wales (Hampden Park), 24 May 1972.
John O'Hare & Archie Gemmill for Scotland, Alan Durban & Terry Hennessey for Wales.

Wales v England (Ninian Park), 11 May 1974.
Rod Thomas for Wales, Roy McFarland, Colin Todd & David Nish for England.

Scotland v England (Hampden Park), 15 May 1976
Archie Gemmill & Bruce Rioch for Scotland, Roy McFarland & Colin Todd for England.

MOST INTERNATIONAL CAPS (Whilst with Derby)

Peter Shilton	34	9 Sep 1987 to 7 Jul 1990
Roy McFarland	28	3 Feb 1971 to 17 Nov 1976
Alan Durban	27	18 May 1966 to 27 May 1972
Colin Todd	27	23 May 1972 to 28 May 1977
Sammy Crooks	26	5 Apr 1930 to 2 Dec 1936
Mark Wright	24	17 Feb 1988 to 12 Jun 1991
Archie Gemmill	22	3 Feb 1971 to 7 Sep 1977
Steve Bloomer	21	9 Mar 1895 to 1 Apr 1905
Charlie Morris	21	2 Mar 1901 to 11 Apr 1910
Rod Thomas	19	11 May 1974 to 12 Oct 1977
Bruce Rioch	18	13 May 1975 to 11 Jun 1978
Tommy Cooper	15	22 Oct 1927 to 29 Sep 1934
Dean Saunders	15	8 Feb 1989 to 5 Jun 1991
Gerry Daly	14	30 Mar 1977 to 16 May 1980
Dally Duncan	14	26 Oct 1932 to 30 Oct 1937
Billy Steel	14	4 Oct 1947 to 27 May 1950
Leighton James	13	24 Apr 1976 to 20 Sep 1977
John O'Hare	13	18 Apr 1970 to 24 May 1972
Ben Warren	13	17 Feb 1906 to 13 Jun 1908
Jack Barker	11	29 Sep 1934 to 17 Oct 1936
Geraint Williams	11	11 Nov 1987 to 11 Oct 1989
John Goodall	10	7 Mar 1891 to 28 Mar 1898
Archie Goodall	8	4 Mar 1899 to 28 Mar 1903
Terry Hennessey	8	18 Apr 1970 to 15 Nov 1972
Raich Carter	7	28 Sep 1946 to 18 May 1947
Billy Caskey	6	29 Nov 1978 to 17 Oct 1979
Paddy Fagan	6	30 Mar 1960 to 7 May 1961
Vic Moreland	6	29 Nov 1978 to 21 Nov 1979
Frank Stapleton	6	23 Mar 1988 to 18 Jun 1988
David Nish	5	12 May 1973 to 18 May 1974
Errington Keen	4	7 Dec 1932 to 2 Dec 1936
David Langan	4	5 Apr 1978 to 16 May 1980
Alf Quantrill	4	15 Mar 1920 to 14 Mar 1921
Arthur Stewart	4	28 Feb 1968 to 11 Dec 1968
George Thornewell	4	21 May 1923 to 21 May 1925
Jack Bowers	3	14 Oct 1933 to 14 Apr 1934
Jack Howe	3	16 May 1948 to 9 Oct 1948
Don Masson	3	13 May 1978 to 3 Jun 1978
John Mercer	3	12 Mar 1904 to 18 Mar 1905
Johnny Morris	3	18 May 1949 to 21 Sep 1949
Bert Mozley	3	21 Sep 1949 to 16 Nov 1949
Mark Pembridge	3	18 Nov 1992 to 10 Mar 1994
Sid Reid	3	14 Oct 1933 to 19 Oct 1935
Dai Astley	2	22 Oct 1938 to 9 Nov 1938
George Davis	2	29 Feb 1904 to 12 Mar 1904
Kevin Hector	2	17 Oct 1973 to 14 Nov 1973
George Kinsey	2	7 Mar 1896 to 16 Mar 1896
Dave McCulloch	2	9 Nov 1938 to 7 Dec 1938
Charlie Napier	2	31 Oct 1936 to 9 May 1937
Mick O'Brien*	2	9 Apr 1927 to 23 Apr 1927
John Robertson	2	21 Sep 1983 to 12 Oct 1983
Jack Robinson	2	20 Feb 1897 to 3 Apr 1897
George Stephenson	2	17 May 1928 to 19 May 1928
Harry Storer	2	17 May 1924 to 22 Oct 1927
Tim Ward	2	21 Sep 1947 to 10 Nov 1948
Jimmy Bagshaw	1	25 Oct 1919 to 25 Oct 1919
Frank Buckley	1	14 Feb 1914 to 14 Feb 1914

Jack Cox	1	5 Mar 1892 to 5 Mar 1892
Peter Doherty	1	28 Sep 1946 to 28 Sep 1946
Ronnie Dix	1	9 Nov 1938 to 9 Nov 1938
Hughie Gallacher	1	6 Apr 1935 to 6 Apr 1935
Charlie George	1	8 Sep 1976 to 8 Sep 1976
Billy Halligan	1	28 Jan 1911 to 28 Jan 1911
Jack Lee	1	7 Oct 1950 to 7 Oct 1950
Tony Macken	1	9 Feb 1977 to 9 Feb 1977
Harry Maskrey	1	15 Feb 1908 to 15 Feb 1908
Jimmy Moore	1	21 May 1923 to 21 May 1923
George Richards	1	1 Jun 1909 to 1 Jun 1909
Gerry Ryan	1	5 Apr 1978 to 5 Apr 1978
Reg Ryan	1	27 Nov 1955 to 27 Nov 1955
Ernald Scattergood	1	17 Mar 1913 to 17 Mar 1913
Jimmy Turner	1	5 Mar 1898 to 5 Mar 1898

Mick O'Brien's two caps were one each for Northern Ireland and the Republic of Ireland.

Archie Goodall's debut for Ireland was their 51st game. It was the first time they had included a player from a Football League club. Bill Taggart (Walsall) and Tom Morrison (Burnley) also played from the League.

Jack Barker made his England debut in the same game as 19-year-old Stanley Matthews of Stoke City. Tommy Cooper's second cap came exactly one year (22 Oct) after his international debut in 1927, against the same team, Northern Ireland.

Roy McFarland played 16 times for England before being on the losing side.

As Archie Gemmill made his international debut, so Tommy Gemmell (Celtic) appeared for the last time in a Scotland shirt.

In a five-match sequence for Wales, Alan Durban pulled on five different numbered shirts - 4, 10, 8, 11 and 7.

INTERNATIONAL GOALSCORERS (Whilst with Derby)

ENGLAND
Bloomer 27, Goodall J. 9, Crooks 7, Carter 5, Morris 3, Bowers 2, Stephenson 2, Davis 1, Dix 1, Lee 1, Moore 1, Quantrill 1, Storer 1, Thornewell 1, Warren 1, Wright 1.

SCOTLAND
Duncan 7, Rioch 6, O'Hare 5, Steel 3, Gemmill 2, Napier 1, Robertson 1, Todd 1 (own-goal).

WALES
Saunders 6, James 4, Astley 3, Durban 2.

IRELAND
Goodall A. 2, Halligan 1.

NORTHERN IRELAND
Caskey 1, Moreland 1.

REPUBLIC OF IRELAND
Fagan 5, Daly 4.

Steve Bloomer scored in each of his first ten appearances for England netting 19 goals. He failed to score in only five of his 23 games.

Two Rams stars pictured in an England team of the 1890s. Back row (left to right): N.L.Jackson (linesman), L.V.Lodge (Cambridge University), J.Reynolds (Aston Villa), J.Reid (referee), J.Holt (Everton), J.W.Sutcliffe (Bolton Wanderers), E.Needham (Sheffield United), J.Crabtree (Burnley), R.Molyneux (FA official), C.J.Hughes (linesman). Front row: W.Bassett (West Brom), S.Bloomer (Derby County), J.Goodall (Derby County), R.C.Gosling (Old Etonians), S.Smith (Aston Villa).

Long Serving Players

The player who has served Derby County the longest in unbroken service is Sammy Crooks, who spent 19 years and 18 days with the Rams. He also spent another four years at the club as Chief Scout.

Steve Bloomer, who spent nearly 17 years as a player at Derby in two spells, also had another 21 years with the Rams in various occupations, including odd-job man.

Current Derby County manager, Roy McFarland, is another who has continued working for the club after his playing career. He played for just under 14 years and has continued for another ten years in other capacities.

S.D.Crooks	**19 years 18 days**
J.T.Nicholas	18 years 100 days
S.Bloomer	16 years 312 days
J.Parry	16 years 182 days
R.Webster	15 years 173 days
A.Latham	15 years 173 days
J.Methven	15 years 152 days
J.D.Stamps	14 years 272 days
D.Duncan	14 years 202 days
J.T.Atkin	14 years 118 days
G.Barrowcliffe	14 years 55 days
S.McLachlan	14 years 1 day
R.L.McFarland	13 years 352 days
A.L.Goodall	13 years 231 days
S.Powell	13 years 182 days
J.R.Howe	13 years 175 days
P.A.Daniel	13 years 75 days
T.Powell	13 years 68 days
G.H.Lawrence	13 years 68 days
J.J.Bagshaw	13 years 47 days
T.V.Ward	13 years 47 days
K.J.Hector	12 years 274 days

Geoff Barrowcliffe receives a gold watch from chairman Harry Payne to mark Barrowcliffe's 500th first-team appearance for Derby County. Watching is manager Tim Ward, himself high in the list of the club's long-serving players.

Jack Nicholas leads out the Rams followed by Peter Doherty. Nicholas is second, behind Sammy Crooks, in the list of long-serving Rams players.

Player Count

Derby County have used 752 players in League and Cup competitions since their inception up to the 1994 Play-off Final. Haydn Morley was the first player to be signed by the Rams but, of course all 11 who played in Derby's first match were debutants. By the end of the 1993-94 season Derby County had used 752 players, the last of which was Gordon Cowans.

On average they turn out 50 new playes every 6.93 years, the longest span between fifties being from when Ron Webster (550) made his debut on 24 March1962 to playing Charlie George (600) on 9 August 1975 in the FA Charity Shield. That is an average of just under four players a season compared with the high score of 13 new players in each of Tommy Docherty's two seasons and 14 in Arthur Cox's first term.

50.	John Goodall	7 Sep 1889
100.	John Paul	12 Dec 1894
150.	George Davis	1 Dec 1900
200.	Fred Cleaver	24 Feb 1906
250.	Shirley Abbott	27 Jan 1912
300.	Harry Storer	12 Mar 1921
350.	George Mee	27 Mar 1926
400.	Hughie Gallacher	10 Nov 1934
450.	James McGill	3 May 1947
500.	Peter Cresswell	21 Aug 1954
550.	Ron Webster	24 Mar 1962
600.	Charlie George	9 Aug 1975
650.	Mick Coop	29 Aug 1981
700.	John Gregory	16 Nov 1985
750.	John Harkes	18 Aug 1993

Above: Ron Webster, number 550 in the list of Rams debutants. He began under Harry Storer and went on to enjoy great success with Brian Clough's team.

Left: John Gregory on the day he made his Rams debut to become the 700th player used by Derby County.

Transfers

Derby County broke the British record several times when purchasing players (*denotes). They have also broken the Scottish record once when selling, Billy Steel featuring in that and a British record when joining Derby.

Tables below shows who and when Derby's club signing and selling fees were broken:

Fee	Player	From	Year
£50	Alf Bentley	Alfreton Town	1906
£1,500	Jimmy Moore	Glossop	1913
£4,500	Harry Storer	Grimsby Town	1921
£5,000	Charlie Napier	Glasgow Celtic	1935
£9,500	Dave McCulloch	Brentford	1938
*£15,500	Billy Steel	Greenock Morton	1947
*£24,500	Johnny Morris	Manchester United	1949
£40,000	Kevin Hector	Bradford	1966
£60,000	Willie Carlin	Sheffield United	1968
£100,000	Terry Hennessey	Nottingham Forest	1970
£170,000	Colin Todd	Sunderland	1971
*£225,000	David Nish	Leicester City	1972
£300,000	Leighton James	Burnley	1975
£330,000	Derek Hales	Charlton Athletic	1976
£350,000	Alan Biley	Cambridge United	1980
£410,000	David Swindlehurst	Crystal Palace	1980
£760,000	Mark Wright	Southampton	1987
£1,000,000	Dean Saunders	Oxford United	1988
£1,000,000	Marco Gabiadini	Crystal Palace	1992
£1,300,000	Paul Kitson	Leicester City	1992
£1,375,000	Tommy Johnson	Notts County	1992
£2,500,000	Craig Short	Notts County	1992

Fee	Player	To	Year
£225	James Stevenson	Newcastle United	1898
*£2,500	Horace Barnes	Manchester City	1914
£2,500	Randolph Galloway	Nottingham Forest	1924
£4,000	Harry Bedford	Newcastle United	1930
£8,000	Tommy Cooper	Liverpool	1934
†£23,000	Billy Steel	Dundee	1950
£50,000	Barry Butlin	Luton Town	1972
£90,000	John Robson	Aston Villa	1972
£135,000	Roger Davies	Club Brugge KV	1976
£180,000	Bruce Rioch	Everton	1976
£180,000	Leighton James	Queen's Park Rangers	1977
£300,000	Colin Todd	Everton	1978
£400,000	Charlie George	Southampton	1978
£500,000	Nigel Callaghan	Aston Villa	1989
£800,000	Paul Goddard	Millwall	1989
£2,300,000	Mark Wright	Liverpool	1991
*£2,900,000	Dean Saunders	Liverpool	1991

Alan Biley cost a Derby County record fee of £350,000 when he joined the Rams from Cambridge United in 1980. The Rams were soon relegated, however, and Biley joined Everton in July 1981.

Billy Steel, a record British signing when he joined the Rams from Morton in 1947, and a record signing by a Scottish club when Derby sold him to Dundee three years later.

Dean Saunders, a great favourite at the Baseball Ground after joining the Rams as their first million pound player. When he was transferred to Liverpool in a double deal with Mark Wright, Saunders was valued at £2.9 million, another Rams record.

Youngest and Oldest

The youngest player ever to play for Derby County is Steve Powell who was aged 16 years and 30 days when he made his debut against Stoke City in the Texaco Cup on 20 October 1971. He is the youngest of four players to have played for the Rams while still 16, Roy Patrick, Fred Flanders and Mark Stallard being the others.

S.Powell	**16 years 30 days**
R.Patrick	16 years 277 days
F.Flanders	16 years 287 days
M.Stallard	16 years 329 days
A.T.Lewis	17 years 62 days
J.Clayton	17 years 62 days
B.Scarborough	17 years 135 days
A.J.Reid	17 years 187 days
J.D.Robson	17 years 230 days
P.A.Blades	17 years 256 days
D.D.Paul	17 years 268 days
W.Cholerton	17 years 273 days
J.Parry	17 years 273 days
C.A.Place	17 years 281 days
G.M.Tate	17 years 282 days
A.M.Gibson	17 years 322 days
H.J.Linacre	17 years 327 days
W.Lievesley	17 years 335 days
A.E.Quantrill	17 years 339 days
J.Hagan	17 years 342 days
A.Garner	17 years 345 days
P.Bartlett	17 years 350 days

Fred Flanders, the former captain of Derby Boys and a junior international, who is third in the list of the youngest players ever to represent the Rams. He later played for Newport County and Hartlepool United.

The oldest player ever to play for Derby County is Peter Shilton who was aged 42 years and 164 days when he played his last game for the club on 29 February 1992 against Watford at the Baseball Ground. He was also the oldest debutant when he played against Luton Town (h) on 15 August 1987 aged 37 years 331 days.

OLDEST DEBUTANTS		OLDEST PLAYERS	
P.L.Shilton	**37 years 331 days**	**P.L.Shilton**	**42 years 164 days**
D.V.Watson	36 years 354 days	A.Latham	40 years 116 days
J.M.Wallace	36 years 306 days	H.M.Maskrey	40 years 65 days
V.R.Woodley	36 years 25 days	S.Bloomer	40 years 19 days
G.S.Cowans	35 years 129 days	J.T.Atkin	39 years 14 days
J.Pye	34 years 291 days	A.L.Goodall	38 years 317 days
S.Fazackerley	33 years 301 days	S.D.Crooks	38 years 264 days
R.Jones	33 years 278 days	J.Methven	38 years 64 days
D.C.Mackay	33 years 259 days	D.V.Watson	37 years 228 days
M.T.O'Brien	33 years 218 days	K.J.Hector	37 years 202 days
K.Ratcliffe	33 years 71 days	J.M.Wallace	37 years 27 days
M.A.Coop	33 years 57 days	D.Duncan	36 years 357 days

England schoolboy international Steve Powell, the youngest player ever to appear in a senior competitive match for the Rams. He also won youth and under-23 honours and went on to enjoy a long career with Derby, as had his father before him. His son, also Steve, is currently on the Rams' books.

Rams Career Records
1884-1994

Below are the career records (League, FA Cup and League Cup) of every Rams first-team player since the club's first FA Cup match in 1884. The years given are the first years of seasons. Thus, 1946 means 1946-47. In the 'Others' list are all the competitions not accounted for in the rest of the table. This list contains figures for the 1894-95 Test Match, 1975 FA Charity Shield, Texaco Cup, European Cup, UEFA Cup, Freight/Rover Trophy, Full Members' Cup and 1991-92, 1993-94 League Play-offs. It should be noted that in 1889-90 the Rams fielded only ten men at Preston. Substitute appearances are given to the right of full appearances (e.g. 26/2).

Player	Played	League App	League Gls	FA Cup App	FA Cup Gls	Lg Cup App	Lg Cup Gls	Others App	Others Gls	TOTAL App	TOTAL Gls
ABBOTT S.W.	1911	1	0	0	0	0	0	0	0	1	0
ABBOTT W.L.	1893	4	1	0	0	0	0	0	0	4	1
ABDALLAH T.	1920-21	15	1	0	0	0	0	0	0	15	1
ABLETT G.I.	1984	3/3	0	0	0	0	0	2	0	5/3	0
ACKERMAN A.A.E.	1954-56	36	21	0	0	0	0	0	0	36	21
ADLINGTON T.	1956-61	36	0	1	0	4	0	0	0	41	0
AINSWORTH C.	1908	8	0	0	0	0	0	0	0	8	0
AINSWORTH F.	1919	1	0	0	0	0	0	0	0	1	0
ALDERMAN A.E.	1928-33	21	5	3	1	0	0	0	0	24	6
ALLAN J.	1893-94	36	8	4	1	0	0	0	0	40	9
ALLEN H.	1898-99	15	3	5	2	0	0	0	0	20	5
ALTON T.W.	1937	3	0	0	0	0	0	0	0	3	0
ANTONIO G.R.	1946-47	18	2	0	0	0	0	0	0	18	2
ARKESDEN T.A.	1898-1900	50	14	1	0	0	0	0	0	51	14
ARMSTRONG A.	1906-07	4	1	0	0	0	0	0	0	4	1
ASTLEY D.J.	1936-38	93	45	5	4	0	0	0	0	98	49
ATKIN J.T.	1907-21	308	3	17	0	0	0	0	0	325	3
ATTLEY B.R.	1981-83	54/1	1	2	0	4	0	0	0	60/1	1
BACON A.	1925-27	8	3	1	0	0	0	0	0	9	3
BAGSHAW J.J.	1906-19	226	6	14	0	0	0	0	0	240	6
BAILEY A.D.	1971	1	0	0	0	0	0	2/1	0	3/1	0
BAILEY H.P.	1909	3	0	0	0	0	0	0	0	3	0
BAILEY L.A.	1937-38	26	0	2	0	0	0	0	0	28	0
BAKER J.	1890	8	0	2	0	0	0	0	0	10	0
BAKER W.E.	1914-20	44	7	0	0	0	0	0	0	44	7
BAKEWELL G.	1884-90	49	9	15	3	0	0	0	0	64	12
BALKWILL A.	1901	11	1	0	0	0	0	0	0	11	1
BANOVIC V.	1981-83	35	0	0	0	3	0	0	0	38	0
BARBOUR T.	1908-20	273	3	21	0	0	0	0	0	294	3
BARCLAY R.	1928-30	61	23	3	3	0	0	0	0	64	26
BAKER F.C.	1903-04	4	2	0	0	0	0	0	0	4	2
BARKER J.W.	1928-38	326	2	27	0	0	0	0	0	353	2
BARKER R.	1967-68	30/8	12	0	0	7	2	0	0	37/8	14
BARNES H.	1908-13	153	74	14	4	0	0	0	0	167	78
BARNES J.	1921	4	0	0	0	0	0	0	0	4	0
BARROWCLIFFE G.	1951-65	475	37	22	1	6	1	0	0	503	39
BARTLETT P.	1977-79	7/6	0	0	0	0	0	0	0	7/6	0
BARTON J.S.	1981-83	68/1	1	8	0	5	0	0	0	81/1	1
BAUCHOP J.R.	1909-12	126	68	9	4	0	0	0	0	135	72
BAYLISS H.H.R.	1920	1	0	0	0	0	0	0	0	1	0

Player	Played	League		FA Cup		Lg Cup		Others		TOTAL	
		App	Gls	App	Gls	App	Gls	App	Gls	App	Gls
BEDFORD H.	1925-30	203	142	15	10	0	0	0	0	218	152
BELL C.	1950-54	77	2	2	0	0	0	0	0	79	2
BELL D.	1934-38	52	0	3	0	0	0	0	0	55	0
BELLHOUSE E.W.	1888	2	0	0	0	0	0	0	0	2	0
BENFIELD T.C.	1914	38	15	1	0	0	0	0	0	39	15
BENTLEY A.	1906-10	151	99	17	13	0	0	0	0	168	112
BESTWICK T.H.	1886-88	1	0	6	0	0	0	0	0	7	0
BETTS A.C.	1911-13	71	0	3	0	0	0	0	0	74	0
BEVAN F.W.	1907-09	51	17	1	1	0	0	0	0	52	18
BIGGINS S.J.	1984-85	8 /2	1	1	0	0	0	1 /1	0	10 /3	1
BILEY A.P.	1979-80	47	19	2	0	2	0	0	0	51	19
BIRD D.W.C.	1934-35	5	2	0	0	0	0	0	0	5	2
BIRDSALL G.	1921	8	0	0	0	0	0	0	0	8	0
BLACKETT J.	1900	17	1	0	0	0	0	0	0	17	1
BLADES P.A.	1982-89	157 /9	1	12	0	9 /3	0	8 /2	0	186 /14	1
BLESSINGTON J.	1899	2	0	0	0	0	0	0	0	2	0
BLOCKLEY J.P.	1977	0	0	1	0	0	0	0	0	1	0
BLOOMER P.	1895	1	0	0	0	0	0	0	0	1	0
BLOOMER S.	1892-1905										
	1910-13	474	293	50	38	0	0	1	1	525	332
BLORE V.F.	1933-34	15	0	0	0	0	0	0	0	15	0
BOAG J.	1896-1903	117	27	23	10	0	0	0	0	140	37
BOSWORTH S.	1898	2	1	0	0	0	0	0	0	2	1
BOULTON C.D.	1964-77	272	0	29	0	16	0	27	0	344	0
BOULTON F.P.	1938-45	39	0	7	0	0	0	0	0	46	0
BOURNE J.	1970-76	35 /14	9	7 /3	2	1 /1	0	5 /6	3	48 /24	14
BOWDEN O.	1932-33	10	1	0	0	0	0	0	0	10	1
BOWER T.A	1886	0	0	1	0	0	0	0	0	1	0
BOWERS J.A.	1959-65	65	19	0	0	3	1	0	0	68	20
BOWERS J.W.A.	1928-36	203	167	17	16	0	0	0	0	220	183
BOWLER G.H.	1912	1	0	0	0	0	0	0	0	1	0
BOXLEY H.	1919	7	0	0	0	0	0	0	0	7	0
BOYD J.M.	1935-36	9	1	0	0	0	0	0	0	9	1
BRADBURY J.J.L.	1899	7	1	0	0	0	0	0	0	7	1
BRAND R.	1890	3	0	0	0	0	0	0	0	3	0
BRINTON J.V.	1937	8	2	0	0	0	0	0	0	8	2
BRISCOE R.D.	1989-90	10 /3	1	0	0	4 /1	0	0	0	14 /4	1
BROLLY M.J.	1982	41 /1	4	3	0	5	1	0	0	49 /1	5
BROMAGE E.	1888-89	17	0	1	0	0	0	0	0	18	0
BROMAGE E.	1923-26	4	2	2	1	0	0	0	0	6	3
BROMAGE H.	1899-1901	5	0	0	0	0	0	0	0	5	0
BROOKS G.	1914	33	0	1	0	0	0	0	0	34	0
BROOKS J.T.	1894	3	0	0	0	0	0	0	0	3	0
BROOME F.H.	1946-49	112	45	7	0	0	0	0	0	119	45
BROWN G.	1956-59	53	20	1	0	0	0	0	0	54	20
BROWN H.T.	1949-50	37	0	3	0	0	0	0	0	40	0
BUCHANAN J.	1954-56	32	12	0	0	0	0	0	0	32	12
BUCKLEY F.C.	1911-13	92	3	5	0	0	0	0	0	97	3
BUCKLEY S.	1977-85	323	21	19	1	21	3	3	0	366	25
BULLIONS J.L.	1945-47	17	0	12	0	0	0	0	0	29	0
BUNYAN C.	1889-91	9	0	2	0	0	0	0	0	11	0
BURNS K.	1982										
	1983-84	36 /2	2	3	0	4	0	0	0	43 /2	2

Player	Played	League App	League Gls	FA Cup App	FA Cup Gls	Lg Cup App	Lg Cup Gls	Others App	Others Gls	TOTAL App	TOTAL Gls
BURRIDGE J.	1984	6	0	0	0	2	0	0	0	8	0
BURTON J.H.	1897-98	10	3	0	0	0	0	0	0	10	3
BURTON N.	1919-20	56	16	5	2	0	0	0	0	61	18
BUTLIN B.D.	1967-72	4	0	0	0	2	0	3	1	9	1
BUTTERWORTH C.E.	1891	1	0	0	0	0	0	0	0	1	0
BUXTON I.R.	1959-67	144/1	41	2	0	11	2	0	0	157/1	43
CALLAGHAN N.I.	1986-88										
	1990	88	11	4	1	3	0	5	1	100	13
CALLAN W.	1921	1	0	0	0	0	0	0	0	1	0
CALLENDER R.H.	1913	5	0	0	0	0	0	0	0	5	0
CAMPBELL R.M.	1983	11	4	0	0	1	0	0	0	12	4
CARGILL D.A.	1958-60	56	8	2	2	1	1	0	0	59	11
CARLIN W.	1968-70	89	14	5	0	14	2	0	0	108	16
CARR W.P.	1925-32	102	0	7	0	0	0	0	0	109	0
CARRUTHERS E.	1976	0/1	0	0	0	0	0	0	0	0/1	0
CARTER H.S	1945-47	63	34	20	16	0	0	0	0	83	50
CARTER S.C.	1978-79	32/1	1	1	0	1	0	0	0	34/1	1
CASKEY W.T.	1978-79	26/2	3	1	0	1	0	0	0	28/2	3
CHALK M.P.G.	1991	4/3	1	3	1	0	0	0/1	0	7/4	2
CHALMERS B.	1890	20	1	2	0	0	0	0	0	22	1
CHANDLER A.	1919-24	169	0	14	0	0	0	0	0	183	0
CHANDLER J.G.	1985-86	45/1	9	7	4	7	3	2/1	0	61/2	16
CHARLES G.A.	1993	43	1	1	0	2/1	0	5	0	51/1	1
CHATTERTON W.	1884-88	5	1	1	0	0	0	0	0	6	1
CHERRY S.R.	1979-83	77	0	8	0	5	0	0	0	90	0
CHESTERS C.W.	1977-78	6/3	1	0	0	0/1	0	0	0	6/4	1
CHIEDOZIE J.O.	1988	2	0	0	0	0	0	0	0	2	0
CHOLERTON W.	1966	1	0	0	0	0	0	0	0	1	0
CHRISTIE T.	1984-85	65	22	7	3	5	0	2	1	79	26
CLAMP E.	1948	1	0	0	0	0	0	0	0	1	0
CLARK B.	1954-57	16	0	1	0	0	0	0	0	17	0
CLARK J.	1978-80	48/5	3	4	0	4	0	0	0	56/5	3
CLAYTON J.	1978-81	21/3	4	1	0	1/1	0	0	0	23/4	4
CLEAVER F.L.	1905-06	11/1	3	1	0	0	0	0	0	12	3
CLEEVELY N.R.	1964-66	15/1	3	1	0	1	0	0	0	17/1	3
CLIFTON G.	1886-88	1	0	2	0	0	0	0	0	3	0
COLEMAN S.	1991-93	62/8	2	5/1	0	5	0	12	0	84/9	2
COLLIN G.	1927-35	309	9	25	0	0	0	0	0	334	0
COMYN A.J.	1991-92	59/4	1	3/1	1	7	0	9	2	78/4	4
CONWELL A.	1959-61	98	1	2	0	7	0	0	0	107	1
COOKE J.A.	1898-99	11	2	0	0	0	0	0	0	11	2
COOP M.A.	1981	17/1	0	1	0	2	0	0	0	20/1	0
COOPER G.F.	1885	0	0	3	0	0	0	0	0	3	0
COOPER L.	1885-91	50	23	8	4	0	0	0	0	58	27
COOPER T.	1925-34	248	1	18	0	0	0	0	0	266	1
CORISH R.	1977	0/1	0	0	0	0	0	0	0	0/1	0
COWANS G.S.	1993	19	0	0	0	0	0	3	1	22	1
COWELL W.	1926	1	0	0	0	0	0	0	0	1	0
COX J.D.	1890-99	212	7	25	0	0	0	1	0	238	7
CRAWFORD A.	1977-79	16/5	4	0/2	0	1/1	1	0	0	17/8	5
CRAWFORD J.	1900-01	42	1	1	0	0	0	0	0	43	1
CRESSWELL P.F.	1954-56	12	2	2	0	0	0	0	0	14	2

Player	Played	League App	League Gls	FA Cup App	FA Cup Gls	Lg Cup App	Lg Cup Gls	Others App	Others Gls	TOTAL App	TOTAL Gls
CRILLY T.	1922-27	197	0	14	0	0	0	0	0	211	0
CROOKS S.D.	1927-46	408	101	37	10	0	0	0	0	445	111
CROPPER W.	1886	0	0	1	0	0	0	0	0	1	0
CROSS S.C.	1986-91	42 /31	3	3 /2	0	4 /4	0	3 /5	2	52 /42	5
CROWSHAW A.A.	1956-57	18	6	0	0	0	0	0	0	18	6
CRUMP F.	1899	6	1	0	0	0	0	0	0	6	1
CULLEN M.J.	1962-64	24	5	1	0	1	0	0	0	26	5
CURRAN E.	1977	26	2	3	0	0	0	0	0	29	2
CURRY W.M.	1960-64	148	67	8	4	8	5	0	0	164	76
CUSHLOW R.	1948-49	2	0	0	0	0	0	0	0	2	0
DAFT T.	1890	3	0	0	0	0	0	0	0	3	0
DALY G.A.	1976-79	111 /1	31	5	2	5	1	0	0	121 /1	34
DALZIEL I.	1981-82	22	4	1 /1	0	3 /1	0	0	0	26 /2	4
DANIEL P.A.	1965-78	188 /7	7	18 /1	0	16 /1	0	15	1	237 /9	8
DARWIN G.H.	1957-60	94	32	3	1	0	0	0	0	97	33
DAVIDSON J.S.	1989-91	7 /5	0	0 /2	0	1	0	0 /1	0	8 /8	0
DAVIES F.	1902	1	0	0	0	0	0	0	0	1	0
DAVIES G.	1953-61	200	5	9	0	4	0	0	0	213	5
DAVIES R.	1971-75										
	1979	120 /16	34	12 /4	8	5	1	7 /2	1	144 /22	44
DAVIS G.H.	1900-07	134	27	21	2	0	0	0	0	155	29
DAVIS J.W.	1904-09	138	9	15	4	0	0	0	0	153	13
DAVISON R.	1982-87										
	1991	213 /3	91	11	7	18	6	4	2	246 /3	106
DAVISON T.R.	1925-30	83	5	2	0	0	0	0	0	85	5
DAYKIN R.B.	1959-61	4	1	0	0	0	0	0	0	4	1
DEACY E.S.	1983	5	0	0	0	0	0	0	0	5	0
DEVINE S.B.	1983-84	10 /1	0	0	0	0	0	0	0	10 /1	0
DEVONSHIRE W.J.	1914	7	1	0	0	0	0	0	0	7	1
DILLY T.	1907	10	2	0	0	0	0	0	0	10	2
DIX R.W.	1936-38	94	35	2	0	0	0	0	0	96	35
DOBBS A.	1933	3	1	0	0	0	0	0	0	3	1
DOCHERTY J.	1893-94	35	0	3	0	0	0	0	0	38	0
DOCKERY G.	1893	5	0	0	0	0	0	0	0	5	0
DOHERTY P.D.	1945-46	16	7	10	10	0	0	0	0	25	17
DONAGHY E.	1926	6	0	0	0	0	0	0	0	6	0
DONALD D.M.	1909-11	45	2	0	0	0	0	0	0	45	2
DRAPER D.	1966	8	1	0	0	1	0	0	0	9	1
DUNCAN D.	1931-46	261	63	28	6	0	0	0	0	289	69
DUNCAN J.P.	1978-80	35 /1	12	0 /1	0	2	0	0	0	37 /2	12
DUNN G.	1890	1	0	0	0	0	0	0	0	1	0
DUNN J.	1952-54	57	21	1	0	0	0	0	0	58	21
DURBAN W.A.	1963-72	336 /10	93	16 /3	10	30 /1	8	6 /1	1	388 /15	112
EADIE W.P.	1914	31	0	0	0	0	0	0	0	31	0
EDWARDS J.W.	1908	2	1	0	0	0	0	0	0	2	1
EGGLESTON T.	1945	0	0	1	0	0	0	0	0	1	0
EKINS F.G.	1891-92	18	3	0	0	0	0	0	0	18	3
EMERY S.R.	1979-81	73 /2	4	3	0	2	0	0	0	78 /2	4
EMSON P.D.	1978-82	112 /15	13	1 /3	0	4 /3	0	0	0	117 /21	13
EVANS G.	1884-86	0	0	5	6	0	0	0	0	5	6
EVANS W.	1907	1	0	0	0	0	0	0	0	1	0

Player	Played	League		FA Cup		Lg Cup		Others		TOTAL	
		App	Gls	App	Gls	App	Gls	App	Gls	App	Gls
EXHAM P.G.	1884	0	0	1	0	0	0	0	0	1	0
FABIAN A.H.	1931-32	12	1	4	2	0	0	0	0	16	3
FAGAN F.	1959-60	24	6	0	0	1	0	0	0	25	6
FAIRCLOUGH A.	1924-26	37	26	0	0	0	0	0	0	37	26
FAZACKERLEY S.N.	1925	3	2	0	0	0	0	0	0	3	2
FELLOWS P.J.	1913	2	1	0	0	0	0	0	0	2	1
FEREDAY D.T.	1928-29	16	2	1	0	0	0	0	0	17	2
FERGUSON A.	1888-90	49	0	2	0	0	0	0	0	51	0
FERGUSON R.B.	1962-65	121	0	4	0	4	0	0	0	129	0
FIFE	1889	2	0	0	0	0	0	0	0	2	0
FINDLEY J.W.	1983	1	0	0	0	0	0	0	0	1	0
FINDLAY T.	1922-23	4	0	0	0	0	0	0	0	4	0
FISHER W.	1896	11	5	4	3	0	0	0	0	15	8
FLANDERS F.	1910	13	0	3	0	0	0	0	0	16	0
FLETCHER F.	1894	3	0	0	0	0	0	0	0	3	0
FLETCHER T.	1904-06	33	8	2	1	0	0	0	0	35	9
FLOWERS J.	1885	0	0	2	0	0	0	0	0	2	0
FORD D.	1898	6	0	0	0	0	0	0	0	6	0
FORDHAM N.M.	1913-14	13	5	1	1	0	0	0	0	14	6
FORMAN F.	1894	8	0	0	0	0	0	0	0	8	0
FORMAN F.R.	1892	4	3	0	0	0	0	0	0	4	3
FORSYTH M.E.	1986-93	302 /1	8	15	0	33	1	28	1	378/1	10
FOSTER G.W.	1982	30	0	3	0	5	0	0	0	38	0
FOX W.	1925	1	0	0	0	0	0	0	0	1	0
FRAIL J.	1897	10	0	0	0	0	0	0	0	10	0
FRANCIS K.D.M.	1989-90	0 /10	0	1 /2	1	1 /2	0	0 /1	0	2/15	1
FRANCIS P.O	1893-95	16	6	3	1	0	0	1	0	20	7
FRITH R.W.	1910	1	0	0	0	0	0	0	0	1	0
FRYER J.S.	1897-1902	173	0	26	0	0	0	0	0	199	0
FULTON W.	1901	13	1	0	0	0	0	0	0	13	1
FUTCHER P.	1982-83	35	0	4	0	1	0	0	0	40	0
GABBIADINI M.	1991-93	95 /8	28	6	2	6	4	14	8	121 /9	42
GALLACHER H.K.	1934-35	51	38	4	2	0	0	0	0	55	40
GALLOWAY S.R.	1922-24	66	25	10	5	0	0	0	0	76	30
GAMBLE F.	1981-82	5 /1	2	1	0	1	0	0	0	7/1	2
GARDEN H.W.	1902	1	0	0	0	0	0	0	0	1	0
GARDNER W.	1920	5	1	0	0	0	0	0	0	5	1
GARNER A.	1983-87	48 /23	17	4 /3	2	1 /4	0	5	1	58/30	20
GARRY E.	1907-12	120	18	9	1	0	0	0	0	129	19
GEE P.J.	1985-91	107 /17	26	6 /1	2	11 /2	3	7 /1	0	131/21	31
GEMMILL A.	1970-77										
	1982-83	324	25	35	6	20	1	25	1	404	33
GEORGE C.F.	1975-78										
	1981	117	36	11	6	10	4	9	10	147	56
GIBSON A.M.	1980-81	0 /2	0	0	0	0 /1	0	0	0	0/3	0
GILCHRIST L.	1904	11	0	0	0	0	0	0	0	11	0
GILL J.	1925-27	65	35	1	0	0	0	0	0	66	35
GILLETT L.F.	1884	0	0	1	0	0	0	0	0	1	0
GODDARD P.	1988-89	49	15	1 /1	0	7	2	5	1	62/1	18
GOLBY J.A.	1922	1	0	0	0	0	0	0	0	1	0
GOODALL A.L.	1889-1902	380	48	43	4	0	0	1	0	423	52
GOODALL J.	1889-98	211	76	26	9	0	0	1	0	238	85

Player	Played	League		FA Cup		Lg Cup		Others		TOTAL	
		App	Gls	App	Gls	App	Gls	App	Gls	App	Gls
GOODCHILD G.	1896	2	0	0	0	0	0	0	0	2	0
GORHAM C.	1884	0	0	1	0	0	0	0	0	1	0
GOULOOZE R.	1992	7 /5	0	1	0	0 /1	0	3	1	11 /6	1
GRANT A.F.	1946-47	12	0	3	0	0	0	0	0	15	0
GREEN J.	1894	7	0	0	0	0	0	0	0	7	0
GREEN L.	1968-70	107	0	5	0	17	0	0	0	129	0
GREEN R.E.	1931	1	0	0	0	0	0	0	0	1	0
GREENWOOD R.T.	1978-79	26 /5	1	1	0	1	0	0	0	28 /5	1
GREGORY J.C.	1985-87	103	22	9	1	8	0	4 /1	0	124 /1	23
GRIMES W.J.	1909-14	161	11	8	0	0	0	0	0	169	11
GROVES A.	1933-35	64	17	5	1	0	0	0	0	69	18
GWYNNE Revd L.H.	1887	0	0	1	0	0	0	0	0	1	0
HADDOW D.	1890	16	0	0	0	0	0	0	0	16	0
HAGAN J.	1935-38	30	7	1	0	0	0	0	0	31	7
HAIG J.	1898	3	0	0	0	0	0	0	0	3	0
HALES D.D.	1976-77	22 /1	4	6	2	1	1	0	0	29 /1	7
HALEY W.T.	1924-26	9	1	2	0	0	0	0	0	11	1
HALFORD D.	1935	6	3	3	1	0	0	0	0	9	4
HALL B.	1903-10	245	11	24	3	0	0	0	0	269	14
HALL I.W.	1959-61	44	13	1	0	6	3	0	0	51	16
HALLIGAN W.	1909-10	22	8	0	0	0	0	0	0	22	8
HAMILTON J.	1894	12	2	0	0	0	0	0	0	12	2
HAMPTON J.W.	1927-29	12	0	0	0	0	0	0	0	12	0
HANDLEY G.	1897-98	15	2	0	0	0	0	0	0	15	2
HANN R.	1932-38	115	0	5	0	0	0	0	0	120	0
HANNAY J.	1920	1	0	0	0	0	0	0	0	1	0
HANNIGAN J.L.	1958-60	72	19	3	0	0	0	0	0	75	19
HARBEY G.K.	1983-86	35 /5	1	1 /2	0	5	1	2 /1	0	43 /8	2
HARBOARD	1888	1	0	0	0	0	0	0	0	1	0
HARDCASTLE D.S.	1905	5	1	1	0	0	0	0	0	6	1
HARDMAN J.A.	1913-14	14	0	1	0	0	0	0	0	15	0
HARDY A.	1891-92	3	1	0	0	0	0	0	0	3	1
HARDY J.J.	1924	3	0	0	0	0	0	0	0	3	0
HARFORD M.G.	1989-91	58	15	1	0	7	3	2	0	68	18
HARKES J.A.	1993	31 /2	2	0	0	2	0	4	1	37 /2	3
HARRISON K.	1954-55	15	3	1	0	0	0	0	0	16	3
HARRISON R.F.	1945-54	254	52	27	7	0	0	0	0	281	59
HARRISON T.W.	1901	1	0	0	0	0	0	0	0	1	0
HART J.L.	1925-26	4	3	0	0	0	0	0	0	4	3
HARVEY J.A.H.	1894	5	0	0	0	0	0	0	0	5	0
HASLAM H.B.	1900-01	8	0	0	0	0	0	0	0	8	0
HAVENHAND K.	1961	26	14	3	0	0	0	0	0	29	14
HAWDEN K.	1953	2	0	0	0	0	0	0	0	2	0
HAYWARD S.L.	1989-93	12 /11	1	1	0	0 /2	0	2 /4	0	15 /17	1
HAYWOOD F.	1906	1	0	0	0	0	0	0	0	1	0
HAZELDINE D.	1952-53	26	6	2	0	0	0	0	0	28	6
HAZELDINE G.	1953	1	0	0	0	0	0	0	0	1	0
HEBBERD T.N.	1988-90	70 /11	10	5	2	13	2	7	0	95 /11	14
HECTOR K.J.	1966-77										
	1980-81	478 /8	155	34	12	42	15	27	19	581 /8	201
HENNESSEY W.T.	1969-72	62 /1	4	3 /2	0	2	1	12	0	79 /3	5
HICKINBOTTOM E.	1888-93	50	0	3	0	0	0	0	0	53	0

Player	Played	League App	League Gls	FA Cup App	FA Cup Gls	Lg Cup App	Lg Cup Gls	Others App	Others Gls	TOTAL App	TOTAL Gls
HICKLING W.	1903	9	0	0	0	0	0	0	0	9	0
HIGGINS A.F.	1888-89	42	2	5	3	1	0	0	0	45	26
HILL A.R.	1981-83	19/3	2	3	1	3	1	0	0	25/3	4
HILL G.A.	1977-79	22/2	5	1	0	2	1	0	0	25/2	6
HINCHLIFFE T.	1938	6	1	0	0	0	0	0	0	6	1
HIND F.	1889	1	0	0	0	0	0	0	0	1	0
HINDMARCH R.	1984-89	164	9	13	1	13	0	6	0	196	10
HINTON A.T.	1967-75	240/13	64	18/2	3	23/1	11	14/5	5	295/21	83
HOGKINSON W.H.	1903	16	9	0	0	0	0	0	0	16	9
HODGSON W.	1965-67	78	17	2	0	6	3	0	0	86	20
HOFFMAN E.H.	1922	1	0	0	0	0	0	0	0	1	0
HOLMES S.	1889-90	21	8	1	0	0	0	0	0	22	8
HOLYOAKE J.E.	1901	1	0	0	0	0	0	0	0	1	0
HOOKS P.	1982-84	46/2	4	3	0	6	0	1/1	0	56/3	4
HOPE J.	1926-29	9	2	0	0	0	0	0	0	9	2
HOPEWELL W.	1888	5	0	0	0	0	0	0	0	5	0
HOPKINS W.	1890	8	0	0	0	0	0	0	0	8	0
HOPKINSON M.E.	1960-67	112/3	4	6	1	10	1	0	0	128/3	6
HOUNSFIELD R.E.	1904-05	23	4	3	0	0	0	0	0	26	4
HOWARD E.	1899	1	0	0	0	0	0	0	0	1	0
HOWARD F.J.	1919	5	0	0	0	0	0	0	0	5	0
HOWE J.R.	1935-49	223	2	21	0	0	0	0	0	244	2
HUGHES A.	1934	2	1	0	0	0	0	0	0	2	1
HUGHES G.	1963-67	184	22	4	0	13	2	0	0	201	24
HUGHES W.	1977	17/2	8	0	0	1	0	0	0	18/2	8
HUNT A.	1904-05	15	1	0	0	0	0	0	0	15	1
HUNT D.	1977	5	0	0	0	0	0	0	0	5	0
HUNT J.	1901-03										
	1905	5	0	0	0	0	0	0	0	5	0
HUNT R.A.R.	1958	24	10	0	0	0	0	0	0	24	10
HUNTER G.I.	1954	19	0	0	0	0	0	0	0	19	0
HURST W.	1922	3	0	0	0	0	0	0	0	3	0
HUTCHINSON F.	1886	0	0	1	0	0	0	0	0	1	0
HUTCHINSON J.B.	1960-63	107	51	3	2	6	4	0	0	116	57
HUTCHISON D.	1931-33	29	4	1	0	0	0	0	0	30	4
IMLACH J.J.S.	1954	36	2	1	0	0	0	0	0	37	2
JACKSON J.H.	1921	13	4	1	0	0	0	0	0	14	4
JAMES L.	1975-77	67/1	15	11	2	7	1	4	3	89/1	21
JARDINE R.J.	1889	1	1	0	0	0	0	0	0	1	1
JEFFRIES A.	1936-38	15	1	0	0	0	0	0	0	15	1
JESSOP F.S.	1930-37	84	7	9	0	0	0	0	0	93	7
JOHNSON T.	1991-93	77/7	23	5	1	5/1	2	15	5	102/8	32
JOHNSTON J.M.	1923	1	0	0	0	0	0	0	0	1	0
JONES N.E.	1922	3	0	0	0	0	0	0	0	3	0
JONES R.	1980-81	59	0	3	0	3	0	0	0	65	0
JONES V.	1937	2	0	0	0	0	0	0	0	2	0
KAVANAGH J.C.	1990-93	46/19	0	5	0	1/1	0	8/4	0	60/24	0
KEAY W.	1893-94	24	7	5	0	0	0	0	0	29	7
KEEN E.R.L.	1930-37	219	4	18	1	0	0	0	0	237	5
KEETLEY F.	1921-25	76	8	6	0	0	0	0	0	82	8
KELHAM H.	1908	1	0	0	0	0	0	0	0	1	0

Player	Played	League App	Gls	FA Cup App	Gls	Lg Cup App	Gls	Others App	Gls	TOTAL App	Gls
KELLY D.	1926-27	5	0	0	0	0	0	0	0	5	0
KIDD J.	1919-21	20	0	1	0	0	0	0	0	21	0
KIFFORD J.	1898-99	6	0	0	0	0	0	0	0	6	0
KING F.O.	1937	3	0	0	0	0	0	0	0	3	0
KING J.	1975-77	12 /2	0	1 /1	0	1/ 2	0	0 /2	0	14 /7	0
KING W.G.	1905	1	0	0	0	0	0	0	0	1	0
KINSEY G.	1895-96	36	0	5	0	0	0	0	0	41	0
KIRBY J.	1929-37	173	0	18	0	0	0	0	0	191	0
KITSON P.	1991-93	97	34	5	1	7	3	12 /1	5	121 /1	43
KNOWLES F.E.	1921	3	1	0	0	0	0	0	0	3	1
KNOX J.J.	1886	0	0	2	1	0	0	0	0	2	1
KUHL M.	1992-93	59	1	6	0	5	0	2	1	72	2
LAMB S.	1905-06	30	1	3	0	0	0	0	0	33	1
LAMPH T.	1919-20	16	0	1	0	0	0	0	0	17	0
LANE M.A.E.	1924	0	0	1	0	0	0	0	0	1	0
LANE S.B.	1983	1	0	0	0	0	0	0	0	1	0
LANGAN D.F.	1976-79	143	1	6	0	6	0	0	0	155	1
LANGLAND A.	1889	2	0	0	0	0	0	0	0	2	0
LATHAM A.	1886-90										
	1901	48	1	8	0	0	0	0	0	56	1
LAW C.R.	1952-53	33	2	0	0	0	0	0	0	33	2
LAWRENCE G.H.	1910-23	137	0	8	0	0	0	0	0	145	0
LAWRENCE S.E.	1887	0	0	4	0	0	0	0	0	4	0
LEACH S.	1897	1	0	0	0	0	0	0	0	1	0
LECKIE C.T.	1898-1904	126	1	13	0	0	0	0	0	139	1
LEE F.H.	1974-75	62	24	5 /2	1	4	1	10	4	81 /2	30
LEE J.	1950-53	93	54	6	2	0	0	0	0	99	56
LEES J.	1888-89	10	2	0	0	0	0	0	0	10	2
LEIGH A.S.	1919	2	0	0	0	0	0	0	0	2	0
LEIPER J.	1892-99	157	0	20	0	0	0	1	0	178	0
LEONARD H.D.	1911-19	144	72	6	1	0	0	0	0	150	73
LEONARD J.	1897	1	1	2	1	0	0	0	0	3	2
LEUTY L.H.	1945-49	131	1	27	0	0	0	0	0	158	1
LEWIS A.T.	1971-72	2	0	0	0	0	0	1	0	3	0
LEWIS M.	1984-87	37 /6	1	0 /1	0	2	0	4	0	43 /7	1
LEWIS W.L.	1931	8	3	0	0	0	0	0	0	8	3
LIEVESLEY W.	1920	1	0	0	0	0	0	0	0	1	0
LILLIS M.A.	1986-87	6 /9	1	0 /1	0	2 /1	0	0	0	8 /11	1
LINACRE J.H.	1898	2	0	0	0	0	0	0	0	2	0
LITTLE T.	1892-93	16	1	1	1	0	0	0	0	17	2
LLOYD A.	1903	1	0	0	0	0	0	0	0	1	0
LLOYD G.H.	1901-02	10	1	2	0	0	0	0	0	12	1
LONG J.	1906-07	61	18	4	1	0	0	0	0	65	19
LOVATT J.	1981	2 /2	0	0	0	0	0	0	0	2 /2	0
LOWELL E.J.	1953	1	1	0	0	0	0	0	0	1	1
LUNTLEY W.	1885	0	0	3	0	0	0	0	0	3	0
LYLE R.C.	1910	7	0	0	0	0	0	0	0	7	0
LYONS J.	1919-22	80	31	6	2	0	0	0	0	86	33
McALLE J.E.	1981-83	51 /7	1	3/ 1	1	4	0	0	0	58 /8	2
McALLISTER A.	1904	24	0	0	0	0	0	0	0	24	0
McANDREW R.	1963	1	0	0	0	0	0	0	0	1	0

Player	Played	League		FA Cup		Lg Cup		Others		TOTAL	
		App	Gls	App	Gls	App	Gls	App	Gls	App	Gls
McCAFFERY A.	1978-79	31 /6	4	0	0	4	0	0	0	35/6	4
McCANN J.	1962-63	55	2	3	0	0	0	0	0	58	2
McCLAREN S.	1985-87	23 /2	0	0	0	5	1	2	0	30/2	1
McCORD B.J.	1987-89	3 /2	0	3	0	1	0	0 /1	1	7/3	1
McCORMICK H.	1946-47	7	0	0	0	0	0	0	0	7	0
McCULLOCH D.	1938	31	16	1	0	0	0	0	0	32	16
MacDONALD W.J.	1898-99	23	4	6	3	0	0	0	0	29	7
McDONNELL M.	1955-57	93	0	6	0	0	0	0	0	99	0
MacDOUGALL A.L.	1928	2	0	0	0	0	0	0	0	2	0
McFARLAND R.L.	1967-80										
	1983	437 /5	44	33	0	37	1	18	3	525/5	48
McGILL J.	1946-47	8	0	0	0	0	0	0	0	8	0
McGOVERN J.P.	1968-73	186 /4	16	18	0	15	2	14	2	233/4	20
McINTYRE J.M.	1921-31	349	9	20	0	0	0	0	0	369	9
MACKAY D.C.	1968-70	122	5	7	0	16	2	0	0	145	7
McKELLAR D.	1978-79	41	0	2	0	0	0	0	0	43	0
MACKEN A.	1975-77	20 /3	1	4 /1	0	3 /2	0	2 /2	0	29/8	1
McLACHLAN J.	1890-94	63	17	3	0	0	0	0	0	66	17
McLACHLAN S.	1938-52	58	1	5	1	0	0	0	0	63	2
McLAREN H.	1949-53	119	53	12	3	0	0	0	0	131	56
MacLAREN R.	1985-87	113 /9	4	9	0	13	1	4	0	139/9	5
McLAVERTY B.	1920-27	115	1	2	0	0	0	0	0	117	1
McLEAN T.	1892	2	0	0	0	0	0	0	0	2	0
McMILLAN J.S.	1890-95	116	45	9	4	0	0	1	1	126	50
McMILLAN S.T.	1914	1	0	0	0	0	0	0	0	1	0
McMINN K.C.	1987-92	108 /15	9	6 /1	1	11	3	11	1	136/16	14
MACONNACHIE A.	1897	23	9	3	0	0	0	0	0	26	9
McQUEEN H.	1895-1900	150	18	18	4	0	0	0	0	168	22
McQUILLAN D.	1952-55	18	1	0	0	0	0	0	0	18	1
MALLOCH G.C.	1927-31	93	0	4	0	0	0	0	0	97	0
MANN H.H.	1928	4	0	2	0	0	0	0	0	6	0
MARSHALL J.	1888	16	0	0	0	0	0	0	0	16	0
MARTIN B.	1919	6	0	0	0	0	0	0	0	6	0
MARTIN R.	1955-59	81	0	4	0	0	0	0	0	85	0
MASKREY H.M.	1902-09										
	1920	202	0	20	0	0	0	0	0	222	0
MASSON D.S.	1977	23	1	3	2	0	0	0	0	26	3
MATTHEWS R.D.	1962-67	225	0	7	0	14	0	0	0	246	0
MATTHEWS W.	1912	1	0	0	0	0	0	0	0	1	0
MAY H.	1902	6	0	0	0	0	0	0	0	6	0
MAY J.	1898-1903	179	17	21	0	0	0	0	0	200	17
MAYCROFT D.	1884	0	0	1	0	0	0	0	0	1	0
MAYS A.E.	1949-59	272	21	9	0	0	0	0	0	281	21
MEE G.W.	1925-31	148	15	7	0	0	0	0	0	155	15
MERCER J.T.	1903-04	26	1	6	0	0	0	0	0	32	1
METCALF R.	1966	1	0	0	0	0	0	0	0	1	0
METHVEN J.	1891-1906	458	0	52	0	0	0	1	0	511	0
METHVEN J.Jnr	1913	1	0	0	0	0	0	0	0	1	0
MICKLEWHITE G.	1984-92	223 /17	31	8 /3	4	23 /3	2	8 /3	6	262/26	43
MIDDLETON F.	1901-05	65	3	3	0	0	0	0	0	68	3
MIDDLETON J.	1977-79	73	0	3	0	4	0	0	0	80	0
MIDDLETON R.	1951-53	116	0	4	0	0	0	0	0	120	0
MILARVIE R.	1889	14	4	1	0	0	0	0	0	15	4

Player	Played	League App	Gls	FA Cup App	Gls	Lg Cup App	Gls	Others App	Gls	TOTAL App	Gls
MILLER D.	1947	1	0	0	0	0	0	0	0	1	0
MILLER J.	1895-97	62	20	9	5	0	0	0	0	71	25
MILLIN A.	1955	1	0	0	0	0	0	0	0	1	0
MILLS G.R.	1982	18	2	3	0	2	0	0	0	23	2
MILLS S.	1891-92	45	7	2	0	0	0	0	0	47	7
MINNEY G.	1920	2	0	0	0	0	0	0	0	2	0
MITCHELL H.	1905	1	0	0	0	0	0	0	0	1	0
MITCHELL J.D.	1958-59	6	0	0	0	0	0	0	0	6	0
MONEY R.	1981	5	0	1	0	0	0	0	0	6	0
MONKS I.	1887-88	3	0	3	2	0	0	0	0	6	2
MOORE J.	1904-05	5	0	0	0	0	0	0	0	5	0
MOORE J.	1913-25	203	75	15	7	0	0	0	0	218	82
MOORE J.L.	1957-63	144	3	7	0	5	0	0	0	156	3
MOORE R.	1919	1	0	0	0	0	0	0	0	1	0
MOORE W.C.	1906-08	11	0	0	0	0	0	0	0	11	0
MORAN J.	1954	2	0	0	0	0	0	0	0	2	0
MORELAND V.	1978-79	38/4	1	1	0	1/1	0	0	0	40/5	1
MORLEY H.A.	1884-88	4	0	6	0	0	0	0	0	10	0
MORRIS C.R.	1900-09	276	1	35	1	0	0	0	0	311	2
MORRIS J.	1948-52	130	44	10	3	0	0	0	0	140	47
MORRISON A.C.	1945-47	52	21	16	1	0	0	0	0	68	22
MORTON W.H.	1920-21	24	1	1	0	0	0	0	0	25	1
MOSELEY G.	1972-76	32	0	4	0	4	0	4	0	44	0
MOZLEY B.	1946-54	297	2	24	0	0	0	0	0	321	2
MURPHY L.	1921-27	221	46	14	3	0	0	0	0	235	49
MURRAY W.	1920	31	3	3	1	0	0	0	0	34	4
MUSSON W.U.	1945-53	246	0	34	0	0	0	0	0	280	0
MYNARD L.D.	1949-50	14	2	0	0	0	0	0	0	14	2
NAPIER C.E.	1935-37	80	24	8	2	0	0	0	0	88	26
NASH R.W.	1885-87	0	0	3	1	0	0	0	0	3	1
NEAL R.M.	1931	10	1	2	2	0	0	0	0	12	3
NEEDHAM G.W.	1919	5	0	0	0	0	0	0	0	5	0
NEEDHAM T.	1887-89	15	3	5	3	0	0	0	0	20	6
NELSON E.	1926	2	0	0	0	0	0	0	0	2	0
NELSON J.	1890	4	2	0	0	0	0	0	0	4	2
NEVE E.	1912-13	47	1	2	0	0	0	0	0	49	1
NEWBERY P.J.	1958-60	5	2	0	0	0	0	0	0	5	2
NEWTON H.A.	1973-76	111/6	5	15	1	10/1	0	13	0	149/7	6
NICHOLAS J.T.	1928-46	347	14	36	2	0	0	0	0	383	16
NICHOLAS W.J.	1905-10	130	0	13	0	0	0	0	0	143	0
NICHOLLS H.	1885	0	0	1	0	0	0	0	0	1	0
NICHOLSON S.M.	1992-93	39	1	2	1	0	0	1	0	42	2
NIELSON N.F.	1951-53	57	8	3	1	0	0	0	0	60	9
NISH D.J.	1972-78	184/4	10	16	1	16	1	17	2	233/4	14
OAKDEN H.	1898	9	5	3	0	0	0	0	0	12	5
O'BRIEN M.T.	1926-27	3	0	2	0	0	0	0	0	5	0
O'BRIEN R.C.	1983	4	0	0	0	0	0	0	0	4	0
O'HARE J.	1967-73	247/1	65	17	3	28/2	8	13	5	305/3	81
OLIVER J.A.	1947-49	16	2	1	0	0	0	0	0	17	2
OLIVER J.H.K.	1949-57	184	1	9	0	0	0	0	0	193	1
OLNEY B.A.	1920-27	223	0	17	0	0	0	0	0	240	0
O'RIORDAN D.J.	1976-77	2/4	1	0	0	0/1	0	0	0	2/5	1

Player	Played	League		FA Cup		Lg Cup		Others		TOTAL	
		App	Gls	App	Gls	App	Gls	App	Gls	App	Gls
ORMONDROYD I.	1991	25	8	3	1	3	0	0	0	31	9
O'ROURKE J.	1900	5	0	0	0	0	0	0	0	5	0
OSGOOD K.	1979-81	61 /8	10	2	0	3	0	0	0	66/8	10
OSMAN R.C.H.	1953-54	2	0	0	0	0	0	0	0	2	0
OXFORD K.	1957-62	151	0	6	0	5	0	0	0	162	0
PALMER C.A.	1984-85	51	2	1	0	7	0	2	0	61	2
PALMER D.F.	1961	18	6	2	0	1	0	0	0	21	6
PARKIN A.G.	1949	9	0	0	0	0	0	0	0	9	0
PARKIN R.	1936	1	0	0	0	0	0	0	0	1	0
PARNELL G.F.	1903-04	9	0	0	0	0	0	0	0	9	0
PARR J.	1945-52	112	0	22	0	0	0	0	0	134	0
PARRY A.J.	1971-72	4 /2	0	0	0	0	0	1	0	5/2	0
PARRY J.	1948-65	482 /1	105	20	5	14	0	0	0	516/1	110
PATERSON R.	1897-99	19	0	2	0	0	0	0	0	21	0
PATERSON W.	1920-23	66	24	2	0	0	0	0	0	68	24
PATON T.H.	1904-05	35	4	3	0	0	0	0	0	38	4
PATRICK R.	1952-55	49	0	1	0	0	0	0	0	50	0
PATTERSON M.	1988-92	41 /10	3	4	0	5 /2	0	5 /1	2	55/13	5
PATTISON J.W.	1921	15	2	0	0	0	0	0	0	15	2
PAUL D.D.	1953-55	2	0	0	0	0	0	0	0	2	0
PAUL J.	1894-97	28	9	1	0	0	0	1	0	30	9
PAYNE F.E.	1947	0	0	1	0	0	0	0	0	1	0
PEART J.G.	1919	9	1	0	0	0	0	0	0	9	1
PEART R.	1946	1	0	0	0	0	0	0	0	1	0
PEMBRIDGE M.A.	1992-93	81 /2	19	6	3	7	1	13	4	107/2	27
PENNEY D.M.	1985-88	6 /13	0	1	1	2 /3	1	1 /3	1	10/19	3
PHILBIN J.	1934	1	0	0	0	0	0	0	0	1	0
PHILLIPS J.L.	1990	3	1	0	0	0	0	0	0	3	1
PICKERING N.	1988-91	35 /10	3	3	0	7 /1	0	3	0	48/11	3
PITMAN R.	1888-89	5	0	2	0	0	0	0	0	7	0
PLACE C.A.	1955	2	0	0	0	0	0	0	0	2	0
PLACKETT H.	1888	16	2	0	0	0	0	0	0	16	2
PLACKETT L.	1886-88	22	7	8	1	0	0	0	0	30	8
PLACKETT S.	1921-26	140	3	16	0	0	0	0	0	156	3
PLUMMER C.A.	1983	23 /4	3	3 /1	1	2	0	0	0	28/5	4
POPPITT J.	1946-49	16	0	0	0	0	0	0	0	16	0
POWELL B.I.	1979-81	86	7	2	1	4	0	0	0	92	8
POWELL K.	1946	13	0	0	0	0	0	0	0	13	0
POWELL S.	1971-84	342 /10	20	31 /1	0	24	1	12	0	409/11	21
POWELL T.	1948-61	380	57	24	7	2	0	0	0	406	64
PRATLEY R.G.	1983-86	29 /2	1	0 /1	0	4	0	4	0	37/3	1
PUMFORD G.L.	1924	2	0	0	0	0	0	0	0	2	0
PYE J.	1954-56	61	24	4	3	0	0	0	0	65	27
PYNEGAR A.	1904	1	0	0	0	0	0	0	0	1	0
QUANTRILL A.E.	1914-20	72	5	4	0	0	0	0	0	76	5
RAISBECK W.	1901	3	0	3	0	0	0	0	0	6	0
RAMAGE A.	1980-81	32 /1	2	2	0	3	0	0	0	37/1	2
RAMAGE C.D.	1989-93	33 /9	4	3 /1	1	6 /1	2	0 /3	0	42/14	7
RAMAGE P.	1928-36	233	55	22	5	0	0	0	0	255	60
RAMSELL E.A.	1905	5	0	0	0	0	0	0	0	5	0

Player	Played	League		FA Cup		Lg Cup		Others		TOTAL	
		App	Gls	App	Gls	App	Gls	App	Gls	App	Gls
RANCE C.S.	1920-21	23	0	0	0	0	0	0	0	23	0
RANDALL L.	1930-34	52	4	0	0	0	0	0	0	52	4
RANSFORD J.	1906	15	3	2	1	0	0	0	0	17	4
RATCLIFFE E.	1902-05	16	0	0	0	0	0	0	0	16	0
RATCLIFFE K.	1993	6	0	0	0	0	0	0	0	6	0
RAYBOULD S.	1894	5	2	0	0	0	0	0	0	5	2
READER A.R.	1913	4	0	0	0	0	0	0	0	4	0
REID A.J.	1980-82	27 /3	1	1 /1	0	2	0	0	0	30 /4	1
REID S.E.	1931-35	16	0	0	0	0	0	0	0	16	0
REVELL C.H.	1950-51	22	2	0	0	0	0	0	0	22	2
RHODES J.A.	1964-70	5	0	0	0	1 /1	0	0	0	6 /1	0
RICHARDS F.	1898	2	0	0	0	0	0	0	0	2	0
RICHARDS G.H.	1901-13	284	33	25	4	0	0	0	0	309	37
RICHARDS J.P.	1982	10	2	0	0	0	0	0	0	10	2
RICHARDS W.	1979-81	16 /3	0	3	0	0 /1	0	0	0	19 /4	0
RICHARDSON J.	1962-70	118	4	3	1	12	0	0	0	133	5
RICHARDSON P.A.	1984	7 /7	0	1	0	0 /2	0	0	0	8 /9	0
RICHMOND J.F.	1957-62	6	0	0	0	0	0	0	0	6	0
RIDDELL F.W.	1907-08	6	1	0	0	0	0	0	0	6	1
RIOCH B.D.	1973-76										
	1977-79	146 /1	38	12	7	11	5	14	4	183 /1	54
RITCHIE A.	1920-26	87	1	6	0	0	0	0	0	93	1
RITCHIE D.	1913	2	0	0	0	0	0	0	0	2	0
RITCHIE W.	1919	4	1	0	0	0	0	0	0	4	1
ROBERTS E.	1935	4	0	0	0	0	0	0	0	4	0
ROBERTS W.	1890	5	0	0	0	0	0	0	0	5	0
ROBERTSON J.N.	1983-84	72	3	5	0	6	1	2	0	85	4
ROBINSON A.	1909	1	0	0	0	0	0	0	0	1	0
ROBINSON J.W.	1891-96	163	0	16	0	0	0	1	0	180	0
ROBINSON T.C.	1927-29	9	0	2	0	0	0	0	0	11	0
ROBINSON W.	1909	3	0	0	0	0	0	0	0	3	0
ROBSON J.C.	1928-31	38	10	2	0	0	0	0	0	40	10
ROBSON J.D	1967-72	170 /1	3	12	1	19	0	9	1	210 /1	5
ROBSON J.W.	1921	3	0	0	0	0	0	0	0	3	0
ROBSON N.	1930-32	35	6	0	0	0	0	0	0	35	6
ROBSON W.	1927-31	13	0	3	0	0	0	0	0	16	0
ROBY D.	1961-64	70	6	5	0	6	1	0	0	81	7
ROSE C.H.	1891-92	5	0	0	0	0	0	0	0	5	0
ROSE W.	1891-92	5	0	0	0	0	0	0	0	5	0
ROULSTONE F.	1888	1	0	0	0	0	0	0	0	1	0
ROULSTONE W.	1887-94	118	4	11	0	0	0	0	0	129	4
ROUND S.J.	1991-92	8 /1	0	0	0	0	0	0	0	8 /1	0
ROWE G.W.	1925	1	0	0	0	0	0	0	0	1	0
ROWE V.N.	1951	2	0	0	0	0	0	0	0	2	0
RUDDY T.	1928-31	22	9	0	0	0	0	0	0	22	9
RUSSELL J.	1898	2	0	0	0	0	0	0	0	2	0
RUTHERFORD J.B.	1898	1	1	0	0	0	0	0	0	1	1
RYAN G.J.	1977-78	30	4	2	1	2	0	0	0	34	5
RYAN R.A.	1955-58	133	30	6	1	0	0	0	0	139	31
SAGE M.	1986-91	137 /3	4	4	0	22 /1	0	8	0	171 /4	4
SAUNDERS D.N.	1988-90	106	42	6	0	12	10	7	5	131	57
SAUNDERS S.	1904-05	8	0	0	0	0	0	0	0	8	0
SAVIN K.A.	1950-55	65	0	1	0	0	0	0	0	66	0

Player	Played	League		FA Cup		Lg Cup		Others		TOTAL	
		App	Gls	App	Gls	App	Gls	App	Gls	App	Gls
SAWYER T.E.	1894	2	0	0	0	0	0	0	0	2	0
SAXTON R.	1964-67	94 /2	1	3	0	9	0	0	0	106/2	1
SCARBOROUGH B.	1958-60	4	0	0	0	0	0	0	0	4	0
SCATTERGOOD E.O.	1907-14	182	3	10	0	0	0	0	0	192	3
SCATTERGOOD K.	1936-37	22	0	3	0	0	0	0	0	25	0
SCOTT A.T.	1927-33	27	0	5	0	0	0	0	0	32	0
SCOTT K.	1950	2	0	0	0	0	0	0	0	2	0
SEAL C.E.	1905	1	0	0	0	0	0	0	0	1	0
SELVEY S.	1888	1	0	0	0	0	0	0	0	1	0
SELVEY W.	1888	1	0	0	0	0	0	0	0	1	0
SHANKS T.	1898-1900	27	9	1	0	0	0	0	0	28	9
SHARMAN D.W.	1950	2	0	0	0	0	0	0	0	2	0
SHARPE I.G.L	1911-12	54	12	3	0	0	0	0	0	57	12
SHEPHERD G.	1919-20	2	0	0	0	0	0	0	0	2	0
SHERIDAN F.M.	1980-81	41 /2	5	0	0	1	0	0	0	42/2	5
SHILTON P.L.	1987-91	175	0	10	0	18	0	8	0	211	0
SHINER A.J.	1920	1	0	0	0	0	0	0	0	1	0
SHIRTCLIFFE E.	1901	4	0	0	0	0	0	0	0	4	0
SHORT J.C.	1992-93	81	6	6	4	7	0	5	0	99	10
SIMPSON P.D.	1991-93	75 /10	28	2 /1	0	6	3	11 /2	2	94/13	33
SIMS J.	1972	2 /1	0	0	0	0	0	0 /1	0	2/2	0
SKIVINGTON G.	1980-82	39 /7	2	0	0	4	1	0	0	43/7	3
SMITH A.	1884-85	0	0	4	2	0	0	0	0	4	2
SMITH F.	1909	5	0	0	0	0	0	0	0	5	0
SMITH F.E.	1947	1	0	0	0	0	0	0	0	1	0
SMITH H.	1906	1	0	0	0	0	0	0	0	1	0
SMITH J.	1888-89	12	0	0	0	0	0	0	0	12	0
SMITH J.	1914	6	0	0	0	0	0	0	0	6	0
SMITH J.W.	1903-06	9	0	1	0	0	0	0	0	10	0
SMITH M.J.	1957-60	22	0	0	0	1	0	0	0	23	0
SMITH S.J.	1922	1	0	0	0	0	0	0	0	1	0
SMITH V.	1925-26	4	0	0	0	0	0	0	0	4	0
SOAR T.A.	1902	2	0	0	0	0	0	0	0	2	0
SPILSBURY B.W.	1885-88	1	1	8	7	0	0	0	0	9	8
SPOONER S.A.	1978-81	7 /1	0	0	0	0	0	0	0	7/1	0
SPRINGTHORPE J.A.	1907	2	0	0	0	0	0	0	0	2	0
STALEY J.	1891-1900	128	0	12	0	0	0	1	0	141	0
STALLARD M.	1991-92	3 /5	0	1 /2	0	0	0	1	1	5/7	1
STAMPS J.D.	1938-53	233	10	29	26	0	0	0	0	262	126
STAPLETON F.A.	1987	10	1	0	0	0	0	0	0	10	1
STEEL W.	1938	11	0	0	0	0	0	0	0	11	0
STEEL W.	1947-49	109	27	15	8	0	0	0	0	124	35
STEELE E.G.	1984-86	47	0	1	0	2	0	3	0	53	0
STEPHENSON G.R.	1961-62	11	1	1	0	2	0	0	0	14	1
STEPHENSON G.T.	1927-30	111	53	9	3	0	0	0	0	120	56
STEVENSON J.	1894-98	73	31	11	1	0	0	0	0	84	32
STEWART A.	1967-69	29 /1	1	1	0	4	1	0	0	34/1	2
STEWART F.H.	1899	2	1	0	0	0	0	0	0	2	1
STOCKILL R.R.	1934-38	66	29	3	1	0	0	0	0	69	3
STOKOE J.	1922	8	1	0	0	0	0	0	0	8	1
STORER H.	1920-28	257	60	17	3	0	0	0	0	274	63
STORER W.	1891-92	25	10	2	1	0	0	0	0	27	11
STRAW R.	1951-57	94	57	4	3	0	0	0	0	98	60

Player	Played	League App	League Gls	FA Cup App	FA Cup Gls	Lg Cup App	Lg Cup Gls	Others App	Others Gls	TOTAL App	TOTAL Gls
STREETE F.A.	1984-85	35	0	1	0	4	0	1	0	41	0
STURRIDGE D.C.	1991-92	9 /2	0	0	0	0	0	0	0	9 /2	0
SUGG F.H.	1884	0	0	1	0	0	0	0	0	1	0
SUMMERS J.L.	1935	2	0	0	0	0	0	0	0	2	0
SUTTON S.J.	1984										
	1991-92	49	0	2	0	4	0	9	0	64	0
SWALLOW R.	1958-63	118	21	4	1	6	0	0	0	128	22
SWINDLEHURST D.	1979-82	110	29	6	0	9	3	0	0	125	32
SYLVESTER T.	1908	2	0	0	0	0	0	0	0	2	0
TAFT D.	1948	6	1	3	1	0	0	0	0	9	2
TATE G.M.	1955	1	1	0	0	0	0	0	0	1	1
TAYLOR K.	1984	22	2	0	0	4	0	1	1	27	3
TAYLOR M.J.	1989-93	82	0	4	0	5	0	6	0	100	0
TAYLOR R.C.	1921	2	0	0	0	0	0	0	0	2	0
THOMAS A.M.	1982	0 /1	0	0	0	0	0	0	0	0 /1	0
THOMAS E.	1964-67	102 /3	43	2	0	6	6	0	0	110 /3	49
THOMAS M.R.	1985	9	0	0	0	0	0	0	0	9	0
THOMAS R.J.	1973-77	89	2	10	0	9	0	10	0	118	2
THOMPSON C.A.	1948-49	16	3	0	0	0	0	0	0	16	3
THOMPSON G.A.	1908-10	46	5	9	1	0	0	0	0	55	6
THOMPSON G.H.	1920	4	0	0	0	0	0	0	0	4	0
THOMPSON J.	1897	1	0	0	0	0	0	0	0	1	0
THOMPSON P.	1958-61	52	19	2	2	1	1	0	0	55	22
THOMS H.	1922-27	179	4	16	0	0	0	0	0	195	4
THORNEWELL G.	1919-27	275	23	20	3	0	0	0	0	295	26
TINKLER A.	1909	2	0	0	0	0	0	0	0	2	0
TODD C.	1970-78	293	6	30	2	20	1	28	1	371	10
TODD T.B.	1955	4	3	1	0	0	0	0	0	5	3
TOOTLE J.	1924-25	7	0	0	0	0	0	0	0	7	0
TOWIE T.	1893	8	1	0	0	0	0	0	0	8	1
TOWNSEND W.	1945-52	79	0	14	0	0	0	0	0	93	0
TRAVIS H.	1936-38	12	4	0	0	0	0	0	0	12	4
TREMELLING S.	1905-07	2	0	0	0	0	0	0	0	2	0
TRUEMAN R.	1908-09	16	0	3	1	0	0	0	0	19	1
TURNER A.D.	1902	21	1	0	0	0	0	0	0	21	1
TURNER J.A.	1896-97	51	2	10	0	0	0	0	0	61	0
UDALL E.W.	1934-36	81	0	7	0	0	0	0	0	88	0
UPTON F.	1954-60										
	1965-66	259	17	8	1	5	0	0	0	272	18
VANN B.W.	1906	3	0	0	0	0	0	0	0	3	0
VARNEY H.	1901-02	2	0	0	0	0	0	0	0	2	0
WALKER C.	1948-54	25	0	0	0	0	0	0	0	25	0
WALKER J.A.	1889-90	11	0	2	0	0	0	0	0	13	0
WALKER J.H.	1911-19	84	4	4	0	0	0	0	0	88	4
WALKER J.M.	1967-73	35 /7	3	0 /1	0	8	0	2 /2	2	45 /10	5
WALLACE J.M.	1947	16	0	3	0	0	0	0	0	19	0
WALLER P.	1961-67	102 /2	5	3	0	8	0	0	0	113 /2	5
WALLINGTON F.M.	1985-86	67	0	8	0	11	0	3	0	89	0
WALSH W.	1946	1	0	0	0	0	0	0	0	1	0
WALTON G.	1905	1	0	0	0	0	0	0	0	1	0

Player	Played	League		FA Cup		Lg Cup		Others		TOTAL	
		App	Gls	App	Gls	App	Gls	App	Gls	App	Gls
WALTON J.	1921	7	0	1	0	0	0	0	0	8	0
WARD C.	1884	0	0	1	0	0	0	0	0	1	0
WARD T.V.	1937-50	238	4	22	1	0	0	0	0	260	5
WARMBY H.	1885-87	0	0	9	0	0	0	0	0	9	0
WARREN A.R.	1901	8	2	0	0	0	0	0	0	8	2
WARREN B.	1899-1907	242	19	27	14	0	0	0	0	269	33
WARRINGTON J.	1901-03	29	7	9	4	0	0	0	0	38	11
WASSALL D.P.J.	1992-93	49	0	3	0	6	0	7	0	66	0
WATERHOUSE F.	1919-20	26	0	2	0	0	0	0	0	28	0
WATSON A.F.	1990	5	0	0	0	0	0	0	0	5	0
WATSON D.V.	1983	34	1	3/2	0	2	0	0	0	39/2	1
WAUGH R.	1912-14	28	0	1	1	0	0	0	0	29	1
WEBB D.J.	1978-79	25/1	1	1	0	2	0	0	0	28/1	1
WEBB G.H.	1921	2	0	0	0	0	0	0	0	2	0
WEBB J.A.	1929-36	25	0	0	0	0	0	0	0	25	0
WEBSTER R.	1961-77	451/4	7	30	0	34	0	15/1	0	530/5	7
WEBSTER T.C.	1948-57	172	0	6	0	0	0	0	0	178	0
WHEATCROFT F.G.	1903-04										
	1905										
	1906-07	25	8	0	0	0	0	0	0	25	8
WHEATLEY S.P.	1951-52	4	0	0	0	0	0	0	0	4	0
WHEELER W.	1910	1	0	0	0	0	0	0	0	1	0
WHITE A.	1927-31	4	0	0	0	0	0	0	0	4	0
WHITE W.	1955	3	0	0	0	0	0	0	0	3	0
WHITEHOUSE J.C.	1923-28	186	82	14	4	0	0	0	0	200	85
WHITTAKER W.	1903	12	0	0	0	0	0	0	0	12	0
WHYMARK T.J.	1979	2	0	0	0	0	0	0	0	2	0
WICKS S.J.	1978-79	24	0	0	0	0	0	0	0	24	0
WIGHTMAN H.	1919-27	180	9	9	0	0	0	0	0	189	9
WIGNALL F.	1968-71	29/16	15	3	1	4/2	0	3	1	39/18	17
WILCOX G.E.	1937-46	12	0	0	0	0	0	0	0	12	0
WILEMAN S.	1933-36	9	1	2	0	0	0	0	0	11	1
WILKES H.T.	1927-32	208	0	12	0	0	0	0	0	220	0
WILKINS R.J.H.	1949-53	30	11	0	0	0	0	0	0	30	11
WILLIAMS D.G.	1984-91	276/1	9	17	0	26/1	1	11	0	330/2	10
WILLIAMS P.D.	1989-93	116/7	23	7	3	6/1	1	2/1	1	141/10	28
WILLIAMS P.J.	1952	2	0	0	0	0	0	0	0	2	0
WILLIAMSON A.	1885-90	41	0	12	1	0	0	0	0	53	1
WILLIAMSON M.	1961-63	12	0	1	0	1	0	0	0	14	0
WILSON A.	1898	1	0	0	0	0	0	0	0	1	0
WILSON A.	1936	1	0	0	0	0	0	0	0	1	0
WILSON C.K.	1922	1	0	0	0	0	0	0	0	1	0
WILSON I.W.	1990	11	0	0	0	0	0	0	0	11	0
WILSON K.J.	1979-84	106/16	30	8	3	8/3	8	0	0	122/19	41
WOMACK A.R.	1957	2	0	0	0	0	0	0	0	2	0
WOMBWELL R.	1899-1901	85	17	10	1	0	0	0	0	95	18
WOOD A.E.	1905-06	60	2	6	1	0	0	0	0	66	3
WOOD J.	1905-06	37	7	3	0	0	0	0	0	40	7
WOODHEAD D.	1955-58	94	24	3	0	0	0	0	0	97	25
WOODLEY V.R.	1945-46	30	0	4	0	0	0	0	0	34	0
WOOLLEY A.	1894	6	3	0	0	0	0	0	0	6	3
WRIGHT H.	1910-11	15	2	1	0	0	0	0	0	16	2
WRIGHT H.E.	1937-38	25	0	1	0	0	0	0	0	26	0

Player	Played	League		FA Cup		Lg Cup		Others		TOTAL	
		App	Gls	App	Gls	App	Gls	App	Gls	App	Gls
WRIGHT L.G.	1888	4	1	0	0	0	0	0	0	4	1
WRIGHT M.	1987-90	144	10	5	0	15	0	7	0	171	10
WRIGHT P.D.J.	1967	12/1	0	0	0	0	0	0	0	12/1	0
WYER P.W.	1956	2	1	0	0	0	0	0	0	2	1
YORK C.H.	1902-03	24	6	3	0	0	0	0	0	27	6
YOUNG G.R.	1953-65	253/1	5	6	0	9	0	0	0	268/1	5

The Rams fall behind at Stockport on 1 December 1956 and went on to lose 3-2 but at the end of the season were crowned Third Division North champions. Rams players left to right are goalkeeper Terry Webster, full-backs Roy Martin and Geoff Barrowcliffe, centre-half Martin McDonnell (on ground) and left-half Glyn Davies (partly hidden).

Subscribers
Presentation Copy:
DERBY COUNTY FOOTBALL CLUB

1	Pip Southall	37	Dennis Ruston
2	Andrew Ward	38	Ben Ruston
3	Anton Rippon	39	Philip Ruston
4	John Grainger	40	Howard Bettany
5	Alan Flintoff	41	Mr Eric J Rose
6	Brian Simpson	42	Alun Owen
7	Ian Simpson	43	Mr K C Saunders
8	John Harris	44	P A Church
9	Mick Derby	45	K & R J Jackson
10	Neil A Beresford	46	Mr Christopher Eaton
11	Shane Sanghera	47	Peter Stephens
12	S M Kelly	48	Liam James Clamp
13	Max Bladon/Stella Barkley	49	A John Newton
14	Clive Moorcroft	50	Barry Snaith
15	Stephen Hawley	51	Deryck Burns
16	Peter Rusbridge & Jenny Smith	52	Jörg-Peter Bartling
17	Alan Beresford	53	Sid Slater
18	Brian Flint	54	Anthony Michael Johnson
19	Adrian Eley	55	Andrew Jarrett
20	Mrs J M Ball	56	David Earnshaw
21	Mrs J M Ball	57	David Sheldon
22	Martin du Sautoy	58	Harold Preston
23	Nick Allgood	59	Colin Grimley
24	Paul Trembirth	60	Steve Cooke
25	Paul Barlow	61	Clery Henderson
26	Andrew Annison	62	David Clowes
27	Graham M Bolam	63	Judy & Harold Draycott
28	Bryan Linden Peach	64	Andy & Mandy Garner
29	Michael Rickwood	65	Jonathan Naden
30	David W Slater	66	Simon A Brown
31	L W Campbell	67	Mark Thompson
32	J B & Miss C A Stevenson	68	Andrew Rowbotham
33	Gary Holman	69	Richard H Sprenger
34	Andrew John Ellis	70	Mr A J Froggatt
35	Leonard Matthews	71	Leonard E Dormer
36	David Rudkin	72	C-Stander, Derby County Fanzine

73	Richard Fletcher	115	Phyllis Eleanor Meakin
74	R Watson	116	Anthony John Peach
75	Jason Madeley	117	Mr Christopher George Boss
76	James R Woolley	118	W Gordon Lee
77	Liam Kelly	119	Christine Gee
78	Steven Newiss	120	Mrs Edith Alice Bolstridge
79	C J A Frost	121	Roberto Forchino
80	Matt Morris	122	Clive Smith
81	Michael Brett	123	Frank Burton
82	Tony Bridges	124	Philip J Ryde
83	Finn Morten Steen	125	Philip Brewin
84	Ken Hales	126	Mr & Mrs R A Shaw
85	Richard J Pope	127	Stephen Francis Rowlinson
86	Paul Riley	128	Mr Adrian Greenwood
87	James Andrew Warren	129	Brian Redfern
88	Elaine Toon	130	David C Atkinson
89	Gary Bowen	131	Stuart Burnett
90	Stephen J Marshall	132	Dale Allan Jones
91	Simon Baker	133	Alisa Dawn Cade
92	David Phillips	134	John E Lake
93	Andrew Phillips	135	S C Bridges
94	George I Phillips	136	Raymond Neal
95	Paul Stanley Rowley	137	John A Harvey
96	David Lomas	138	Lee Lawrence
97	Michael Lomas	139	Neal Roy Johnson
98	J Ringrose	140	G K Stone
99	Glyn Mellor	141	Chris Kendall
100	Chris Cohen	142	Chris Kendall Football Programmes
101	Michael Cohen	143	Shirley A Paterson
102	K J Orpe	144	Steven Rankin
103	Mark Thompson	145	Michael Wilson
104	Andrew Cudworth	146	Michael Wilson
105	Philip Cudworth	147	Mr Andrew Miller
106	Gavin Dean Perry	148	Wallace Scott
107	Keith James Sims	149	Lindon Brown
108	Kevin John Sims	150	Charles Ross
109	Helen Jane Sims	151	Steven Else
110	Victoria Ann Saunders Sims	152	Andrew Hallam
111	Mick, Brigid, Hannah & Natasha Yates	153	C S Pritchard
112	Jonathan N Prime	154	Ian Cartwright
113	Harry Prime	155	Andrew Pickering
114	Andy Pickers	156	Frederick Gilmartin

157	Anna & James Beeson		199	Steve Kinsey
158	Shane Madeley		200	Mark Tyrer
159	Jonathan Gallimore		201	Michael Clarke
160	Michael T O'Neill		202	Marsha Limbert
161	Trevor J Whetton		203	Gareth Alun Jones
162	Harry Malcolm Shelley		204	James Paterson
163	Michael Harrison		205	Arto Tuominen
164	J R G Sutcliffe		206	Sophie Brookes
165	Andrew Duff		207	Tony Cracknell
166	Tom Bestwick		208	Mr John Stewart Marshall
167	Kevin Large		209	Michael Webb
168	Martin Kent		210	Mr Steven Robert Greenhough
169	Stephen Kent		211	Malcolm Turner
170	Paul Burgess		212	Simon Cooper
171	Peter John Lockhart		213	Brian Lawton
172	Gary Keith Shapcott		214	Philip Lawton
173	Barry Walker		215	John Timmins
174	Geoffrey Burd		216	Richard Hardwick
175	Harry Lewis		217	Roy & Pam Eley
176	Darren A England		218	Brian Woodall
177	Antony K Crossman		219	Phil & Carol Nicklin
178	Christopher Taylor		220	Michael G Robinson
179	Maurice John Freestone		221	David Lambert
180	Richard Bagshaw		222	Jonathan W House
181	John D Anthony		223	Gerald Hill
182	Ruth, Edward & Julian Hill		224	Phil Aiken
183	Alan Cooke		225	Mr M L Hall
184	Arthur Frank Pearson Jnr		226	John Spencer
185	Richard Hill		227	Neil Paul Rhodes
186	Bryan Edward Walton		228	Paul R Lester
187	Ralph McSeveney		229	Paul Wright
188	Paul Green		230	Richard Stuart Twells
189	Roger Green		231	Pat Thomas
190	David M Watson		232	Dennis Hawes
191	Andrew J Watson		233	David Moore
192	Daniel Luke Spencer		234	S Wood
193	David Gregg		235	Mr J Peter Davis
194	William D Gosling		236	Inge Haagensen
195	William D Gosling		237	Mark Childs
196	Darren Taylor		238	Mr R Bradley
197	J E Harrison		239	Andrew Bell
198	Jack Wilmot		240	Adam Page

241	Charles H B Clark	264	Michael Briggs
242	Nigel Wright	265	Barry Walker
243	Sue Hyett	266	Ken Smith
244	Adam Ireland	267	Duncan M Chambers
245	David Rigley	268	Matthew Michael Sanders
246	Jeremy Webb	269	Ivan Hodkinson
247	C A Simpson	270	Mr Vernisse Sylvain
248	M E W Litting	271	David C Beck
249	K G W Litting	272	Paul Adrian Munro
250	John & Robert Beresford	273	Judith Margaret Peel
251	James Hilton	274	Chris Neal
252	John R Clarke	275	William Faizal Beck
253	Graham Mason	276	Steve Shaw
254	Anthony Holman	277	Geoff Webb
255	Richard Holman	278	John Hackman
256	Steve Eyre	279	S C Glaister
257	Jack Statham	280	Anthony Russell
258	Steven McGhee	281	John Hudson
259	Beverley Murden	282	Paul Walker
260	Ziggy Fugiel	283	Dennis James Chapman
261	Andrew James Dawson	284	Paal Illevold
262	Christopher Wood	285	Susan Grainger
263	Revd G Horan		